DOUGLAS JOHN HALL

DOUGLAS JOHN HALL

COLLECTED READINGS

DAVID B. LOTT, EDITOR

Fortress Press
Minneapolis

DOUGLAS JOHN HALL: COLLECTED READINGS

Unless otherwise noted, scripture quotations are from the New Revised Standard Version Bible, copyright © 1989 by the Division of Christian Education of the National Council of Churches of Christ in the USA, and are used with permission.

Cover design: Tory Herman
Cover image © iStockphoto / Aptyp_koK

Library of Congress Cataloging-in-Publication data is available
Print ISBN: 978-0-8006-9986-4
eBook ISBN: 978-1-4514-6516-7

The paper used in this publication meets the minimum requirements of American National Standard for Information Sciences—Permanence of Paper for Printed Library Materials, ANSI Z329.48-1984.

Manufactured in the U.S.A.

This book was produced using PressBooks.com, and PDF rendering was done by PrinceXML.

CONTENTS

A Friendship of Shared Memories

Phyllis Trible

A few years ago Douglas John Hall returned to Union Theological Seminary, New York, where he had earned a doctorate in 1963. Alone he wandered through the impressive stone buildings. He visited the library, whose world-renowned collection endures; the chapel, whose renovation in the late 1970s did not eliminate totally its sacred space; and the refectory, whose elegant architecture invites the breaking of bread in the sharing of community.

After these wanderings, Doug sat in the courtyard, there to reflect upon his student life. Professorial figures dominated. From John Bennett to Henry Pitney Van Dusen (alas, the male spectrum only), they surrounded Doug like a great cloud of witnesses. As he returned to that past, that past returned to him. But how is it that I, who was not present at this re-creation, can write about it? The answer comes through a letter Doug shared. We remember.

When I reflect on the shared memories, my mind travels to a seminar on Deuteronomy that Doug, I, and others took with Professor Samuel Terrien. A single incident surfaces—as amusing now as it was then. Each of us made an oral report to the class. As a student in Theology, not in Bible, Doug offered a somewhat different approach. Soon thereafter, a few of us happened to meet Professor Terrien in the hallway. He was ecstatic. Apparently unaware of the irony, he let us biblical students know that Doug's paper was the model to emulate.

Outside this incident, Deuteronomy provides a way to view Doug's theological pilgrimage. That way links past, present, and future. As ancient Israel celebrated the harvest festival, it recounted its past—a story stretching from the ancestor Jacob to settlement in "a land flowing with milk and honey" (Deut. 26:5-9). In the retelling, the ancestors became "we" and "us." Past and present intertwined. Another passage continued the linkage by including "those who are not here with us today" (Deut. 29:14-15). Present stretched into future.

Not unlike Deuteronomy, Doug's writings embrace past, present, and future. From the citing of biblical references, he moves through centuries, continents, and characters: Anselm of Canterbury to Zwingli in the male environments of Europe past; McFague, Ruether, Soelle with contemporary feminist voices in North America and Europe; Endo, Kitamori, Koyama, and Song with Asian contributions. And if by itself, the act of writing nods toward the future—toward readers yet to come—there is more. In the lovely "Dedication" of *What Christianity Is Not* (2013)—a book he "intends" to be his last—Doug addresses his grandchildren. Ever the teacher, he commends to them the Word and the Spirit that illuminate his life and work. Their future enters his present even as the past endures.

The ancestor Jacob informs Doug's theology in another way. Scoundrel that he was, Jacob wrestled mightily in deep darkness with a stranger from whom he demanded a blessing (Gen. 32:22-32). He got the blessing but walked away limping. Scoundrel that he is not, Doug wrestles mightily in deep darkness with mysteries of faith. He knows wound and blessing. If, for our former classmates, this Jacob story reads as "the magnificent defeat" (Frederick Buechner) versus "the crippling victory" (Walter Brueggemann), for Doug it leads to "the theology of the cross."

"Lighten our darkness" became the title of one of Doug's compelling books. In it he writes of struggles and sufferings, of mystery and paradox, of abandonment, defeat, and death—all without a triumphal ending. He wrestles with the cross as deep darkness spreads over the land (cf. Mark 15:33). He knows that blessing comes not on his terms, or ours. Hardly by chance, then, does Doug's "last" book, the one dedicated to his grandchildren, conclude with the piercing and italicized affirmation: "*and him crucified*" (1 Cor. 1:23). Beginning with the ancestors, the theology of the cross illuminates our way and spreads to those to come.

From his student years at Union Theological Seminary through decades of professorial activities to continuing literary pursuits in retirement, Douglas John Hall offers no dramatic turns, no attention-grabbing proclamations, no facile theologies but rather the wisdom of a pilgrim of faith in a turbulent world. For a steady sharing of mystery, meaning, and memories, my appreciation extends across years of friendship.

Phyllis Trible
Baldwin Professor of Sacred Literature, Emerita, Union Theological Seminary

Introduction

David B. Lott

> *The theologian is charged with the*
> *responsibility of interpreting for his or her*
> *own time and place the very core of the*
> *faith—gospel for the here and now. . . .*
> *The theological vocation, then, requires a*
> *courage that is more than natural—the*
> *courage of being, in Paul's language, a "fool*
> *for Christ," a courage that darkly suspects,*
> *however, that most of the time it is just*
> *playing the fool.*
> *—Douglas John Hall (2005:22, 24)[1]*

"Gospel for the here and now"—these five words could well sum up the writing and teaching career of Douglas John Hall, which has spanned nearly five decades. In twenty-five books and countless essays, he has repeatedly courted the risk of "playing the fool" in order to press the church and Christians to a more disciplined, intellectually engaged faith that takes seriously the gospel imperative to "confess Christ and him crucified" in our contemporary context. The "dark suspicion" that the theologian often plays the fool demonstrates Hall's typical modesty while belying the bold and invigorating message of his theological project. In addressing both the hopes and the hubris of the church and the discipline of theology, his words are sharp but never barbed, pleading and urgent without making room for despair or cynicism.

Given his appreciation for the apophatic approach in theology—the *via negativa*—one might best begin to describe Hall's contribution to the discipline of theology by first saying a few things about what he is *not*.[2] Douglas John Hall has not been the founder of any particular school or movement in theology, nor is he an exemplar for any such school or movement. He does not easily wear an ideological label, such as "postliberal" or "neo-orthodox" or "process" theologian. In spite of his explicitly Canadian roots, he is not especially concerned with exploring his social location as a theologian. He does not show uncritical devotion to any of his formidable teachers or influences: Paul Tillich, Reinhold Niebuhr, Karl Barth, and a host of others. Nor is he regarded as a theological spokesperson for particular issues of social justice and political import.

It is important to highlight approaches that Hall does *not* exemplify because, stated positively, these are terms that have been used to describe many of his esteemed friends and contemporaries. Indeed, one might well think it extraordinary that Hall has garnered a dedicated following without embracing a school, label, social location, cultus, or issue, the self-identifications that are often *de rigueur* for attracting an audience. If anything, Hall explicitly eschews ideological impulses in theology, even as he sympathizes with and vocalizes support for many so-called liberal or progressive directions in theological thought and political action. Without being a gadfly, he defies efforts to pigeonhole his thought, at times locating himself somewhere between Barth and Tillich!

For Douglas John Hall, "interpreting for his own time and place the very core of the faith" is the key to his vocation as a theologian. That is to say, the particular theological issues to which he has given special attention—suffering and the theology of the cross, stewardship, the disestablishment of the churches—fall under the umbrella of his concern for contextuality in theological thought. He writes in a *Christian Century* article, "I think I was among the first to employ this by-now-overworked term in theological discourse,"[3] and it is his work on contextuality that arguably is his chief, and most original, contribution to the discipline. Contextuality is what shapes and conditions all those other, aforementioned concerns; nearly every one of his books touches on this matter, even when its primary focus is some other topic. Describing the responsibility to interpret the core of the faith for this time and place, he writes,

> . . . it cannot be done without daring to think that one has grasped, in some authentic sense the character of one's own epoch, one's own *Sitz im Leben* or zeitgeist, one's own context or historical moment. . . . It is no theology that merely announces what was said and done in the past—what questions people asked in the Middle Ages, what answers theologians gave in the sixteenth century, or what concerns are held by Christians living in some other part of the world. Yes, theology has an indispensable historical component. But to become theology, not just historical doctrine or religious erudition, Christian

thought must have been pierced to the heart by the pathos of the human condition *here* and *now*. (2005:23)

Hall's concern for context is distinct from contemporary theologians who conceive of contextuality in terms of social location—that is, they assert it is the theologian's conscious engagement with his or her own geographical location, race, ethnicity, gender, sexual orientation, and so forth that is the primary context for shaping one's theological constructions. Hall is hardly unaware or inattentive to his social location but, rather than self-consciously privilege social location, which puts the theologian first, he insists on the preeminence of *theology*—and thus to that "core of the faith." To understand why this is so, it is important to look at his personal biography.[4]

Biographical Sketch

Born in 1928 and raised in the village of Innerkip near Woodstock, Ontario, Hall left his secondary schooling at age sixteen to take a one-year course at a local business college in order to help support his financially strapped family; he was the eldest of six children. He soon found work in the business office of the local newspaper, and four years later was admitted to the Royal Conservatory in Toronto to pursue music composition and piano performance. But a year later he sensed the call to Christian ministry and was admitted to the University of Western Ontario on a probationary basis because he lacked a high school diploma.

Despite these precarious educational beginnings, Hall's academic success generated offers of graduate study from the most prestigious theological institutions in North America. He opted for Union Theological Seminary in New York City, where his teachers included such luminaries as Reinhold Niebuhr, John Coleman Bennett, and Paul Tillich. He met Karl Barth, one of his early theological heroes, when the great Swiss theologian came to the United States on a lecture tour. Hall also crossed paths with the likes of Phyllis Trible, Frederick Buechner, Malcolm Boyd, Walter Brueggemann, Edward Farley, and Rhoda Palfrey, who would become his wife in 1960, as well as international figures like M. M. Thomas, V. C. Samuel, and Masao Abe.

Leaving Union Seminary in 1960 (and receiving his Th.D. from there in 1963), he served for two years as pastor to a United Church of Canada congregation in northern Ontario, and then was called to teach at the newly established University of Waterloo in southern Ontario. In 1965 he was appointed to the MacDougald Chair of Systematic Theology in St. Andrew's

College at the University of Saskatchewan, in Saskatoon, before moving finally in 1975 to McGill University in Montreal as professor of systematic theology.

Hall was launching his teaching and writing career during a time of enormous political, cultural, and theological ferment. Books such as Jürgen Moltmann's *Theology of Hope* and J. A. T. Robinson's *Honest to God* were roiling theological and church circles, even as the feminist movement, the sexual revolution, and student protests against the Vietnam War were overturning academic and political practices and institutions. These seminal works and events helped shape Hall's thought, moving it beyond the assumptions of his seminary education and early teaching efforts. Despite an initial resistance, he writes,

> I realized after four or five years that my students had a point: theology made in Europe, however beautifully and persuasively articulated, cannot be promulgated in Canada or the United States as though it were immediately applicable, with perhaps only a few local illustrations.
>
> I began to see how imperceptibly I, though thoroughly a child of this "New World" myself, had been swept into the powerful narrative of European Protestant neo-orthodoxy, so called. My own nation's geography, history, sociology, politics and culture had played a very small part in the evolution of my Christian understanding. What had occurred in patristic, medieval, Reformation and modern Europe had had a greater voice in my theology than had the struggle of my own ancestors for a place in the sun. Like most North American writers and preachers, I had borrowed my theology ready-made from the sufferings of others.[5]

Thus, as Hall began to pursue writing and publishing as part of his theological vocation, one can see him contending with his theological mentors and heroes, breaking from Karl Barth—or at least the later Barth, whose *Christian Dogmatics* seemed to Hall too closed a system for the times—and embracing more closely Tillich, with whom he had earlier struggled, as well as Niebuhr. The theme of Hall's first book, published in Japan, *Hope Against Hope* (1971), anticipated the first of his books to receive wide attention in the United States, *Lighten Our Darkness* (1976). The subtitle used in both books was *Towards an Indigenous Theology of the Cross.* That reiterated modifier "indigenous" highlights the emphasis on contextuality as the driving force behind his thought, even as the theology of the cross supplies his theological hermeneutic. (He frequently cites Jürgen Moltmann's statement that the theology of the cross is the "key signature" of the whole of Christian thought.)

For the next decade, Hall's many books would focus heavily on two other key themes. First, in *The Steward: A Biblical Symbol Come of Age* (1982/90); *The Stewardship of Life in the Kingdom of Death* (1985/88); and *Imaging God: Dominion as Stewardship* (1986), he rethinks stewardship for a post-Christendom age. His reframing of this classic Christian topic relates directly to his second major theme, the disestablishment of the churches (as in, for instance, 1980's *Has the Church a Future?* and 1989's *The Future of the Church*). He applies the theology of the cross directly to issues of theodicy in *God and Human Suffering: An Exercise in the Theology of the Cross* (1986), which proved to be one of Hall's most widely read books. Together, these books proved popular with theological faculties, pastors, as well as general audiences and thus helped establish him as a favorite lecturer at seminaries and churches in the United States.

In 1989, Hall launched one of the most ambitious theological publishing projects of the final decades of the twentieth century: a three-volume systematic theology published with the common, overarching subtitle *Christian Theology in a North American Context*. The first volume, *Thinking the Faith*, focuses on theological method, and is Hall's most extended and in-depth exploration of the place of contextuality in theological thought. It is here that he works out most explicitly how Christian theological ideas and traditions derived primarily from northern Europe change when they are set within the context of the United States and Canada. The content and implications of Hall's argument are further developed in the trilogy's second and third volumes, *Professing the Faith* (1993) and *Confessing the Faith* (1995). These latter books look more specifically at classic theological topics such as the Christian doctrine of God, anthropology, Christology, ecclesiology, mission, and ethics.

Many reviewers misunderstood *Thinking the Faith* when it first appeared, arguing that a book on theology "in a North American context" should naturally examine the diversity of contemporary nonwhite, non-European theologians. They were puzzled when Hall deliberately focused on the admittedly mostly white-male European heritage shaping Western Christian thought in North America, and some were angered by his relative inattention to feminist thought, African American religion, and liberation theology. But Hall was guilty of neither oversight nor ignorance. Rather, he was arguing that such critical examination of our "immigrant" theological roots within the North American context is essential if we wish to construct theologies fit for postmodern Christians in an era of disestablishment, diversity, and pluralism, while remaining true to the cross of Christ. Thus, *Thinking the Faith* is arguably the pivotal book in Hall's catalog, the volume most essential to understanding his overall theological project.

Although one does not detect great shifts in his thought over the years, his books do demonstrate how his key concerns adapt specifically to the events, movements, and cultural circumstances contemporaneous with the time of their writing. For instance, in *Lighten Our Darkness*, written in the mid-1970s, he examines the theology of the cross in the light of Watergate, Vietnam, nuclear threats, and the communist bloc. Later, in *The Cross in Our Context* (2003), Hall analyzes the theology of the cross in light of the 9/11 terrorist attacks, the Iraq and Afghanistan wars, American imperialism, the collapse of the communist state, and the climate crisis. Both books offer a common understanding of the cruciform nature of Christian existence, but one refracted through a changing context.

Following completion of the trilogy, Hall's subsequent books have been shorter and more thematic, including several collections of essays and lectures, such as *Bound and Free* (2005) and *Waiting for Gospel* (2012). One notable exception is *Why Christian? For Those on the Edge of Faith* (1998), in which Hall attempts a Christian apologetics through the conceit of a quasi-epistolary dialogue between a searching student and his theology professor. Here we see Hall as he is best known to many of his readers, as a beloved mentor gently and unapologetically prodding his protégés to deliberate, disciplined theological thought. One of the reasons Hall is so popular with pastors and many mainline seminary professors is his profound respect for his audience; he has a way of making his reader feel smart without ever stooping to cheap flattery or overt ingratiation. It is clear that his humble roots prompt him to identify deeply with his interlocutors in the churches.

Organization of This Book

In highlighting the role of contextuality in Douglas John Hall's theological project, I in no way discount those concerns for which he is best known, most particularly the theology of the cross or disestablishment of the churches. Indeed, many recognize him first and foremost as a "theologian of the cross" or a "prophet of disestablishment," and discount the place of contextuality relative to those. Hall surely does not immediately embrace those labels, though he cannot utterly disavow them either. But his concern for theological accountability always drives him back to the *hic et nunc*, to that which conditions how we read.

Thus *Douglas John Hall: Collected Readings* does not attempt to be a comprehensive overview of his thought or publishing oeuvre. It focuses solely on his works published by Fortress Press. Moreover, it does not aim to summarize his ideas or serve as a general introduction to them. Rather, it attempts to show how contextuality governs Hall's principal concerns, particularly the theology of the cross and church disestablishment. Thus the readings put fresh attention on his theological method. While several excerpts from *God and Human Suffering* and *Professing the Faith* emphasize theological "content," many more are taken from *Thinking the Faith, Confessing the Faith,* and *The Cross in Our Context,* which highlight the contours and implications of disciplined theological thought, and press readers to devote themselves more wholeheartedly to that discipline. The excerpts have been lightly edited, mostly to remove irrelevant phrases, add clarifying words, or delete unnecessary notes. The introductions to each piece attempt to put the excerpt in context, both within Hall's thought, and within the plan of the book itself. In some cases, the selections may leave the reader with more questions, in which case I hope they will feel prompted to revisit—or discover anew!—the original works, which remain fresh years beyond their publication. The closing bibliography provides a complete list of Hall's published books, but does not include articles or volumes to which he was a contributing author.

Part 1, "Thinking and Knowing: Theology as Contextual Practice," explains why such disciplined theological thought remains crucial in our day and age, considers the relationship of theology to faith, and begins to describe the context in which we are engaging it in that praxis. The closing chapters in this first section examine the relationship of thinking to knowing, revealing the various "modes" of knowing and how such knowing is part and parcel of our spiritual being.

Part 2, "The Crucified God and the Suffering Christ: Theology in the Context of the Cross," delves more explicitly into theological topics, such as the place of tradition, the theology of the cross, the relationship of suffering between God and Jesus, and soteriology.

Part 3, "Ecclesiology and Ethics: Theology in the Context of Disestablishment," looks more closely at the place of the church in our modern context, and the purpose of disestablishment. Hall has always asserted that theology and ethics are inseparable, and so the final essays in the book focus on that relationship, closing with a chapter on the Christian vocation as "Stewards of the Mysteries of God."

Together, these excerpts also paint a selective, impressionistic portrait of one of the most beloved and influential North American theologians of the past forty years. Douglas John Hall's accomplishment is marked by the gracious eloquence with which he urges us to think—carefully, deliberately, expansively—and thus to bring our own contextualized voices to proclaim the gospel that the church—and the world—has been waiting for. He has gifted us with an enduring method for doing that essential work, and a canon that deserves our ongoing attention, for its concerns will surely not disappear anytime soon.

ACKNOWLEDGMENTS

I am grateful first to the staff of Fortress Press for their invitation to edit this volume, and for their efforts to help me gather the various chapters from books whose original electronic files disappeared many years ago. In particular I thank Will Bergkamp, Scott Tunseth, Marissa Wold, and intern Kate Crouse, who handled the heavy lifting of scanning many, many pages of aged books into word-processing files, with sometimes amusing results. Michael West, who acquired and edited many of Hall's Fortress Press books, was a helpful conversation partner as I tried to discern the direction and focus of this collection. My partner, Robert Huberty, not only gave me editorial tips on making the introductions more engaging, he also listened patiently as I talked about what I was reading and my struggles to form this into a volume worthy of its subject and worthwhile to serious students of his discipline. The ecumenical lectionary study group I attend weekly here on Capitol Hill in Washington, D.C., was also both forbearing and encouraging as I repeatedly brought Hall's thoughts to bear upon the week's preaching texts. For this and their ongoing friendship, this marvelous group of pastors, priests, and laity deserve mention by name: Rose Beeson, David Deutsch, Bill Doggett, Rebecca Justice ("Justi") Schunior, Cara Spaccarelli, Andy Walton, and Michael Wilker.

And last, but most importantly, I thank Douglas John Hall himself for his friendship and inspiration as well as his eager support for my taking on this project. I was a novice editor at Augsburg Books in 1988 when I was asked to proofread *Thinking the Faith*; if any book has had a life-changing effect on me, it is this one. Even though I had over six years of seminary training in my back pocket, Hall's work was in many ways the real beginning of my theological education. Over the next ten years, Hall and I worked together on several more books, and in the process we formed a friendship that has now lasted for a quarter-century. I am deeply grateful for the legacy he leaves us, to which I feel compelled to return again and again.

Notes

1. Quotes from Hall's books will be cited with in-text references, using the publication year and pages, and keyed to the bibliography that follows the final chapter.

2. Hall's latest book, *What Christianity Is NOT: An Exercise in "Negative" Theology* (Eugene, OR: Cascade, 2013), which he says will be his last, explicitly addresses the apophatic approach.

3. Douglas John Hall, "Cross and Context: How My Mind Has Changed," *The Christian Century* 127, no. 18 (September 7, 2010), http://www.christiancentury.org/article/2010-08/cross-and-context.

4. For more extensive autobiographical sketches, see *Bound and Free*, esp. ch. 1, "A Theologian's Journey: Where I Have Been" (32–50); "Cross and Context"; and idem, *The Messenger: Friendship, Faith, and Finding One's Way* (Eugene, OR: Cascade, 2010).

5. Hall, "Cross and Context."

PART I

Thinking and Knowing: Theology as Contextual Practice

1

Invitation to Theology

Hall opens Thinking the Faith, the first volume in his systematic trilogy, with what he calls "A Summons to Contextualization," and moves from there to ponder "The Meaning of Contextuality in Christian Thought" and how we might discern our current context. Here, however, leading with Hall's argument for the necessity of theological thought in the first place will help us understand better how he understands the nature of such thinking and how it functions in Christian life—particularly in a context that is often content to try to eschew the disciplined practice of theological thought. For Hall, theology is in many ways a reactive discipline, which must respond to the needs of the moment, which are often recognized in the questions being asked. As he writes just prior to this selection, "Perhaps theology will become possible only when we have developed a distaste for answers, i.e., when we have come to know better the depths of the questions. Yet for those who are prepared for such an exposure to our context, there exists today—and in a way unique in our history—not only a summons but also an invitation to theology" (1989:169).

Source: Hall 1989:169–77.

SOCIAL EXTREMITY/THEOLOGICAL OPPORTUNITY

The old adage that "man's extremity is God's opportunity" has been applied in questionable and even despicable ways—for instance, by "evangelists" who operate on the principle that you must first break the human spirit and then offer it the "balm of Gilead." If the proverb is understood in a descriptive rather than a prescriptive sense, however, it makes considerable sense. It is the same kind of sense Jesus made when he said, "Only the sick have need of a physician." Those who are in good physical and mental health, with money in the bank, a promising career, and two lovely children, may have some additional comfort from the "consolations of religion"; but they are not likely to cry out for help, forgiveness, salvation! The same thing may be said of societies. Surely the reason why Christianity has operated in our society primarily as a "culture religion" (Peter Berger), a blend of religious denominationalism and nationalism, is that few have needed it for what it really is—a religion of radical grace. The dominant culture of our society has felt no overwhelming need for the realistic reading of the human situation that is presupposed by a theology of radical grace.

It does not lie within the power of the disciple community to *engineer* such need in its host society. However fervently prophetic spirits within the disciple community may wish for the kind of depth and vitality of faith and theology that great social transitions have often evoked, they cannot cause such transitions to occur. All the admirers of the pivotal Christian figures of such epochs (Augustine, Aquinas, Luther, the young Barth), who want the world always to be ready for such ringing messages as those epochs called forth—all such persons are frustrated, because the world will move at its own pace. Its crises cannot be ordered up by prophets! In this sense, theology is dependent upon society, upon the world. It has to take what is there, what is given in the moment, including what may indeed be hidden and should be brought to light. It cannot manufacture shakings of the foundation.

But when such shaking occurs; when in the course of society's unfolding the thinly veiled chaos that its "culture" just managed to cover begins to show through and the ancient unrest of *homo sapiens* is no longer contained by the careful conventions of the ages, *then* the disciple community must prepare itself to wake from its dogmatic slumbers, reach more deeply into the resources of its tradition than it has been accustomed to do, and see what can be found there for the healing of the nations. In *this* sense, the extremity of a human community is the *opportunity* for a new attempt at telling God's story of the world.

THE SITUATION

This, I believe, is how we should regard the context in which we find ourselves on this continent today. The worldview out of which our society has evolved has reached its extremity. It is a theologically evocative situation, and for our province of the universal church it is the first situation of this kind that we have experienced. For that reason alone it is difficult enough, of course. Christians in North America have known hardships—for instance, the hardship associated with the settlement of this vast continent. But on the whole ours has been one of those "peaceful" epochs, during which a certain domestication of the faith occurs. Religion has been a comforting and comfortable thing, imbibed in the quietness of small-town Sunday mornings.

Moreover, we are the products of an age which thought that upheavals of the kind that is now brewing in our midst were things of the past. There are, to be sure, tens of thousands who would be content to have us play our conventional role as pacifiers and alleviators of the little pains of existence. The disciple community is always under this temptation in such times—to preach "peace, peace, where there is no peace" (Jer. 6:14; 8:11). But, on the other hand, there are problems of such enormous proportions that no amount of pacification will make them disappear: the crisis of resources and the environment, of population, of economic and social injustice, of violence, of the threat of nuclear war, and other specific issues. . . . And beneath and in them all there is a monumental shift in the mood of our society at large which, if we have ears to hear, sounds like the clear announcement of human corporate extremity. This mood is articulated, not only by historians, anthropologists, political philosophers, but in widely circulated literature and the most accessible forms of art. Even Hollywood movies are no longer "Hollywood." A popular journalist describes the mood shift in the following provocative statement:

> The entire American proposition has been built upon the premise of ever expanding opportunity, upon a vision of the future as a territory open-ended and always unfolding, upon ascendant history. "We are the heirs of all time," said Herman Melville. What happens if the future seems to be closing down, to be darkening? If nature, first an enemy to be subdued and then a resource to be exploited, is now an endangered victim of technology? The classic American salvation (clear the land! build! disembowel the mountains!) threatens to invent damnation . . .
>
> All the furniture of the American myths is being dismantled and stored. Psychologically, if not yet financially, a stale air of foreclosure has wafted around . . . , Americans feel themselves sliding towards triviality, and beyond that toward an abyss that might swallow the whole experiment like a black hole . . .
>
> . . . Many of them remain sunnily confident. But the old interpretations, the old American theology, no longer works very well. Americans invented themselves in the first place, and then were interminably reinvented by the rest of the world. Perhaps more than most peoples, they need to possess an idea of themselves, a myth of

themselves, an explanation of themselves. It is time for them to start inventing and imagining again.[1]

The sense of dislodgment is also the tone adopted by Sydney E. Ahlstrom in the final chapter of his monumental work, *A Religious History of the American People*. "The Turbulent Sixties," he writes, witnessed "the sense of national failure and dislocation [which] became apparent to varying degrees in all occupational groups and residential areas."[2]

> Americans, whether conservative, liberal, or radical, found it increasingly difficult to believe that the United States was still a beacon and blessing to the world. . . . One could only be assured that radically revised foundations of belief were being laid, that a drastic reformation of ecclesiastical institutions was in the offing, and that America could not escape its responsibilities as the world's pathbreaker in the new technocratic wilderness.[3]

For a historian of American religion and life, Ahlstrom concludes, to contemplate our society in the sixties and beyond is to consider "a time of calamities."[4] To reflect on the American experience in such a time, "whether as amateur or as professional," is to know oneself to be "a pioneer on the frontiers of post-modern civilization."[5]

The question that this situation poses for thoughtful participants in it is whether the "postmodern" society that may come to be will be worthy of the lofty term "civilization." Many of our contemporaries have already concluded in their hearts, if not openly, that we are witnessing the inauguration of a new barbarism in the Western world generally.[6] There is indeed a growing feeling among us—almost a popular expectation—that neither the meek nor the strong will inherit the earth, that "of these cities, all that will remain is the wind that blew through them" (Bertolt Brecht). For the extremity of modernity is not like the extremities of earlier civilizations. We can pull down the whole world along with us into the abyss.

Apocalyptic, it has been said, is the mother of religion.[7] Christianity not only finds human endings evocative, but it dares to announce that real *beginnings* are made only at the point where endings are experienced, or anticipated. Can this "logic of the cross" (Reinhold Niebuhr) apply also to the extremity of our civilization? Let us attempt to explore that possibility, and to see what it may hold for us by way of detailing the character of the invitation to theology implicit in our context.

ALTERNATIVES FOR A SOCIETY IN DESPAIR

The life of a society undergoing the collapse of the system of meaning upon which its laws, institutions, moralities, and unspoken values have been based presents to those within it a choice among three rudimentary *types* of response: they can capitulate to the hopelessness entailed in such an event; they can refuse to admit its occurrence; or they can look for ways to be realistic without becoming immobilized.

(*a*) The first alternative is the most fearful, and for that reason is less common a response than the second. For it means the more or less conscious abandonment of hope. At least hope *for the society* is abandoned, and whether personal hope can be sustained without the support of a system of meaning which transcends the individual is a matter of grave doubt. That a significant number of people in our society have found it impossible to maintain hope for their personal destinies is borne out by recent statistics concerning suicide (especially the rate of suicide among the young) and mental collapse. That the line between personal and social hope is at best a fine one is verified by the necessity of regarding very private matters like suicide and mental health as special *social* phenomena on account of their frequency. The resort to self-destruction, whether through deliberate acts or in more subtle ways, is only a final resort—the tip of a very large iceberg. It must be assumed (and most social analysts do assume) that a much larger number of persons in our society experience the same symptoms which lead their contemporaries to such drastic "solutions," though not in as acute forms . . .

Hopelessness of an advanced and pathological sort also expresses itself in the violence and vandalism marking our cities, highways, and entertainment world. But the most common and most fearsome dimension of this phenomenon is neither overt self-destruction nor the spoliation of the environment, but a pervasive cynicism.

Cynicism can be adopted by the respectable citizen who would not go in for graffiti on the surfaces of public monuments, and for whom madness and suicide are constitutional improbabilities. The cynic does not even have to voice his or her cynicism. The cynic can carry on nicely within the officially optimistic society, mouthing the necessary platitudes and going through the motions of business, professional, and social life. An unspoken convention in the public realm anticipates and even encourages these attitudes in persons. The open articulation of cynicism is contrary to the social code. But the *living* of cynicism is a well-documented phenomenon in North America today. Its most familiar garb is shallow hedonism: the jogger who concentrates on physical well-being and whose devotion to the cult of the body has the convenient bonus of squelching persistent questions of the mind; the tourist who is able to find Calcutta and Mexico City "interesting"; the spectator who can observe life's pathos with eyes as dry as the protective glass covering of his television screen. It is very difficult to gauge the extent and the consequences of the covert cynicism in our society, for we have come to expect so little.[8] One can glimpse something of its hold upon us, however, if one compares a typical Hollywood film of the 1940s or 1950s with most films produced in North America today.

(*b*) Overt hopelessness, however, requires a certain daring, and therefore the second alternative open to persons in communities whose foundational beliefs are being eroded is without question the more common among *us*: repression and the nurture of false hope.

Repression, as psychiatry since Freud has shown, is an automatic defense mechanism of the human psyche. The subconscious intuits dimensions of reality that the conscious mind cannot bear, and stifles them. It is natural and necessary.[9] We could not bear "naked exposure to anxiety," said Tillich (in the context of his discussion of the Christ's cry of dereliction from the cross).[10]

Yet the repressive mechanism, however necessary, can never be utilized without cost; and when it is adopted as a way of coping with very sizable segments of experience, perhaps even the most decisive segments, then the cost is very great. A person or a collectivity that draws upon the repressive mechanism consistently and deeply is probably expending more emotional energy in this activity than in any other. For it requires a great deal of psychic energy to blot out unpleasant or unbearable realities.[11]

Part of this psychic energy is expended on exaggerated tokens of belief in that which is not spontaneously believable, but which must be believed in order to reduce the threat of what *is*. The cost of such an exercise is not just the draining of personal and public resourcefulness which it necessarily entails. It is also the forfeiture of the quest for truth, and the suppression of things (and persons) through whose presence unwanted truth continues to assert itself.

This alternative is the apparent choice today, not only of a vociferous minority in our society—persons and groups whose noisy insistence upon the retention of old values and ways is too ostentatious to be true; it is the pattern of many who are less demonstrative—perhaps, indeed, "the silent *majority*." It is not accidental that observers representative of a wide variety of expertise have dubbed our society "the repressive society." Nor is it accidental that this alternative becomes more popular the more conspicuously the "old" values and ways are harried by events. The advocates of this path have become increasingly defensive, one-sided, and militant. Repression under intense pressure expresses itself in suppressive activities. The consequences are seen today in the face of governments that promise a speedy return to rhetorical virtues and verities, are elected to office on the strength of these promises, and then can make their promises appear practicable only by adopting economic and international policies that further victimize oppressed minorities and endanger the peace of the larger human community.

And by outright lies! The way of repression pursued as a way, especially on the part of a collectivity, is the tacit decision that false hope is better than no hope. And in theory this may be so. But false hope defending itself as true can be as dangerous as cynical despair in retreat from public life. It is in fact only so far removed from cynicism as the subconscious is from the conscious mind. As a temporary measure, it may seem to succeed. But under continued and prolonged duress, its truly cynical aspect will become increasingly visible.

(c) Neither of these alternatives commends itself to a reflective and responsible Christian faith. The Christian can recognize in certain types of hopelessness (for instance, in the classical pessimism of a Camus) the advantage of a preference for realism. But because the realism of the pessimist or the cynic is no longer goaded by any persistent vision of the good, its honesty about evil is finally, literally, meaningless. The second path—repression and the pursuit of unworthy hopes—wards off the threat of meaninglessness and despair temporarily, but only at the expense of truth. The faith it saves is "bad faith" (Sartre), and its hope is cheap hope—hope as a shield from life. The first alternative makes it necessary to dispose of the questions of being and meaning which *will* assert themselves and can be silenced only through prolonged and concentrated effort; the second makes it necessary to lie about the world in order to believe in "the System." The one courts the night, the other throws up artificial light before it has really experienced real darkness.

This leaves a third alternative, and we can infer from the analysis of the first two, *via negativa*, what requirements it has to meet: It must provide the possibility of being truthful about what is happening in the world, to the self, to society. Persons must be able to feel a certain permission to orientate themselves towards the truth. At the same time it must hold out the prospect of a good which transcends this present reality, and permits the spirit to explore it without falling victim to ultimate despair.

Both of these things are necessary: The human spirit needs, on the one hand, the freedom to be truthful about the perceived realities of its condition. Not only for our intellectual integrity, but for our mental and moral sanity, "we have to be as hard-headed as possible about reality and possibility."[12] Without this capacity, the spirit soon finds itself mired in the constraints of self-deception. Wisdom, as we have already agreed, admits the necessity of repressing some of the truth for the sake of health, even for survival. But if repression becomes the habitual manner of coping with the most conspicuous realities of one's world, then it destroys the self whose happiness it has been invoked to protect. This, surely, is as true of the macrocosm as of the microcosm. A society which silently commits itself to a kind of programmed indifference toward the sorts of life-and-death issues confronting us today in the Western world is engaged on a course of self-destruction. "A society based on happiness cannot survive; only a society based on truth can survive."[13]

On the other hand, the human spirit cannot survive either on sheer unalloyed honesty about the world—especially when "the world" presents bleak and futureless images of itself. In times of social extremity, such truth as thrusts itself into our conscious or subconscious minds can more readily be oppressive and damning than liberating. "There are ultimate problems of life which cannot be fully stated until the answer to them is known. Without the answer to them, men will not allow themselves to contemplate fully the depth of the problem, lest they be driven to despair."[14] The human spirit, then, needs not only the freedom truthfully to contemplate what *is*, but the courage to believe that such contemplation can help to bring about a better state. Indeed, unless they are able to trust that something good can come of truthfulness, most men and women will always prefer half-truth or downright falsification—not, of course, as a conscious ploy, but intuitively, recognizing that the truth which under certain conditions "makes free" under other conditions makes one infinitely sad, or simply terrified.[15]

Thus the invitation to theology sharpens itself and becomes more explicit. It becomes a kind of echo of Job's invitation to his religious advisors, "Oh, that I knew where I might find him!" (Job 23:3). Is it possible to find in this faith tradition a foundation for the spirit and mind to discover the courage to be open to the negating and overwhelming realities of our societal extremity—but without despair? How, under the conditions of a society sliding toward triviality, shall we sustain an orientation toward the truth (*Wahrheitsorientierung*) that is also in some authentic way a theology of hope?

Notes

1. Lance Morrow, "On Reimagining America," *Time* (March 31, 1980), 38–39 (emphasis added).

2. Sydney E. Ahlstrom, *A Religious History of the American People*, vol. 1 (New York: Doubleday, 1975), 609.

3. Ibid., 617.

4. Ibid., 618.

5. Ibid., 620. See also Harvey Cox, *Religion in the Secular City: Towards a Postmodern Theology* (New York: Simon & Schuster, 1984).

6. E.g., Alasdair MacIntyre concludes his book, *After Virtue: A Study in Moral Theory* (Notre Dame: University of Notre Dame Press, 1984), 263, by noting that in many respects there are parallels between our society and the decline of Rome. "What matters at this stage is the construction of local forms of community within which civility and the intellectual and moral life can be sustained through the new dark ages which are already upon us. And if the tradition of the virtues was able to survive the horrors of the last dark ages, we are not entirely without grounds for hope. This time however the barbarians are not waiting beyond the frontiers; they have already been governing us for quite some time." See also Jacques Ellul, *The Betrayal of the West*, trans. Matthew J. O'Connell (New York: Seabury, 1978).

7. In this connection, see J. Christiaan Beker, *Paul's Apocalyptic Gospel: The Coming Triumph of God* (Philadelphia: Fortress Press, 1982).

8. In his disturbing book *The Culture of Narcissism: American Life in an Age of Diminishing Expectations*, Christopher Lasch writes: "After the political turmoil of the sixties, Americans have retreated to purely personal preoccupations. Having no hope of improving their lives in any of the ways that matter, people have convinced themselves that what matters is psychic self-improvement: getting in touch with their feelings, eating health food, taking lessons in ballet or belly-dancing, immersing themselves in the wisdom of the East, jogging, learning how to 'relate,' overcoming the 'fear of pleasure.' Harmless in themselves, these pursuits, elevated to a program and wrapped in the rhetoric of authenticity and awareness, signify a retreat from politics and a repudiation of the recent past" (New York: Norton, 1978), 4–5.

9. "We cannot repeat too often the great lesson of Freudian psychology: that repression is normal self-protection and creative self-restriction—in a real sense, man's natural substitute for instinct" (Ernest Becker, *The Denial of Death* [New York: The Free Press, 1973], 178). Humanity, whose nature and destiny it is not only to be mortal but to be vulnerable to the debilitating consciousness of mortality, must repress a great deal simply in order to function. "The animals don't know that death is happening to them. . . . They live and they disappear with the same thoughtlessness. But to live a whole lifetime with the fate of death haunting one's dreams and even the most sun-filled days—that's something else. . . . I believe that those who speculate that a full apprehension of man's condition would drive him insane are right, quite literally right. . . . 'Men are so necessarily mad that not to be mad would amount to another kind of madness' [Pascal]" (ibid., 27).

10. Paul Tillich, *The Courage to Be* (New Haven: Yale University Press, 1952), 39.

11. "We know very well that to repress means more than to put away and to forget that which was put away and the place where we put it. It means also to maintain a constant psychological effort to keep the lid on and inwardly never relax our watchfulness" (G. Zilboorg, "Fear of Death," *Psychoanalytic Quarterly* 12 [1943]: 467).

12. Becker, *The Denial of Death*, 280.

13. C. F. von Weizsäcker; see *Die Zeit drängt: Eine Weltversammlung der Christen für Gerechtigkeit, Frieden und die Bewahrung der Schöpfung* (Munich and Vienna: Carl Hanser, 1986).

14. Reinhold Niebuhr, *The Nature and Destiny of Man*, vol. 2 (New York: Scribner's, 1964), 75.

15. "Why are groups so blind and stupid?—men have always asked. Because they demand illusions, answered Freud, they 'constantly give what is unreal precedence over what is real.' And we know why. The real world is simply too terrible to admit; it tells man that he is a small, trembling animal who will decay and die. Illusion changes all this, makes man seem important,

vital to the universe, immortal in some way. . . . The masses look to the leaders to give them just the untruth that they need" (Becker, *The Denial of Death*, 133).

2

Theology and Faith

In part 1 of Thinking the Faith, Hall describes "The Disciple Community" by way of explaining the nature of contextuality and the necessity of disciplined theological thought to the church, that is, the disciple community. As he notes, "Discipleship is disciplined thought about the faith." Speaking more specifically of theology as confessional, he writes, "Christian theology is an undertaking of the church, and its mandate is to help the disciple community to make its rightful confession in the world" (1989:69, 107). In part 2, then, Hall looks more specifically at the discipline of theology, and how it relates to seven specific elements: faith, the Bible, doctrinal traditions, experience, prayer, the church, and the world. In explaining the relationship of theology to faith, Hall employs the apophatic approach to describe two alternatives that must be avoided in the doing of theology: fideism and subjectivism. Considering this relationship here allows us to think about the discipline of theology at the very point at which most of us first engage it and the delicate balancing act this requires of us.

Source: Hall 1989:248–57.

DEFINING FAITH

Clearly, faith is an important component of theology. We implied this when we said earlier that theology is *confessional*. One *thinks* the faith because one believes, or is at least curious about belief. But what *is* belief? What is *faith*?

It is necessary, given our North American context in general and the ecclesiastical-religious dimension of that context in particular, to distinguish faith from two distorted conceptions of it. The one is objectivistic and intellectualistic; the other subjectivistic and experiential.

For certain Christian groupings on this continent, to "have faith" means to accept a body of doctrine. One assents to the truth of this doctrine on the authority of the church, or of a creedal tradition, or of the Scriptures, or of some less easily defined (perhaps charismatic or "spiritual") authority. The doctrine may be called "revealed truth"; it may be quite explicitly stated in propositional form; or it may be expressed more nebulously in symbolic, liturgical, or moral practices. Some of those for whom faith means the submission of the mind to established *doctrina* are able to express the content of their belief verbally in almost mathematical formulas and theory; for others, the acceptance of Christian teaching is articulated in more symbolic ways, indicative of a readiness to accept the authority of an impressive tradition and the guardians thereof. The first type is more characteristic of the Protestant and the second of the Catholic appropriation of this interpretation of what faith means. Both, however, share the assumption that faith is assent (*assensus*) to religious truth.

At the opposite extreme, faith is conceived in terms of a subjective mood, a belief-ful attitude. It is not *what* one believes that is important here but the posture of believing as such. President Eisenhower was exemplifying this view of faith when he said, "I don't care what a man [*sic*] believes, only that he believes." If the former type of faith is associated with doctrinal and ecclesiastical "orthodoxy," the latter belongs to circles of less doctrinaire pietism, especially the vaguely liberal and often sentimental sort of pietism which is so prevalent in North American neo-Protestantism.

Against both of these popular conceptions, I am assuming here that faith is a category of relationship. It means in the first place "faith *in*." It is fundamental trust (*fiducia*). At least at the linguistic level, both of the classical ecumenical creeds of the church (the Apostles' and the Nicene) assume this relational posture when they begin with the words, *Credo in* . . .

There is a subjective as well as an objective component in the relational understanding of faith. It is objective in that the "object" of one's *credo* lies outside the self: *Credo in Deum*. It is subjective in the sense that belief involves the decision and commitment of the self: *Credo—I* believe. Faith is what occurs, from the human side, when we know ourselves to be encountered, judged, and accepted by the gracious God. While the object of our faith (God) is different from the objects of ordinary human faith in other persons who have shown themselves trustworthy, the faith itself is not essentially different. When I say that I have faith in my wife, or my friend, or my lawyer, I am using the word "faith" in basically the same way as when, as a Christian, I say that I have faith in God. What is intended is simply: *trust*. Luther would only use the German word *vertrauen* (to trust) as a synonym for faith (*glauben*).

Whether Faith Is a Prerequisite for Theology

The question posed by the juxtaposition of faith and *theology* is whether faith is a necessary *prerequisite* for the doing of theology. The answer to this question depends a good deal on one's preunderstanding of faith, and therefore we have tried first, in a preliminary way, to establish the typical alternatives present in our context. If faith means assent to a body of doctrine, whether in explicit propositional form or more symbolically conceived, it will almost certainly follow that faith will be regarded as an indispensable prerequisite for theology; for in this view, apart from such assent one does not have access to the truths he or she is to explicate, or one's apprehension of those truths would be by definition false or incomplete.

At the other extreme, where faith does not refer to religious data but to a mood or posture (belief-ful-ness), faith may or may not be regarded as a prerequisite to theology; for those assuming this mindset, theology is usually of only secondary importance, and therefore the tendency of communities embracing such a position is to be very open with respect to conditions requisite to the doing of theology.

But what if one insists that faith refers neither to religious data nor to a spiritual attitude, but to a response of trust within the context of relationship with God? How does such a view of faith relate to the theological enterprise as such? We may best arrive at an answer to this question if we proceed *via negativa*. Two alternatives should be avoided:

(*a*) *Fideism:* The suggestion that theology can be undertaken only by believers, and at every level of analysis, is an aspect of Christian fideism, i.e., the assumption that the human intellect is incapable of attaining true knowledge of God. While this position may sometimes be found intermingled with a relational understanding of faith (*fides*), as in the Barthian school, it is normally heavily informed by the dimension of knowledge (*gnosis*). A strict discontinuity is perceived between those who are recipients of revealed truth and those who are not. Without the *gnosis* which is the primary datum of theology, it is naturally impossible to do theology.

But if faith is not the acceptance of revealed truth but trust in the revealing God, the matter comes out differently. For then the lines of demarcation between belief and unbelief, believer and disbeliever, are at least more fluid than fideism supposes.

And, in the post-Christendom, religiously pluralistic situation of our present context, must we not in fact conclude that these lines *are* fluid? On the one hand, the demise of imperial Christianity has left Christians in a state of continuous decision making. It cannot be assumed that one is Christian by birth, or even by a dramatic and once-for-all rebirth. Again and again the line between belief and unbelief is traversed. It is indeed for most of us an invisible line. Absolute distinctions between the states of belief and unbelief are no longer convincing. No biblical verse is more existentially meaningful to post-Constantinian disciples of the Christ than the prayer, "Lord, I believe, help my unbelief!" (cf. Mark 9:24). And while we may sometimes lament the fact that a pure, unalloyed, and childlike belief seems impossible for us, we are on the whole grateful that such a model of belief is no longer mandatory—is no longer, at any rate, the measuring stick by which authenticity of membership in the disciple community is tested. For not only does it seem beyond us in a world "come of age" (Bonhoeffer), and perhaps beyond mature humanity under any conditions, but it appears indistinguishable from mere credulity.[1] What we encounter in the Scriptures, both in the long saga of ancient Israel and in the story of the Christ and his original disciples, is not credulity. It is a trust which struggles with existential distrust and a faith which is in dialogue with doubt. It is faith and not sight (Heb. 11:1). There is a Judas in Peter, too. Knowing, therefore, something of unbelief within ourselves, and of the strangely *positive* contribution of such unbelief to the life of belief, we are skeptical of a fideism which assumes unquestioning assent to allegedly revealed knowledge as the precondition for authentic theological reflection.

At the same time, the plurality of religious, quasi-religious, and humanistic alternatives present in our context also contributes to this experiential refutation of the fideist position. We no longer exist in a world where "Christianity," whether genuine or merely official, holds almost exclusive sway; where concepts and concerns can be identified as "Christian" only because people lack knowledge of the beliefs and practices of other religious traditions; and where "non-Christian" is itself a category defined by Christians. Daily we encounter ideas and deeds, persons and movements, whose ethos lies outside the Christian fold, but whose reality is unmistakably reminiscent of our own. As we find disbelief and doubt within ourselves, so we are apt today to find something akin to what we mean by belief and depth of understanding within others who do not profess *our* creed.

We may find such in those who do not, some of them, profess any overtly religious creed! Many of the persons whose ideas we have employed in the preceding section of this study, for example, either claim not to be believers in God or are more or less silent on the matter of theistic belief. Yet we have learned much from them—from Becker and Arndt and Machoveč and many others—not only about the truth of our common human condition, but also about matters expressly associated with Christian teaching: Jesus, the meaning of suffering, courage, hope, and so on. Can one really draw hard and fast distinctions between theological work emanating from an explicit faith in the triune God and less irrational but perhaps more profoundly theological work? One of the more neglected parables of Jesus might be helpful here: quite possibly there are Christians who assert their willingness to work in the theological vineyard of their Lord but do not actually *do* the work; and perhaps there are also others who refuse to hear any specifically Christian command, yet in the end perform what is in a real way theological work (see Matt. 21:28-32). Such parables should not be confined to the realm of deeds only!

This is not to say that faith—an explicit faith in Jesus Christ—is necessary to theology. It is simply to warn against a false way of making the distinction. Confining relevant theological workmanship to those who confess belief in the Christ means ruling out a great many persons who throughout the history of the church as well as in our own time contribute very substantially to our understanding of the faith, though they themselves remain outside or on the periphery of the community of belief. All of us who confess the name of Jesus as Christ do so in language that is full of indebtedness to persons who did not or do not believe in Jesus Christ. One name alone is enough to secure the point: Plato.[2] Instead of making the distinction in such a way as to eliminate a priori this whole company of co-workers, let us say that theology done from within a specific faith stance within the disciple community differs from the theological or paratheological work of the co-workers in that it involves the decision to commit oneself to an explicit confessional posture, and to attempt to interpret the world from the perspective of that commitment.

It is in this sense, I believe, that we should understand the famous dictum of St. Augustine, *Credo ut intelligam* (I believe in order that I may understand). Belief here means trust in God, in the sense discussed above. But it is not simply a vague openness to deity or transcendence; rather, it is a trust directed toward *that* God who has been revealed in the Christ and is testified to by the Scriptures and the apostolic tradition. *Trusting* God is the prerequisite for the disciplined attempt to understand the meaning of this God's self-manifestation. When Augustine goes immediately to say, "Indeed, unless I believed I should not understand," he is not intending to assert (as fideism is wont to do) that nonbelievers can understand nothing of God or the things of God. That would be wholly inconsistent with Augustine's essentially Platonic epistemology. He is saying, rather, that apart from belief—that is, apart from the relationship of faith in God—fullness of comprehension is impossible; for this relationship, and the trust that characterizes it, is the existential basis of theology. It would be at least as impossible to achieve depth of understanding outside the relationship with God as it is to achieve such depth apart from personal relationship with another human being about whom "knowledge" is claimed . . .

(b) *Subjectivism:* The second position that should be avoided in the attempt to understand how theology and faith are related may be called subjectivism or religious introversion. It consists in the supposition that faith *by itself* is sufficient for the theological task, or that theology is essentially if not exclusively the articulation of personal religious feeling. In reality much more is involved in the discipline of theology than my personal belief. Belief is, we have said, requisite for depth of understanding: to understand is to stand under, to know oneself to be dependent upon the outcome of that which one beholds. A sustained concentration upon the claims of the tradition requires the kind of struggle of spirit and intellect which can occur only if the outcome truly matters. But faith is oriented toward something, Someone, beyond itself: it is faith *in*. A faith which manifests an inordinate interest in itself is a contradiction in terms.

All the same, precisely this contradiction is a conspicuous factor in our particular context. Traditional forms of pietism, aided and abetted by modern psychologism and the flight into subjectivity on the part of generations doubtful of objective meaning, have ensured that Christianity in our society should become a popular vehicle for a type of self-preoccupation. The narcissism that secular persons manifest in the care of their bodies or their houses is equally evident in the religious whose attention is devoted to the cultivation of their own private spirituality.

In such subjectivistic circles of Christian spirituality, it is faith itself that is celebrated: the fact of faith, the experience of faith, the ecstatic or agonizing moods and emotions belonging to the life of faith. Theology then becomes the articulation of "my" or "our" faith—our spiritual ups and downs, our religious feelings, our prayer life, our fellowship, our life "with Jesus" or "in the Spirit," etc. Everything is centered in the believing subject or subjects.

It is interesting to note that St. Paul, who has more to say about the meaning of faith than any other writer of the Newer Testament, never speaks of faith in the first person, except rhetorically. Nor does he ever tell his readers about his famous "Damascus road experience," the subsequent model for so much that has transpired along these lines! The account of the "conversion" of Paul comes to us from the Luke-Acts tradition. Only once does Paul himself give himself as it were the luxury of personal religious reflection—and that in a cloaked way and in a context full of irony (2 Corinthians 12). Similarly, John Calvin never provides any detail about his "sudden conversion." This is because faith, for Calvin as for Paul, however indispensable, is no end in itself but only a means. It is that gift of God which enables us to see—to *glimpse*, rather, "as through a mirror dimly" (1 Cor. 13:12)—what is infinitely more worthy of contemplation than our own selves, and apart from which our self-knowledge is stunted and neurotic.

The habits of doctrine impel us to name that upon which faith opens the human spirit to God, but that convention does not do justice to Paul or to biblical religion generally, because, while faith is *in* God, what this existential trust enables us to "see" is much more inclusive than what the word *God* normally signifies. Trust in God opens us to a whole new world. It is a window onto all of reality. Everything appears in another light—our own kind, the other creatures, nature, work, time, and (yes, of course!) God.

Precisely this *end* of faith, namely, its reorientation of the human spirit *toward the other*, is why a faith which finds *itself* interesting is a contradiction in terms. The intention of that grace which makes faith possible is exactly to *free the self from preoccupation with itself and to turn it toward the other*—God, the neighbor, the world. *Theology*, which faith enables and which can only, at depth, be enabled by faith, is the attempt of the mind that is being liberated from the prison house of self to give expression to the great universe of meaning that through the grace of belief in God it has begun to intuit. Subjectivistic theology has mistaken the means for the end, the window for that upon which the window allows us to fix our gaze.

FAITH AS LOVE IN UNDERSTANDING

To say that faith "opens us" to the other is in reality not yet linguistically strong enough. It would be more accurate to say that faith *drives us* towards the other—or, to state the matter still more accurately, that faith expresses itself *in love*.

In a rudimentary and halting way, we know what this means at the level of Christian ethics: "Faith without works [of love] is dead" (James 2:17). As Luther put it, "Faith is a living, restless thing. It cannot be inoperative. We are not saved by works; but if there be no works, there must be something amiss with faith."[3] But, especially in our North American context, where knowledge and its pursuit has been conceived in almost exclusively instrumentalist terms, we hardly ever think of applying the dictum that faith expresses itself in love to the human quest for understanding—for *sophia* (wisdom). To theology! Yet precisely that is what we shall have to discover if we are to meet the challenge and invitation to theology implicit in our context. What *theologia* and *philosophia* have in common is love—the love of truth.[4]

Unlike the word *philosophy*, *theology* does not contain within itself, etymologically, the idea of loving wisdom or truth; but the reality which for Christians lies behind the word *theology*, namely, the God whose love liberates humanity for newness of life, is as insistent upon the quest for understanding as were the ancients who coined the term *philosophia*. In this, Jerusalem and Athens are at one. Their ways of understanding are different, and what is understood is different, but for both of these founding traditions of our civilization the quest for understanding is of the essence—is a matter of love. Both therefore stand in fundamental opposition to modernity, for which the goal of understanding is not love of truth but mastery of the world.

Faith in the God who "is love" (1 John 4:8) moves us to love the other—namely, everything upon which the window of faith opens. The same faith which expresses itself in the love of God and the neighbor impels us to embrace the totality in our understanding. It is this desire for consummate understanding that informs the theological quest—and often, because the desire ceases to be nurtured by love and becomes instead the product of concupiscence and pride, turns to pretension. Theology as the Queen of the sciences! Yet these distortions are distortions of an impulse that inheres in Christian theology as such—the impulse to know what is loved; and no false modesty should deter the disciple community from exploring that impulse, especially not when such assumed modesty is a cloak for intellectual sloth or plain anti-intellectualism, which is too frequently the case in ecclesiastical circles in our context.

Faith expresses itself in the will to comprehend just as insistently as in the will to perform good deeds. The intellectual impetus emanates from the same love, the same thrust-beyond-self, as does the ethical. In fact, the one without the other is inevitably a reduction of itself. It is this insight that has again surfaced in the language of *praxis*, where the deed and the thought are inseparable.

That faith manifests itself in the love of understanding is the meaning of Anselm of Canterbury's famous phrase, *fides quaerens intellectum*, faith seeking understanding. *If it is truly faith*, Anselm insists, it will seek to understand what is believed. We ought to hear the verb "to seek" here in an almost aggressive sense. Like the defiant boldness of a lover, the doing of theology entails a search that will not be deterred by the many obstacles that are certainly in the way of it. The quest into which, by faith, we are initiated is no mild inquiry ("research") but a determined and unquenchable passion to comprehend. It *will know*! It will not be satisfied with simplistic answers to difficult questions. It will be like Jacob wrestling with the angel until dawn, until he is blessed and limps away from the encounter. There is a drive toward understanding built into faith itself, if it is really faith and not just sentimentality.

Of course it will never be fully satisfied! This is Paul's point about the distinction between faith and sight. Faith will not be sated until it has been replaced by sight. That is the eschatological dimension in faith, the hope that keeps the disciple community striving for genuine wisdom and makes it forever dissatisfied with whatever wisdom it thinks it finds though this eschatological dissatisfaction (we must immediately add) held in a dialectical tension with the contentment to which we drew attention earlier, the calm of a discipline which knows from the outset its finitude.

. . . The greater share of those who have been designated Christians throughout the sixteen centuries during which Christianity has served successive empires as their official cultus have not found it necessary resolutely to strive for understanding. Even clergy could be found (in pockets of Christendom they still exist) who could boast that they had no interest in theology. Let us be forthright: what calls itself faith, under the conditions of culture religion, does not necessarily drive to understanding. On the contrary, it may well function to quell ordinary intellectual curiosity and offer people thought-free tranquility! Given the formative character of such a long history, it is not surprising that still today theology can be regarded by many Christians as an esoteric and merely professional activity, conducted on the periphery of the religious life.

But in the diaspora situation in which the earliest Christians lived, which (as we have seen) has again become the norm in many parts of the *oikoumene*, and which promises to become the standard form of the church of the not-so-distant future everywhere, the situation is very different. In that situation, people are not pushed into the Christian community by unthinking forces of social custom, and faith is no merely "natural" response to existence. It is gift and struggle. It is a matter of decision—not a once-for-all decision, but one that must in a real sense be renewed daily, and in the presence of much evidence to the contrary.

Such a context brings us once more to the authentic character both of faith and theology. To commit oneself to the God of the gospel in our present context is to know from the start, and to be made to know again and again, that *the discipline of understanding is inherent within the faith decision.* Without theology, that is, without a continuous, determined, and studied quest for comprehension on the part of the whole people of God, the church of the future will not be able to subsist. In [contemporary] society . . . , the disciple community does not have a choice between faith-by-itself and faith-with-theology. If there is faith in such a context there will be a disciplined passion to understand; and the age-old distinction between "theologians" and "ordinary Christians" will be terminated at last, or at least interpreted in strictly functional terms. For in that context *all* Christians must in some measure become theologians. How else could they give a reason for the hope that is in them (cf. 1 Peter 3:15)? Why else would they remain?[5]

Notes

1. See my article, "Beyond Cynicism and Credulity: On the Meaning of Christian Hope," *The Princeton Seminary Bulletin* 6, no. 3, new series (1985): 201ff.

2. Many Christians from Augustine to C. S. Lewis are conspicuously Platonic in their articulation of what they believe. George Grant . . . describes himself as being "above all a lover of Plato within Christianity" (*Technology and Justice* [Toronto: Anansi, 1986], 90).

3. Quoted by Roland Bainton in *Here I Stand: A Life of Martin Luther* (New York: Abingdon, 1950), 331.

4. On the relation of faith, love, and truth, see Emil Brunner, *The Divine-Human Encounter* (London: SCM, 1944).

5. I am in complete agreement with Edward Farley when he writes that "[e]ducation in the truest and most serious sense of that word (*paideia*) needs to be introduced into the church" (*Theologia* [Philadelphia: Fortress Press, 1983], 196). Behind this assertion lies Farley's profound analysis in an earlier work, *Ecclesial Man: A Social Phenomenology of Faith and Reality* (Philadelphia: Fortress Press, 1975), of what he calls the "reality-loss" in present-day manifestations of Christian faith, which he identifies "largely" as "an intellectual problem." [For the complete text of this note, see Hall 1989: 257.]

3

Defining Contextuality

Moving backwards in Thinking the Faith, we return to near the beginning of the book, where Hall makes the statement that drives this entire project: "Christian theology is contextual by definition." It is interesting to note here Hall's appeal to two of his greatest influences: Karl Barth and Paul Tillich. Hall has said that his awakening to his own context prompted in him "second thoughts about Tillich, the greatest challenger of my seminary musings,"[1] whereas, by contrast, Barth had earlier held more appeal for him. Here, Barth is only named once, relative to his statement about the false split between ethics and theology. But later in the section, Hall refers to Germany in the 1930s, when Barth was involved with the Confessing Church movement against Nazism; it is this period of Barth's work that Hall sees as most contextually driven, whereas later, beginning with Christian Dogmatics, Barth seemed less relevant and more inclined to "timelessness" (a quality he ascribes to both conservative and liberal readings of the tradition)—the false belief that "theology is the study of an assemblage of basically immutable truths—theologia eterna" (1989:71). This passage helps to dismantle such an understanding. Instead, having established the necessity of theology to Christian discipleship and its relationship to Christian faith, we can perhaps hear better Hall's assertion that "Faith is the grace-given courage to engage [the everyday, complicated, beautiful, ugly, and threatened world of our experience, when and where we are]. Theology is a disciplined reflection and commentary upon faith's engagement. Theology therefore is contextual, and that by definition" (1989:74).

Source: Hall 1989:75–93.

DIMENSION OF THE WHOLE TASK

To claim that Christian theology is by definition contextual is to insist that the *engagement* of the milieu in which theology is done is as such a dimension of the doing of theology. The attempt to comprehend one's culture—to grasp at some depth its aspirations, its priorities, its anxieties; to discern the dominant ideational motifs of its history; to distinguish its real from its rhetorical mores—all this belongs to the theological task as such. For example, if it is true that the recurrent *leitmotiv* of Canadian imaginative literature has been that of "survival," as Margaret Atwood has claimed in her perceptive study of the subject,[2] then such a theme cannot be ignored by the Canadian theological community if it intends seriously to pursue theology and is not interested merely in church doctrine and conventional morality. Or again, if "narcissism" accurately describes a way of life that has become prevalent in middle-class America,[3] this is as significant a datum for the discipline of theology as it is for social psychology. . . . [T]o speak about "the First World" . . . is already to speak *theologically*. Such data are not just adjuncts to theology, or preparatory aspects, which can quickly be attended to in an introduction. Nor are they matters that the theologian can happily leave to practical theology or ethics. Karl Barth was at least anticipating the concerns of present-day *praxis* theology, when in the foreword to his first volume of *Church Dogmatics*, he wrote: "Ethics so-called I regard as the doctrine of God's command and do not consider it right to treat it as otherwise than as an integral part of dogmatics, or to produce a dogmatics which does not include it."[4] The split between theology and ethics is not only a false one, but one which has contributed much to the reputation for timelessness earned by a doctrine-centered theology that did not speak both from and to its historical context.

To insist upon the contextual character of Christian "systematic" thought, then, is to claim that at every juncture—in its Christology as in its ethics, in its eschatology as in its pastoralia—Christian intellectual reflection entails serious dialogue with the existing situation of one's world. When this dialogical quality is lacking at the level of the church's doctrinal reflection, no amount of practicality and concreteness at the level of "applied Christianity" will make up for the lack. Indeed, a quite obvious reason why, in North America especially, there has been a perennial rift between theological theory and practical religion, making it necessary for the latter in its various forms to become virtually independent of academic theology, is that what theology we have had is conspicuously deficient in just this dialogical quality. You cannot begin the task of doctrinal speculation on a strictly theoretical plane and expect it to evolve quite naturally into a discussion of the most practical issues besetting church and society.

A Conscious Element

The fact is, of course, that in a certain sense all theological thought reflects its context, intentionally or not. We are, after all, creatures of time and space. There is no such thing as noncontextual human thought, including theological thought.

What there is, however (and therefore it is necessary to engage in such a discussion as this), is a form of thought, which *does not regard itself as contextual*, and which for complex reasons is treated by whole segments of the populace of this continent as if it were contextually neutral. What there *is*, to be specific, is a very extensive and deeply entrenched but no less contextual tradition in theology—a tradition comparatively unified, variations on well-rehearsed themes; a tradition, namely, which took shape within the historical experience of a specific people, the Europeans. This de facto contextual theology actually does echo the many and diverse movements of evolving European civilization—as one would expect it to do. To follow, for instance, the development of the doctrine of the atonement, is to be introduced to rudiments of the long history of Europe's anxieties and its ways of coping with those anxieties. The concept of humanity as *imago Dei*, so important for Christian anthropology, is indecipherable without some awareness of the various stages of European humanity's self-understanding. As Hendrikus Berkhof has said, "By studying how systematic theologies have poured meaning into Genesis 1:26, one could write a piece of Europe's cultural history."[5] But, for many reasons . . ., this European theological contextuality in several typical forms (Augustinian, Thomistic, Calvinistic, pietistic, and others) has been permitted to conduct itself throughout the inhabited earth as if it were *not* a thoroughly contextualized statement of the meaning of Christian faith, but something transcendent of history and therefore entirely universal and portable. It could be transplanted in the soils of all the other continents without undergoing any significant metamorphosis—without undergoing the *kind* of metamorphosis, for example, that Christian belief underwent in its translation from the Near East into the "pagan" cultures of ancient and early Medieval Europe itself. And if the soils of those other continents were not hospitable to this Euro-Christian transplant, then European *soil* could be taken abroad as well! (Here we could conduct a very long excursus on the history of Christian missions.)

We shall return to this observation, for more than one comment has to be made in this connection. For the present, our reference to the Europeanization of the Christian theological tradition is intended only to illustrate something of what is at issue in the theological principle of contextuality. It is to point up, namely, that theology will be (in a certain sense of the term) "contextual," even when it does not intend to be so; even when it is considered quite independent of its context. But the observation also illustrates the fact that the most problematic theology, from the standpoint of a faith, which wishes to be in a *purposive and conscious* dialogue with its sociohistorical context, is a theology which hides its de facto contextuality under the guise of universality. Such a theology not only discourages the continuous engagement of the human situation by the representatives of the gospel of Jesus Christ, it carries with it assumptions about the human situation which are either not concretely accurate or (as has frequently happened) are quite patently false. Nor is this inaccuracy and falsehood ever merely harmless. For it functions in the raw environs in such a way as to preclude struggle, on the part of the Christian community, with the actualities of those new environs. It functions, that is to say, as *ideology*.[6]

The lesson being taught us today by the deceptive ideological functioning of religion in so many parts of the world (including our own) is that theological activity must involve a quite *conscious and deliberate* engagement of the context, and must develop a critical awareness of the way the church's witness actually operates in its host society. We cannot assume that this will happen automatically. Unless it is intentionally guarded against, what seems to occur as a matter of course in church doctrine is the perpetuation of religious and other presuppositions which deter and deflect the thrust of the gospel towards a more direct encounter with existing social conditions. In short, the habit of ideological eternalism must be countered today by an explicit demand for historical concreteness and topographical particularity in all theological reflection.

THE CONTEXT AS CONTRIBUTOR TO THEOLOGICAL DISCOURSE

We have said that contextuality in Christian theology means that the social situation in all of its uniqueness informs the reflection of the Christian community, and that it must now do this in a deliberate manner. But to leave the matter there would be to invite the suggestion that the compulsion towards contextualization implicit in the gospel of incarnation and cross would be satisfied if, from its side, the Christian community were to be a sensitive and observant spectator of its historical setting, its habitat. And that would be unfortunate.

For the notion of a Christian disciple community seeking in its solitude to comprehend its historical moment does not yet capture the meaning of contextuality in theology. We have already used the word "dialogue" to describe the relation between the theological community and its social context, and we must be clear that this means *dialogue!* This dialogue is not merely a conversation conducted within the precincts of the *koinonia*. It is not a matter of the disciple community, or some part of it, researching its "world," determining its real condition, and then responding to its own world-analysis from the side of its Christian belief. Such an approach has frequently characterized the various traditions of Christian apologetics, and while it is certainly to be preferred to theological stances which feel no responsibility even to reflect upon the world's condition, it is not yet genuinely contextual in nature. True contextuality means the initiating and nurturing of a *dialogue* with one's culture, a genuine give-and-take, in which the world is permitted to speak for itself, and in which therefore the Christian community opens itself to the *risk* of hearing things that it had not anticipated and to which it cannot *readily* respond. In other words, in a fully contextual approach to its subject, the disciple community sees its sociohistorical habitat, not only as a field to be investigated but as a partner in the investigation—and therefore as contributor to the theological task itself.

What the disciple community has to learn from its context—what it can only learn *from* its context—is something of the spirit of the times (*Zeitgeist*). The dominant mood of an age cannot be discerned only by taking note of current events—a thing which can be done without very much actual contact with the world, particularly in these days of rapid communications. To discover "what time it is" (undoubtedly the most difficult aspect of the whole vocation of theology),[7] the Christian community has to have access to those sources within its host culture which can inform it, not only about what is *occurring* in the world, but about what these (external and internal) occurrences are doing to the human spirit. This knowledge is always in some considerable measure hidden from faith, for the basic and obvious (yet subtle) reason that faith as such *protects the believing community from raw exposure to such knowledge.* Faith itself gives us a sense of meaning that is able to cushion our spirits from the shock of events—events which may well constitute for large numbers of our contemporaries the very stuff out of which despair, cynicism, and nihilism are fashioned. Because it is the vocation of the church to address itself in particular to those who are crushed by life, it is necessary for the disciple community always to achieve a comprehension of reality as it is experienced by such persons. The poor, the unemployed, the handicapped, those whom society ostracizes because they deviate from "the norm," the powerless—such persons are important to the community of belief not only because they are those in and through whom the Christ is concretely present to us, pleading for our care, but also because, without them, we shall almost certainly fail to understand "what time it is."

To speak concretely: It is possible for Christians in the First World today—if they can be delivered from the general state of apathy by which our societies are enthralled—to learn a great deal about the desperate state of famine in parts of the continent of Africa. Quite apart from any contact with those who suffer from these conditions of drought and exploitation, North American churches can (and do) amass large dossiers of information, and, moreover, engage in impressive acts of charity. But all of this can occur without any significant growth in understanding our world, or even this one dimension of the total world-*problématique*. In order to approximate genuine understanding of the context in question, we must open ourselves to those who live at the center of it, its victims. Such growth in understanding can only be attained through participation . . . , that is, through a process of recognizing existentially something of our own responsibility, as First World citizens for this Third World condition—in other words, through a painful confrontation with the realities *of our own specific context.*

An African Christian has stated this in terms more explicit than any that I might devise:

> People are not finally developed by other people. People must develop themselves. Villagers should be talking together to decide what they want and how to get it. This may mean bringing in outside animators for a limited time, people who can help villagers identify their needs and work out appropriate ways of satisfying them. If necessary villagers can consult with people in neighbouring areas, or other Third World countries. . . . [But] the biggest job of the church of the North is in the North, because that is where the problem lies. You must put pressure on the transnational companies to change their exploitative practices, and pressure on the government regarding aid and military spending. Eight hundred billion dollars is spent annually on arms. If the North can be humanized, development is possible.[8]

A theology which knows that it is not time*less* will always need to know what time it is *hic et nunc*. Unless it knows this, this Christian community will not know what form of the Word is appropriate—what is address, gospel, *sermo*. But the Christian community never can know this unless it comes to know—rather intimately—those who are oppressed by the silent but powerful principalities governing the here and now.

CHRISTIAN IMMERSION IN THE CONTEXT

As the above illustration concerning the North/South economic disparity makes very plain, however, the disciple community's understanding of its context requires not only that it invite representatives of the world to enter into the theological dialogue, but also that it should itself be prepared to go out into the world. It is, as Tillich has said, a matter of "participation." Really to *know* one's context means to participate *in* it—not only physically and factually, which in any case is unavoidable, but consciously, deliberately, reflectively. The dialogue with one's world which belongs to Christian faith and theology not only involves an ongoing discussion with those who are able, through their experience or skills, to represent the world; it involves personal immersion in one's world.

To put it in other words, becoming Christian means simultaneously becoming *contemporaneous*. Christian belief may indeed lift one, in some real sense, out of immediate preoccupation with the world. Without this, Christians would lack the *perspective* that is necessary for understanding their "here and now," as well as the prospect of *willing* their participation in it. But it is for the sake of participation that we are lifted out; it is in order to achieve a new status of being "in" the world that we are denied the right to be, simply, "of" it.

We are of course speaking here of a process—an *ongoing* process, and one which cannot be undertaken without pain. When Paul Tillich writes that "the really serious problem for us is participation,"[9] he is not thinking only of an academic or intellectual problem. He is speaking existentially about the suffering that belongs to the community of faith as a whole, and specifically to those within it who are called to the vocation of intensive theological thought. The liturgical paradigm of this pain is baptism, and it is in this sense that the word *immersion* should be heard in the subhead of this section. The disciple community can only become what it is called to be as it is again and again (sacramentally) immersed in the problematic of its context, plunged beneath the threatening waters of the present and impending future, and caused once more to recover its hope in response to the realities of that concrete situation. Tillich has elsewhere poignantly illustrated what such participation means to the theologian, and why it is "the really serious problem for us." The theologian, he writes in the introduction of the second volume of his *Systematic Theology*,

> must participate in the human predicament, not only actually—as he always does—but also in conscious identification. He must participate in man's finitude, which is also his own, and its anxiety, as though he had never received the revelatory answer of "eternity." He must participate in man's estrangement, which is also his own, and show the anxiety of guilt, as though he had never received the revelatory answer of "forgiveness." The theologian does not rest on the theological answer which he announces. He can give it in a convincing way only if he participates with his whole being in the situation of the question, namely, the human predicament. In the light of this demand, the method of correlation protects the theologian from the arrogant claim of having revelatory answers at his disposal. In formulating the answer, he must struggle for it.[10]

Participation is the *sine qua non* of communication: "Where there is no participation there is no communication." If Martin Luther had not been compelled to experience at first hand the terrible anxiety that gripped his age—the anxiety of an almost inescapable judgment by an almost implacable God[11]—he would never have discovered the gospel of "justification by grace through faith." As we know from Luther's biography, however, that discovery cost him a great deal of personal anguish—and not just at the outset of his career. The *Anfechtungen* (times of utter abandonment) remained permanent, periodic features of his Christian life.

Perhaps it is the threat of such abandonment that has deterred the church so consistently from exposing itself to the always-new circumstances of the present and, conversely, has attracted it to past expressions of the faith, which were tried and true. What the Christian community forfeits by adhering so steadfastly to its own established conventions, however, is precisely *communication*. Without communication there is no *gospel*, for gospel cannot be identified with doctrinal treasures hidden under the bushel of ecclesiastical rites and the in-language of professional churchmanship. Gospel means the Word proclaimed and heard—proclaimed in full awareness of what it has to engage, heard therefore as the living Word (*viva vox Dei*) and as good news.

With important exceptions, the Christian church throughout the ages has not distinguished itself by the appropriateness or good timing of its proclamation. It has been much more adept at *profession* than at *confession*.[12] Frequently, perhaps habitually—it has substituted *didache* (teaching) for *euangelion* (gospel), *doctrina* for *theologia*. On account of its commitment to entrenched systems of belief, it has often announced reconciliation where judgment was called for, and exhortation to repentance where sheer acceptance and mercy would have been more fitting. It has comforted the comfortable and chastised the miserable, liberated the oppressors and laid upon the oppressed the additional spiritual burdens of duty and divine decree. It has leaped into Asia with "glad tidings" fashioned in the English countryside, and it has offered sixteenth-century doctrines of salvation for twentieth-century sinners. Persuaded of the universal relevance of an *evangel* made in Europe, missioners both militant and gentle "persuaded" the native people of South and North America to adopt Christianity. With overwhelming regularity, the majority of the missioners manifested no concern whatsoever for the contexts of the indigenous peoples, not even bothering, often, to learn the rudiments of their languages. But *evangelism*, as distinct from indoctrination or the sheer imposition of religion, assumes on the part of the evangelized something approximating freedom of choice. "Where there is no participation there is no communication"—and must we not face the fact that a great deal of what the church militant has considered communication with the world has in reality been a very one-sided affair? Something more aptly designated, perhaps, "transmission"? Because of its position of power under the conditions of Constantinianism, the church did not really have to communicate with the world; it could simply announce, declaim, and legislate. It must be asked very seriously by those who reflect upon the Christian past today, and upon the impact of that past on continuing theological ethical practice, whether the *gospel* in the strictest sense of the term has ever been more than a minority possibility and reality—the exception to the rule.

Context, Form, and Content

The distinction between a contextual theology and a theology which either *is*, or is readily employable *by*, ideology can be illustrated by the juxtaposition of two statements which come out of that period of awesome clarification in Western history to which again and again those who seek to comprehend our civilization have had to turn: Germany in the 1930s. At that time, the dean of the Berlin cathedral, Heinrich Gruber, founder of the so-called *Gruberbüro* (an organization which helped Jews and other threatened persons escape from the Nazis), said very simply: "The gospel in our time is that Jesus Christ was a Jew." The full impact of this statement can only be appreciated, however, if it is contrasted with a contemporary pronouncement: Hitler's so-called *Reichsbischof*, Ludwig Müller, sensing a certain questioning of his orthodoxy, coyly declared, "I can accept all the creeds."

A theology which does not help the church to discern, out of the great riches of its tradition, the *appropriate* word—"the Word from the Lord"—inevitably functions as an ideational construct within which Christians may find refuge from history, and which therefore lends itself to the support of the status quo, whether intentionally (as was certainly the case with the *Reichsbischof*) or by default. The statement of Gruber illustrates that it is precisely immersion in the context, including especially solidarity with the victims of society, that gives the theological community the prospect of such discernment.

To state this in more traditional terms: contextuality in theology means that the *form* of faith's self-understanding is always determined by the historical configuration in which the community of belief finds itself. It is this world which initiates the questions, the concerns, the frustrations and alternatives, the possibilities and impossibilities by which the content of the faith must be shaped and reshaped, and finally confessed. Conscious and thoughtful involvement of the disciple community in its cultural setting is thus the *conditio sine qua non* of its right appropriation of its theological discipline. It cannot be a mere spectator of the world's life, like the man at the window in Elie Wiesel's *The Town beyond the Wall*,[13] who watched as the Jews of his city were rounded up for deportation. The church can become a theologically alive and obedient disciple community only as it permits its thinking to be receptive to and re-formed by the realities of its world.

The statement that the form of the faith is to be determined by the worldly context of the Christian community perhaps suggests that there exists a given content which is in some sense independent of the forms that it assumes historically. Such a suggestion, taken at face value, could lead back to the very assumption that we have been trying to dislodge in this analysis, namely, that there is some immaculate expression of the faith, preceding every concrete articulation of it, and that it is the church's task to protect and preserve this "pure gospel" in the midst of the historical flux. The declaration that theology is by definition contextual, however, precludes entertaining such a notion. For our argument implies that it is a condition of the theological task as such and from the outset of the church's pilgrimage through time that it occurs under the laws of time and place and is inevitably marked by the particularities thereof. I am in complete agreement with Gordon D. Kaufman when he writes, "Theology is human work: theology is done by men and women for human purposes and . . . serves human purposes and needs . . ."[14] More than that, theology is always *theologia viatorum post lapsum*.[15] Even of the Scriptures this must be said—and it has been said now for more than a century, despite the fact that on this continent in particular most of what is claimed for the Bible by Christians seems impervious to this scholarship. God may be above the *fluxus*, but all of our statements about God are conditioned. They are conditioned not only by our historicity but also by our limited intelligence and our sinful inclination. Even if they were not conditioned by these creaturely factors, they would be conditioned by the God about whom they are made, who, being transcendent Person, does not permit description or definition but only *testimony* (the real meaning of the commandment against graven images).

There is then no eternal "text"—no *theologia in se* (ideal theology as distinct from actual theological work)—which it is our duty as Christians to interpret for our context, no abiding "content" that permits itself to be shaped, reshaped, and perhaps inevitably misshapen in response to the molds that time provides. There are only historical testimonies to a Presence, to events in which this Presence was experienced as being very near ("with us"), and to utterances which helped and still help to locate and illuminate the mystery of which this Presence is the center.

On the other hand, the rejection of theological absolutes which could form themselves into an eternally true body of doctrine does not mean that we are forthwith landed into a foundationless relativism. The insistence that any attack upon theological absolutes must imply the abandonment of theology to sheer relativism or capricious historicism is not only a non sequitur; it is usually a spurious argument meant to protect some reputed orthodoxy. Besides flying in the face of what Tillich called, with justification, "the Protestant principle,"[16] such an argument overlooks the fact that the most common situation both in faith and in life generally is neither one which can boast of the possession of absolute certitude nor one which is entirely without intimations of truth, but rather one in which the unknown factor (whether that refers to religious mystery or simply the moving edge of time, the mystery of future) is counterbalanced by certain aids which, while they are by no means flawless, at least serve to insulate and to guide. The "content" side of theology should be understood in this sense. While Christians cannot legitimately indulge in the empty boast of those who claim the possession of absolutes, neither are they wholly abandoned to the spirits and whims of the moment. They have inherited a tradition, a "common heritage" (Robert McAfee Brown). None of this heritage—not the Holy Scriptures themselves—can be assigned the status of the ultimate. To do so would be to usurp the sovereignty of God! On the other hand, neither is it a matter of pure relativity and subjectivism. The tradition is there, and it is there *pro nobis*. It cannot be ignored, set aside, or treated at will; or rather, if this or that faction is ready to treat it in such a manner, other influences within the *koinonia* will see to it that such treatment is challenged. So long as the truth to which we wish to bear witness is bound up with a presence which, however hidden from human sight (*Deus absconditus*) reveals itself to faith within the flux (*Deus revelatus*), the testimony of those who have acknowledged and revered this presence throughout the centuries has to be taken with great seriousness. This of course applies in a special way to the original revelatory events, which though they do not immediately interpret themselves but depend upon a prophetic or spiritual event for their meaning ("Pentecost," in the Newer Testament's mode of understanding), nevertheless are inseparable from the external occurrences as such, and therefore bind us to the testimony of those nearest those occurrences, the so-called eyewitnesses.

The Scriptures and their authority in theology must become a matter for closer examination presently. For the moment we may characterize the whole of our common heritage, including these earliest and most normative testimonies, by insisting that in itself and as such *it would drive us to the specifics of our own context*.

To elaborate: We may certainly—and gratefully—admit that within this common heritage there are recurrent themes, such as the consciousness of sin, the experience of forgiveness, the sense of purpose in a world that often seems purposeless, the joy of fellowship, the hope of the faithful for a society in which justice and peace prevail, and others. But these recurrent themes should not (and when considered in any depth cannot) be turned into a hard-and-fast set of ideas, "great facts," a perennial textbook of true doctrine, *vera theologia*. Indeed, any really careful study of the persons and movements throughout the Christian centuries in whom this common heritage was most profoundly articulated (those who in fact were largely responsible for creating it) will show that it is both a rich and a flexible heritage, one which *developed* and was not delivered whole, one which evolved quite obviously in response to emerging situations in church and society. Few if any of the greatest exponents of the Christian faith (those whose names immediately come to mind when we employ the word "tradition") would ever have desired that their thought should be treated by subsequent generations of Christians as if it were perennially valid.

Most of them, we may confidently surmise, would have agreed with Tillich's statement . . . : "None of us is asked to speak to everybody in all places and in all periods." Irenaeus, Origen, Augustine, Anselm, Luther, Calvin, Kierkegaard, Schleiermacher—the very names of such persons tell us about the quite specific periods of history to which they belong, for they were all firmly rooted in their contexts.

Of course, the great thinkers of the premodern past were not *conscious* of the fact that they were being contextual. We should not expect them to have been conscious of this, for such consciousness belongs to the modern period, the period which discovered history—which discovered, that is, the impact of historical particularity upon the human perception of reality. Luther, the medieval man, did not possess this historical consciousness in our sense. He did not think of himself, therefore, as someone who was doing theology contextually. He simply believed that he was discovering God's "lively Word." Nevertheless, what made his theological work compelling was precisely the fact that, wittingly or unwittingly, he had entered profoundly enough into the problematic of his age to be able (by grace!) to express the faith in a way that could truly address that problematic.

Moreover, in order to speak to their specific contexts, these shapers of the tradition were compelled to modify, and sometimes to reject outright, the power of the theological conventions that *they* had inherited. Thus Augustine had eventually to let go of many of the Neoplatonic influences by which he had at first been enticed, which were powerfully present in his epoch, and which informed much of the Christian tradition to which he was heir. Aquinas, in turn, had to distance himself from significant aspects of the theology that had been dear to Augustine and the whole of the early Middle Ages. Luther found it necessary to rebel against the conventions of Scholasticism which, he believed, could not contain the word of the cross. Barth could only come to terms with his time and place as he let go (not without difficulty) of the liberal commonplaces into which he had been indoctrinated by the memorable teachers of the nineteenth century, Wilhelm Herrmann and von Harnack and the others. And the process continues.

In short, if we turn to the most gifted thinkers of the Christian past for our understanding of what is involved in the doing of theology, this common heritage itself drives us toward contextual thinking. What we inherit as our "blessed tradition" is no fixed, ordered, and consistent deposit of doctrine, but an astonishingly expansive and variegated story—a story sufficiently rich and nuanced to function in very different times and places *with amazing consistency!* Only, the consistency is not to be located in what the tellers of this story said so much as it is in the effects that their quite different ways of enunciating the story had upon their hearers. What is most provocative about our common heritage in its highest and most decisive expressions, in other words, is that despite the diverse and sometimes even antithetical character of their articulations of the faith, a long-range review of the history of Christian thought leaves one with the definite impression that these many witnesses have been pointing toward a single Truth. But since it is a *living* Truth, it must be testified to in a great many *differing* ways, and it can never be captured in any of them or in all of them together.

The message that we receive from this Christian past is therefore not, "Repeat what we have said!" but rather, "Do what we have done!" That is, with feet firmly planted in our own *hic et nunc*, we in our turn should look and listen for this "elusive"[17] but self-giving presence, this truth which our progenitors glimpsed but which, like the collectors of manna in the wilderness, they could not store up for future consumption. The *form* that eternal truth must assume is dependent upon the specifics of historical time. The Word is forever seeking hearers—now! "Today if you will hear my voice . . . !" Hence, theology is an always-unfinished undertaking of the disciple community. There will never be a time when the church can cease *thinking*, and this thinking will have to manifest the trait of originality as long as the Christian movement lasts and even if it accumulates, in the process, ten times the volume of tradition that it now acknowledges.

THEOLOGY AS THE MEETING OF STORIES

We may expand our understanding of the meaning of contextuality in Christian theology through the deployment of this metaphor of story. Story is in fact more than a metaphor in our time; it has become the key concept of a whole methodology. That this has occurred is directly related to our present discussion; for it is precisely because so much of the conventional language of theology too readily suggests a body of timeless information that some Christian thinkers and communicators in our period have turned (or perhaps *returned*) to the language of narration. It is a useful language, and natural to a faith rooted in the Scriptures of the two testaments. The wonder is that Christian theology could so soon and so thoroughly have evolved into conceptual and perceptive expressions which have little in common with either the historical narratives of the Older Testament and parts of the Newer, or the parabolic approach favored by the rabbi Jesus.[18]

What we encounter in the tradition of Jerusalem, especially but not exclusively in the Scriptures themselves, does not resemble a collection of theorems, dogmas, principles, truths, or philosophic arguments so much as it resembles drama, saga, narrative, story. Let us call it "God's Story of the World."[19] Like all stories, it has a beginning (a promising one) and an ending (a happy ending, as J. R. R. Tolkien rightly insists).[20] But the way from the promising beginning to the happy ending—the consummation!—is very complicated, and not simply a foregone conclusion. Presumption is thus constantly ruled out: "Therefore let any one who thinks that he stands take heed lest he fall" (1 Cor. 10:12).

The unpredictability of the course that God's story will follow is largely due to the fact that, in the meantime, another storyteller is at work. Humanity is telling its own story, improvising scenarios, creating roles for itself—for all the other creatures, too, and of course for God! The roles that humanity creates are—in the view of these witnesses to God's story—almost always *not* the roles intended for it. Humanity does not have any real aptitude for the parts that it writes for itself. Yet it seems to be perfectly at liberty to experiment very widely.

There are, of course, certain stock roles, familiar also to Athens and to most other human traditions. Two such standard roles are very common, though they are never quite the same from one moment to another (remember: we are dealing here with a *linear, not a cyclical* view of history). Sometimes humanity tells a very heroic story about itself: Prometheus-like, the human race fancies itself greater than its gods—a feat not terribly difficult, since the roles it creates for its divinities are usually underwritten! The literature of the nineteenth century is full of that particular story. At other times, the race's corporate autobiography is dismal—a genuine pathos: Man as Willy Loman. Low Man.[21] There are, however, many variations on these and other themes, and the combinations are never the same, never quite the same. History does not repeat itself, even though similarities and patterns may certainly be observed. Sin may be as old as Eden, but it appears in ever-new guises. The human creature is a consummate storyteller, a veritable Scheherazade! In fact, says a great Jewish storyteller of our time, "God created man because he likes stories."[22]

Theology lives *between* the stories—God's story of the world, and humanity's ever-changing account of itself and all things. *Theology is what happens when the two stories meet.*

It is of course the particular vocation of the disciple community to keep listening especially for *God's* story. That is the only reason for distinguishing it from any other community, any other reflective human posture. But contrary to those who think that this community has direct and unmediated access to the divine account of reality, we must insist (on biblical grounds) that it is literally impossible to hear God's story *alone*. The reason is elementary: God's story is itself always interacting with, responding to the human story! Even God, in the *Hebraic*-Christian understanding of God, must wait to find out what the strange creature who is the articulate center of creation will do, what new tale the creature will circulate about itself, its environment, its Creator.

Not that the biblical God lacks *preconceptions*! Certainly, like any imaginative artist, any good parent, the God of the Scriptures has designs for what God brings into being. But according to Jerusalem God will not *impose* God's *oikonomia* (economy) upon the creation. God will wait, react, and respond. God will take up into the divine *boule* ("plan"—cf., e.g., Acts 2:23) the (usually frustrating) acts, deeds, words, and thoughts of the creature, causing them, despite their potentiality for permanent evil, to serve the Creator's and therefore also the creation's ultimate good.

The Joseph narrative of Genesis could be regarded as paradigmatic for the *whole* story which this tradition wishes to preserve. With decidedly malevolent intent, the brothers sell their younger, favored sibling into slavery. Nothing prevents their doing this. It is their act, their decision. Yet it is finally—and therefore, says faith, also in some mysterious way originally—God's determination; for it becomes God's means of preserving the people of the covenant. "As for you, you meant evil against me; but God meant it for good, to bring it about that many people should be kept alive . . . ," Joseph tells his brothers at the end of the narrative (Gen. 50:20).

God's story of the world, then, is no fixed drama in which all of the parts have been written and from which there can be no deviation,[23] but an ongoing tale, the comprehension of which makes it mandatory for those who try to follow it to sustain an equally active attempt to comprehend the *human* story. Unless they know something of the latter, in all the uniqueness of the here-and-now, the disciples will not understand God's story (which may be part of the reason why the *original* disciples were perplexed by Jesus' teaching and in particular by his determination to go the way of the cross). For, contrary to certain prosaic interpretations which have their spiritual origins elsewhere than in Jerusalem, God does not have the same "old, old story" to tell, regardless of "the context." God's word to Solomon in all his pomp is not simply a rephrasing of God's word to sick, defeated Saul. The postexilic prophets have a message significantly different both in detail and in tone from those who predicted Israel's captivity. Jesus had something quite different to say to John the beloved disciple from what he had to say to the impulsive and demanding Peter (John

21:20f.). The author of the Apocalypse has conspicuously variant messages from "the Spirit" to the churches addressed in chapters 2 and 3. One could go on.

Similarly, the disciple community must always struggle to discern an appropriate testimony to God's story. A theology which continues addressing itself to nineteenth-century industrial Prometheanism long after Western humanity has cast itself more characteristically in the role of Willy Loman is not only anachronistic; it isn't theology! A theology which offers tried and true remedies for the human anxiety of guilt and condemnation when the regnant anxiety is the anxiety of meaninglessness and despair[24] is no theology; it is probably ideology. God is not so "dead," surely, as to have pronounced the final word on the subject of the meaning of Christ's crucifixion with the publication of Anselm's *Cur Deus Homo?* or Calvin's *Institutes of the Christian Religion*—despite the continuing dominance of the substitutionary theory of the atonement. So long as the human story goes on, the divine story of the world will never be wholly . . . finished.[25]

Notes

1. Douglas John Hall, "Cross and Context: How My Mind Has Changed," The Christian Century 127, no. 18 (September 7, 2010), http://www.christiancentury.org/article/2010-08/cross-and-context.

2. Margaret Atwood, *Survival: A Thematic Guide to Canadian Literature* (Toronto: Anansi, 1972).

3. As Christopher Lasch claims in *The Culture of Narcissism: American Life in an Age of Diminishing Expectations* (New York: Norton, 1978).

4. Karl Barth, *The Doctrine of the Word of God: Prolegomena to Church Dogmatics*, I/1, trans. G. T. Thomson (New York: Scribner's, 1936), xiv.

5. Hendrikus Berkhof, *Christian Faith: An Introduction to the Study of the Faith*, trans. Sierd Woodstra (Grand Rapids: Eerdmans, 1979), 179.

6. Since I shall use the term "ideology" with some regularity in this study, I should like to clarify the connotation that it has for me. I have not found a better definition than the one provided by Dorothee Soelle in her book *Political Theology*, trans. John Shelley (Philadelphia: Fortress Press, 1971), 23. I shall quote the entire context of which her brief definition of ideology is a part: "When we analyze Bultmann's understanding of kerygma, we recover the formal structure typical of and necessary for his thought, which in itself is sufficient to vindicate him. Bultmann makes a fundamental distinction between kerygma and theology, an important fact suppressed by the entire Bultmannian right. Kerygma appears 'as a formidable summary of everything which has to be proclaimed, and now threatens to conceal the real problems facing proclamation under a welter of high-sounding christological terminology.' It becomes a collection of doctrines that can neither be criticized nor questioned, most of which—and this is deemed progress—are no longer formulated mythologically but ideologically. *By ideology I understand a system of propositional truths independent of the situation, a superstructure no longer relevant to praxis, to the situation, to the real questions of life.* The superstructure has lost precisely what Bultmann learned from dialectical theology, the basic relation to life, and thus it is more resistant to transformation and not even interested in working to improve the underlying situation" (emphasis added). Another excellent

and, for me, definitive statement is provided by Gustavo Gutiérrez: "The term *ideology* has a long and varied history and has been understood in very different ways, But we can basically agree that ideology does not offer adequate and scientific knowledge of reality; rather, it masks it. Ideology does not rise above the empirical, irrational level. Therefore it spontaneously fulfills a function of preservation of the established order. Therefore, also, ideology tends to dogmatize all that has not succeeded in separating itself from it or has fallen under its influence. Political action, science, and faith do not escape this danger" (*A Theology of Liberation: History, Politics and Salvation*, trans. Sister Caridad Inda and John Eagleson [Maryknoll, NY: Orbis, 1973], 214–35).Theology, like all intellectual activity, walks very close to ideology. "All human knowledge is tainted with an 'ideological' taint," wrote Reinhold Niebuhr. "It pretends to be more true than it is. It is finite knowledge, gained from a particular perspective; but it pretends to be final and ultimate knowledge. Exactly analogous to the cruder pride of power, the pride of intellect is derived on the one hand from ignorance of the finiteness of the human mind and on the other hand from an attempt to obscure the known conditioned character of human knowledge and the taint of self-interest in human truth" (*The Nature and Destiny of Man: A Christian Interpretation* [New York: Scribner's, 1953], 194–95).Theology is prevented from crossing the invisible line into ideology only by one thing, and that is the very thing we have been discussing here, namely, the necessity, inherent to it, of sustaining an ongoing dialogue with the world, and thus of being continuously judged and connected by the transcendent Word to which it can only bear secondary witness.

7. Cf. Hall 1989:126–41.

8. From "The story behind the story of famine," in *Mandate*, a publication of the United Church of Canada, Toronto (September 1985), 21f.

9. Paul Tillich, *Theology of Culture* (New York: Oxford University Press, 1959).

10. Paul Tillich, *Systematic Theology*, vol. 2 (Chicago: University of Chicago Press, 1957), 15. (Of course, this statement suffers, in the present historical context, from its unfortunate use of exclusive language. It also needs to be revised in such a way as to deliver it from the rather blatant individualism of its conception of "the theologian." Without denying that theology, to be challenging, must usually pass through the filter of an individual life, it needs to be recognized that theology is an undertaking *of the church*. It is for this reason that I most often speak here of "the theological community," awkward as such a phrase may be. Despite these limitations, however, Tillich's essentially humble characterization of "the theologian" is a highly instructive one—and as rare as it is instructive.)

11. What Tillich, in *The Courage to Be* (New Haven: Yale University Press, 1952), calls "the anxiety of guilt and condemnation."

12. See *Thinking the Faith*, 55–56.

13. Elie Wiesel, *The Town beyond the Wall*, trans. from *La ville de la chance* (New York: Avon, 1967).

14. Gordon Kaufman, *Theology for a Nuclear Age* (Philadelphia: Westminster, 1985), 19.

15. A theology of pilgrims "after the fall"—a term frequently employed in the writings of post-Reformation Protestant scholastics.

16. Paul Tillich, *The Protestant Era*, trans. James Luther Adams (Chicago: University of Chicago Press, 1948), 161ff.

17. I have in mind Samuel Terrien's moving work, *The Elusive Presence: Toward a New Biblical Theology* (New York: Harper & Row, 1978), and especially the concluding paragraphs: "In biblical faith human beings discern that presence is a surging which soon vanishes and leaves in its disappearance an absence that has been overcome. It is neither absolute nor eternal but elusive and fragile, even and especially when human beings seek to prolong it in the form of cultus. The collective act of worship seems to be both the indispensable vehicle of presence and its destroyer. Presence dilutes itself into its own illusion whenever it is confused with a spatial or temporal location. When presence is 'guaranteed' to human senses or reason, it is no longer real presence. The proprietary sight of the glory destroys the vision. . . . In biblical faith, presence eludes but does not delude. The hearing of the name, which is obedience to the will and the decision to live now

for an eternal future, becomes the prophetic vision of the glory. Presence is articulated in the Word, but the Word is heard only by those who recognize the promise and already live by its fulfillment. In this sense, Torah is Logos made flesh" (476–77).

18. I am not, however, among those who would advocate dispensing with the conceptual approach in favor of narrative. I have no doubt that concept without story ends in forms of propositionalism which have little in common with the tradition of Jerusalem; but I also fear that a theology which attempts to rely primarily on story produces fragmentation both of belief and of the community of belief. Narrative theology is essential if we are to escape from the confines of doctrinalism, for it preserves the sense of livingness and mystery without which both God and the world become "too small" (P. Watson). Yet story needs commentary—as the rabbinic tradition knows very well—if it is to avoid falling into a thousand mythic pieces, each inviting a plethora of interpretations, thus opening the door to something far worse than the denominationalism that plagues doctrinally divided Christendom. There is no reason why concept and story cannot live together. They do in the Bible. The tradition of Jerusalem (unlike Athens) gives story/history a certain priority. This is because Jerusalem understands and loves the livingness of God and the creation, and celebrates the uniqueness of the particular. But even to do this the biblical faith must also resort to concepts and precepts. The Epistles of Paul must always be secondary to the Gospels; yet the Epistles illuminate the meaning of the Gospels. One would not wish to give the musicologists priority over the Mozart concertos they so laboriously analyze! Yet musicology can help us to hear Mozart better. So it is with theological concepts and ethical precepts: they can enable us to hear more "hearingly" the Story that Christians are, in turn, to tell.

19. In a helpful chapter in his *Truthfulness and Tragedy: Further Reflections in Christian Ethics* (Notre Dame: University of Notre Dame Press, 1978), 71ff., Stanley Hauerwas writes: "It is obvious that whatever else it is the message that appears central to the Christian life is in the form of a story. . . . This does not mean that all theology must itself assume the form of narrative, but rather whatever form theological reflection may take, one of its primary tasks is reminding us of a story." See also Sallie McFague, *Speaking in Parables: A Study in Metaphor and Theology* (Philadelphia: Fortress Press, 1975).

20. J. R. R. Tolkien, "On Fairy Stories," in *The Tolkien Reader* (New York: Ballantine, 1966), 3f.

21. Perhaps the most instructive exercise for anyone wishing to compare nineteenth- and twentieth-century images of the human is to read, in succession, R. M. Ballantyne's *The Coral Island* (London: J. M. Dent, 1949), and William Golding's *The Lord of the Flies* (Harmondsworth: Penguin, 1954). Golding's novel, which ends with a serviceman's expression of astonishment that "English schoolboys" could prove such uncivilized beings, is the considered response of a sensitive twentieth-century artist to the highly positive conception of humanity and society offered in *The Coral Island*, which was first published in 1825 and was read by every English (and colonial) schoolboy.

22. Elie Wiesel, *The Gates of the Forest* (New York: Avon, 1969).

23. It was the error of the supralapsarians that they confused the divine determination of the world with philosophic determinism; and this error can be correlated quite precisely with the substituting of conceptual for narrative or dramatic patterns of thought. It is one thing to regard the world from the perspective of an impersonal Fate which programs history in advance; it is something else to think of history as the scene of a redemptive drama in which the Redeemer incorporates into the redemptive "plan" the very evils ("the wrath," Ps. 76:10) from which creation must be redeemed.

24. See Tillich, *The Courage to Be.*

25. Discussion of this theme, intentionally suggestive of our Lord's last "word from the cross," is continued in Hall 1989:99–106.

4

The Sisyphus Syndrome

In *Professing the Faith*, the second volume of his trilogy on Christian theology in a North American context, Hall uses his contextual approach to examine three major doctrinal areas: the doctrine of God, creaturely being, and Jesus the Christ, Savior. In each case, he first examines the doctrine through the lens of historical theology, which he describes as "the articulation of the belief of the Christian community as it has developed over the centuries" (1993:33). He next takes a critical theological approach, which "cultivates a special awareness of the manner in which, in a given context, religious ideas and practices function" (1993:35). Finally, he turns to constructive theology, which "is the ongoing attempt of the disciple community to shape its theological understanding—and hence the church's kerygma—to meet and shape the realities of the situation" (1993:36). This excerpt, which comes from the critical theology section on creaturely being, not only functions to initiate a Christian understanding of anthropology, but is also descriptive of the context in which such an understanding is formed. As such, it shows how the contextual approach as already described may be applied to a specific theological concern. (Readers should also note that Hall capitalizes the word Theology when he is referring to the Christian doctrine of God, but lowercases it when he is referring to the general discipline.)

Source: Hall 1993:253–62.

A FUNDAMENTAL WEAKNESS

In her moving novel about pioneer days in Nebraska, Willa Cather has her heroine comment, "Isn't it queer; there are only two or three human stories, and they go on repeating themselves as if they had never happened before; like the larks in this country, that have been singing the same five notes over for thousands of years."[1] This sentiment would have to be questioned by Christians were it rendered in absolute terms, for the Judeo-Christian conceptions both of history and of individual life preclude any theory of eternal recurrence. Yet Jerusalem as well as Athens recognizes that there are certain familiar patterns where human stories are concerned; and while each story is unique, it is possible to detect familiar themes, expressed in an indeterminate number of variations, each with its element of novelty and surprise.

One such pattern in particular fascinates the biblical account of the human condition. It is the strange correlation of high and low images of the human: how the one seems to beget, in time, the other; how, like a teeter-totter, human history fluctuates between overly grandiose and overly debased self-perceptions on the part of that creature on whom, as we have maintained, this literature concentrates. Reaching, as it supposes, higher than humanhood, the creature regularly falls—or slinks—into a position far less noble. Seeking knowledge beyond the ken of creaturehood, the pair in the Garden come to know their nakedness. Clamoring for a transcendence above the plains of historical ambiguity and transience, the builders of Babel are reduced to incoherence and mutual alienation. Lusting after absolute power, Ahab and Jezebel and many other sovereigns of ancient Israel are cast back upon the essential vanity (Koheleth) of their condition. Saul the conqueror becomes Saul the melancholic, ineffectual old man. In turn, David, the innocent shepherd king, is corrupted by power and must stand accused: "Thou art the man (2 Sam. 12:7 [KJV]). Wanting to have places "at your right hand and your left hand" (Matt. 20:21), the ambitious apostles finally flee in cowardly disgrace, from the site of their "King's" unholy anointing, their places assumed by thieves (Mark 15:21). Many other examples could be cited.

Whenever the church has permitted the Bible to be its window on the world, both of these themes, as well as their odd but not illogical interaction, have informed Christian anthropology. Thus the church at its best has remembered that humanity is susceptible both to delusions of grandeur and fits of self-deprecatory torpor, both *superbia* and *acedia*—inordinate pride and abysmal, debilitating sloth. Seldom, therefore, has the human sphere of Christian influence been entirely without testimony to the falseness of both sides of this distortion of human creaturehood. In times of rampant and dangerous national, racial, or cultural pride, at least a few Christians have issued the warning: "Let anyone who thinks that he stands take heed lest he fall" (1 Cor. 10:12 [ASV]). And in periods of societal lethargy, fearfulness, or desolation there have been prophetic attempts to "strengthen the weak hands, and make firm the feeble knees" (Isa. 35:3).

All the same, it seems evident, as many Christian feminists have insisted, that historic Christianity has been far more adept at recognizing and addressing humanity's exalted self-images than its low self-esteem. Prometheus and not Sisyphus has been the familiar paradigm of the church's anthropology. Despite a considerable lack of imagination in recognizing the subtler forms of human egoism, at least in the presence of unbridled pride what remains of prophetic zeal in the church normally knows what to say and to do. "He hath put down the mighty from their seats" (Luke 1:52). Part of the appeal of liberationism today is associated with this ancient sense of the wrongness of human *superbia*—the pride of oppressors. Hubris in both individuals and communities evokes from a vigilant Christian minority the courage to confront overbearing rulers and haughty classes and whole arenas full of jeering mobs. It is perhaps the heroic side of faith that is appealed to in such situations. Flagrant boastfulness on the part of mortals calls forth from the *Defensor fidei* a blast from the trumpet of the Lord. Faced with such pretension, humble faith may rise to heights of righteous indignation, entering the theater of worldly pomp with a fierce dignity, like old Polycarp at his martyrdom.

But it is not heroism that is called for when human civilization falls into decline, its citizens restless victims of self-doubt and moral confusion. David was able through heroic courage to slay Goliath and achieve Israel's deliverance, but he could not in such fashion cure the melancholia of King Saul (1 Sam. 16:14ff.).

Who will speak to Sisyphus, comfort him, help him to hope again? Not conviction but compassion must be the posture of such a one, and not strength but wisdom. And, as Job asks, "Where shall wisdom be found?" (Job 28:12).

The wisdom even of recognizing, let alone ministering to, human defeatism and despair is never easily acquired. Yet such wisdom is finally more needful than the courage to confront human arrogance. For beneath the facade of our various experiments in mastery, there is an aboriginal, Babel-awareness of human fragility. This awareness is only barely covered by the pomp of empires, the "irony" (Reinhold Niebuhr) of whose histories is invariably the consequence of their vain attempts to conceal their finitude. No ermine, armor, or designer jeans can prevent the worm of self-doubt from entering the soul of the thinking animal. Thought itself will betray the thinker who endeavors to enhance his security by taking thought. "Fool, this night thy soul shall be required of thee" (Luke 12:20 [KJV]).

The conclusion that we have had to reach in our earlier reflections on the North American context today,[2] to recapitulate them in the metaphoric language of the present discussion, is that the humanity Christians are called to engage in this context resembles Sisyphus more than Prometheus. But to be accurate we should have to devise a more finely nuanced articulation of the ancient myth; for our Sisyphus still parades himself as Prometheus, not knowing any other role. He no longer has the heart to play with conviction the character of Prometheus, stealer of fire from the gods, technocratic hero; for at some unconscious level he is deeply suspicious of his aptitude for that part, having in the meantime discovered how little control he has over the stolen fire. All the same, these are the lines that he has learned, and the character of Sisyphus is wholly foreign to his North American education, which leaves no place for failure. So he continues, year after year, mouthing the old Promethean speeches while silently accumulating the thoughts that have gone into the making of every historical Sisyphus—"thoughts that wound from behind" (Kierkegaard). In the eyes of some observers, he has become an almost comic figure: a fat, drugged, pleasure-seeking, failed, often suicidal Prometheus, chained still to the rock of his well-rehearsed mythology, but no longer believing it. He is Sisyphus playing the part of Prometheus.

As we have received it, the Christian doctrinal heritage concerning creaturely being seems to me ill-equipped to engage such a figure. The present unimpressive performance of Christianity in the two northern nations of this continent, which is in part the consequence of ecclesiastical degeneration and mediocrity, is also partly to be explained by the inadequacy of our received anthropological conventions to comprehend the type of humanity rampant in our social milieu. These conventions have conditioned us to think about the human creature in an exalted fashion; and, intermingled as they are in North America with even less qualified theoretic exaltations of the human coming from the side of the Enlightenment, they prove almost useless in the face of a humanity that is in fact deeply humiliated—but humiliated at a sub- or even unconscious level for lack of any operative paradigms for openly acknowledging its humiliation.

This generalization applies to both conservative and liberal expressions of Christian doctrine in North America. There are, to be sure, exceptions, but the rule, I believe, holds: conservative Christianity, including neo-orthodoxy, knows a good deal about the sin of pride but it is hardly acquainted with sloth.[3] Neo-orthodoxy has been more faithful to the best of the tradition than has theological liberalism, because it remembers enough of the profound traditions of the faith to know that humanity is fundamentally flawed and in need of radical redemption; but it almost invariably defines this distortion in terms of our inordinate quest for superhuman power and significance. Having received the stamp of strong male personalities ancient and modern—Augustine, Calvin, Edwards, and others—who were themselves rather promethean; and having honed its sermon against pride in a life-and-death struggle with the Renaissance, modern orthodoxy in the West understands very little the "absurd" human of the existentialists or the "mass" human of the consumer society.

At the same time, theological liberalism has known better than the orthodox that humanity requires compassion and encouragement, not only chastisement; thus liberalism has gone a little way toward addressing human pathos—but only a little way. Having discarded any hint of "total depravity" in favor of sins more amenable to salvation by enlightenment and forgiveness, liberalism has been incapable of realizing the depths of contemporary alienation.

Directly or indirectly, then, both expressions of Christian theo-anthropology at work in our context have promulgated such high images of the human that it is difficult for people who are suffering under the impact of a barrage of evidence of their lowness to find in the church's testimony any sense of their being addressed. A hundred years of science, including the theory of evolution, having successfully persuaded the majority of their ordinariness; daily contact with people of all races and creeds having all but dispelled the myths of specialness; terrible wars, ecological catastrophes, "symbolic" diseases like AIDS, the failure of institutions and consequent public cynicism having robbed most North Americans of their unsullied pursuit of happiness; a gospel that assumes (even if it does not say so) the superiority of the human species, or understands so little the human suspicion of our inferiority, will hardly engage anyone. Or rather, it will function to prevent such engagement. In addressing itself to a species of humanity accustomed to religious and cultural assumptions of humanity's centrality in the scheme of things, it will confirm those managerial segments of society that will do anything to avoid the existential questioning of their mastery, while failing altogether to speak to the actual passivity of the majority. (If we wonder why Christianity of all varieties in North America is an overwhelmingly middle-class affair, we should pause to ponder that statement.)

FORMULATING OUR HYPOTHESIS

In introducing this . . . subject of creaturely being, it may seem that I have too narrowly circumscribed the tradition. Let me admit at once, therefore, that Christian traditions respecting creaturehood—notably the creature *anthropos*—are widely diverse. Like Theology, Christian anthropology covers an almost incredible array of opinion. To read side by side Augustine and Pelagius, St. Thomas and Luther, Calvin and Wesley, Richard Hooker and John Knox, Albrecht Ritschl and Karl Barth, Carl McIntire and Norman Vincent Peale, Rosemary Radford Ruether and Wolfhart Pannenberg, would be to come away from the exercise thinking that one had been in the presence, if not of another Babel, at least of representatives of many different cults. And it would probably only exacerbate the confusion were one assured that all these commentators on the human condition are professing Christians. It is perhaps presumptuous, therefore, to claim—as I have done in the foregoing—that the Christian tradition concerning human being leaves us more adequately equipped to engage Prometheus than Sisyphus.

It would be presumptuous indeed to register such a hypothesis as though it could account for every exposition of the subject. What I have stressed, however, is that my generalization refers to the tradition *as we have received it*. Here we need to remind ourselves of what has been advanced in the first volume concerning the role of tradition in theological work.[4]

Tradition is not a static thing, a great deposit of inert material, like the archives of some city or university, which remains the same decade after decade, century after century. Tradition as that which the Christian past hands over to us involves not only what is handed over but also those to whom it is handed. Tradition is a living thing because its being received, if it is truly received and not just formally acknowledged, always entails discovery, surprise, nuance, insight, judgment, confirmation, interrogation, and (above all) struggle. We do not hear precisely what our grandparents heard from Tertullian or Thomas Müntzer or Teresa of Avila. Our minds are attuned to other themes, other questions and alternatives. Today's students of theology reading Karl Barth or Paul Tillich are not arrested by the same things that commanded the attention of the generations actually taught by those theologians. The single fact that many of today's theological students are women makes this inevitable.[5] We do not need from the past precisely what our predecessors needed, nor will our successors need precisely what we need as we search for a usable past.

This methodological observation is particularly important when it comes to the anthropological dimensions of Christian thought. The ever-changing face of humanity requires that what the past enjoins of us must be held in tension with new problems and possibilities that were not present, or not decisive, for our predecessors.[6]

An example is the impact of advanced technology in all areas of life. One looks in vain for any sustained critique of technology in Reinhold Niebuhr's magnum opus of fifty years ago, *The Nature and Destiny of Man*. Although the work must be regarded still as a veritable classic of Christian anthropology, and although it provides innumerable insights needed as background for Christian reflection upon high technology, Niebuhr's Gifford Lectures assume a significantly different human context. More than anyone of his generation of theologians, he anticipated so much about what was coming to be on the face of the earth that we may consider him still immediately pertinent—almost a contemporary.[7] But he does not address the problems of ecological catastrophe, Third World indebtedness, North/South disparities, abortion, gender exclusivism, violence against women, and a whole host of other problems with which faith today must wrestle. Nor does he speak to a world, such as ours has recently become, where the long-standing division between First and Second Worlds has broken down; where communism is more severely criticized inside the countries of the former Warsaw Pact than outside of them; where capitalism indulges in empty boasts about its victory and inherent superiority; where many Americans are confused because the old *Feindbilder* (enemy images) that have been used to bolster our own questionable ideology can no longer serve that purpose.

The situation is even more complicated than these specific ethical issues suggest. What one realizes the more one studies Reinhold Niebuhr's earlier works is that this greatest of all North American contextual theologians is addressing himself to a human mentality—an *imago hominis*—that is significantly different from the image of the human that has come to be in more recent decades and looms on the horizon altogether too large for comfort. For Niebuhr, who regularly admitted that he "cut his theological eyeteeth" battling the self-possessed automobile magnate Henry Ford, the *problématique* for which the Christian message must address itself is the sin of pride, or rather sin *as* pride. Henry Ford was, so to speak, his paradigmatic Prometheus. So it is not accidental that of the ten chapters of the first volume of the Gifford Lectures, no fewer than three are devoted to the analysis of sin, and precisely sin as inordinate pride, hubris:

> The truth is that man is tempted by the basic insecurity of human existence to make himself doubly secure and by the insignificance of his place in the total scheme of life to prove his significance. The will-to-power is in short both a direct form and an indirect instrument of the pride which Christianity regards as sin in its quintessential form.[8]

That Niebuhr concentrated, in the first place, on the doctrine of sin and, in the second, understood sin's quintessence to be pride ought not to be construed as a fault or limitation on him.[9] On the contrary, it demonstrates his uncanny sensitivity to what Luther called "the little point where the battle rages." For in the context in which Reinhold Niebuhr was reared and "cut his theological eyeteeth," radical sin was not prominent in either Christian or secular consciousness, and as for pride, it was the very mood of America's dominant classes, the setbacks of depression, racial tension, and wars notwithstanding. The novels of Sinclair Lewis, Theodore Dreiser, John Steinbeck, and many others identify the same *problématique* as does Niebuhr. What remained of the idea that humanity was irrevocably fallen was reduced to trivial, private, and moralistic proportions. In a figure like Ford (and in many more subtle than he) Niebuhr could with perfect right recognize a type of *Homo sapiens* in the grip of Prometheanism, however unsophisticated and naïve.

Moreover, because mainstream Christianity in North America, as in Europe, had allowed itself to be carried along by the bravado of modernity, it had practically lost touch with any of the profound teachings of the tradition on whose basis the tragic, pathetic, and downright evil aspects of the human condition could be recognized, named, and challenged. Conservative Christianity, which remembered the dogmas, was too unimaginative and too implicated with power to apply them. Thus it became the vocation of Reinhold and H. Richard Niebuhr in North America, as of Barth, Brunner, Bonhoeffer, Suzanne de Dietrich, and others in Europe, to recover and enliven ancient wisdom like the dogma of original sin, through which they could derive an alternative perspective on the human situation in the first half of the [twentieth] century, and fashion their gospel accordingly. In short, their (with hindsight, amazingly correct) perception of their own context evoked and was evoked by their struggle with the tradition. If we imitate them methodologically, however, I think that we shall not be able to imitate the specific content of their witness, especially where the predominant mood of our society is concerned. For we find ourselves today, I believe, in a significantly different social milieu. Later history may record that the last decades of the twentieth century in North America were in fact very different from the first five or six decades as far as the spirit of the times (*Zeitgeist*) is concerned.

This is not to imply that there are no threads of continuity between the two periods. When Reinhold Niebuhr's portrait appeared on the cover of *Time* magazine's twenty-fifth anniversary issue in March of 1948, the caption beneath it read: "Man's Story Is Not a Success Story." Niebuhr knew the Bible, and he understood that the inordinate self-regard he felt compelled to denounce was only a slight historical turning removed from debilitating insecurity. Conversely, neither have we seen the end of that mentality to which Henry Ford gave undiluted expression when he quipped that "History is mostly bunk"—the rhetoric of progress. Positive thinkers are still able to achieve a following for their contemporary versions of the early twentieth-century motto invented by Dr. Émile Coué: "Day by day, in every way, I am getting better and better."

Yet today this kind of optimism is forced and often patently hollow. It is the only role that we know well. It is, besides, the part that we feel obligated to play. The very continuation of our society seems dependent upon our playing it. Prometheus American-style is so familiar a model of the human that we are never surprised by it, whether we encounter it in television commercials or in church; and we only find it slightly ridiculous when we see it exhibited in the films of the '40s and '50s. By comparison with present-day cinematography and other art, however, these productions of the middle of the century and earlier seem innocent in the extreme. Nothing indicates so precisely the attitudinal gulf separating the first from the second half of this century as do the films of the two periods; and it is hardly even necessary to specify which films.

To those who have some historical awareness, this observation inevitably invites a comparison with Europe. We have already anticipated that comparison in our use of the Sisyphus/Prometheus typology. These mythological figures have been drawn upon often in twentieth-century European literature. Sisyphus was the very model of contemporary humanity for the existentialists, especially Camus (who may or may not have been an existentialist). Jürgen Moltmann made good use of the two mythic figures in his first influential work, *Theology of Hope*. That work was in fact written over against two attitudes prevalent in postwar Europe, Germany in particular: Marxian *superbia* and existentialist *acedia*—the Sisyphus syndrome.[10]

It is nevertheless impossible to transfer these insights of European philosophic and theological reflection directly into the North American situation, though many attempted to do so in the wake of Moltmann's "theology of hope." The reason for this is simply and profoundly that our context is infinitely more complex than the European, precisely on the question of our public mood respecting the nature and destiny of humanity. As I have characterized it above, we too have become Sisyphus, but a Sisyphus imitating Prometheus. There is no room for losers in this society, despite the notorious fact that, from the standpoint of the pop philosophy of "winning," greater and greater numbers of North Americans have lost—economically, in marriage and family life, in health and self-esteem, and so on. Our public policies insist upon an upbeat approach (reduced to almost vaudevillian proportions in every pre-election party convention), despite the facts of staggering national debts, lingering recessions, and permanent unemployment. Task forces on self-esteem are created. Politicians and educators launch programs designed to "make people feel good about themselves"—despite their actual performance and notwithstanding the underlying sense of confusion and loss of confidence.[11]

However understandable this may be, given the history of European civilization in North America, it is apologetically complicating. No wonder so many younger theologians in our context look longingly to human situations where oppression is straightforward, or try to import into our situation liberationist themes like conscientization. It is one thing to "conscientize" the oppressed and marginalized who are surrounded by concrete evidence of their depressed condition; it is something else to "conscientize" the middle classes of North America. To a Sisyphus who cannot avoid the knowledge of his degradation, one may perhaps speak directly about the hope that can be experienced on the far side of despair, and only there. But how does anyone address a Sisyphus who thinks that he is Prometheus, or thinks that he ought to think that he is Prometheus: a Sisyphus who is so conditioned by simplistic variations of the onward-and-upward way of the "religion of progress" that to persuade him of his need is already almost impossible and perhaps unwise?

Against the backdrop of these reflections, we may formulate our critical hypothesis as follows: The tradition as it has come to us too readily conveys a high conception of the human, which, under the impact of the contemporary loss of purpose, fails to engage the low self-esteem entertained at varying levels of awareness by increasing numbers of people in our context. While biblical and minority traditions could speak to this condition, they have not been imaginatively explored by Christians. The appropriate corrective is not a further ontic elevation of *Homo sapiens* but rather the enucleation of a Christian anthropology that accentuates human creaturehood and develops its teleology in conjunction with a "new" understanding of humanity's vocation within the sphere of creation.

Notes

1. Willa Cather, *O Pioneers!* (Boston: Houghton Mifflin Co., 1913), 119.

2. Hall 1989: chs. 2, 3.

3. I say this in the full knowledge that Karl Barth devoted a large section of his *Church Dogmatics* to sloth, the Sisyphean side of sin. See esp. vol. IV/1, pp. 403ff. and vol. IV/2, pp. 403ff., 483ff., trans. G. W. Bromiley (Edinburgh: T. & T. Clark, 1956, 1958). But precisely this is the aspect of Barth's anthropology that has not been taken up and developed, with appropriate contextual sensitivity, by Barth's North American disciples.

4. Hall 1989:263ff.

5. See Rosemary Radford Ruether's illuminating discussion of this process in *Sexism and God-Talk: Toward a Feminist Theology* (Boston: Beacon, 1983), 12–18.

6. Theology "continues its vital development only to the extent that such thinking remains in touch with depth experience" (ibid., 15).

7. See in this connection Robert McAfee Brown's introduction to his collection, *The Essential Reinhold Niebuhr: Selected Essays and Addresses* (New Haven: Yale University Press, 1986), xx: "To make honest use of Niebuhr in our own time, we must remember what he never forgot, that the gospel speaks different words to different times, and even different words to different participants in the same times."

8. Reinhold Niebuhr, *The Nature and Destiny of Man*, vol. 1 (New York: Scribner's, 1953), 192.

9. As is well known, an important aspect of present-day Niebuhr scholarship is the feminist critique of his conception of sin, which in its concentration on pride seems to many to reflect a highly masculine bias. [The complete text of this note is found in Hall 1993: 259.]

10. Jürgen Moltmann, *Theology of Hope: On the Ground and Implications of a Christian Eschatology*, trans. James W. Leitch (London: SCM, 1967), esp. 24ff.

11. See the essay by Charles Krauthammer, "Education: Doing Bad and Feeling Good," *Time* (Feb. 5, 1990), 56.

5

Modes of Knowing

In the final chapter of Thinking of Faith, Hall turns to the topic of epistemology, which, quoting Paul Tillich, he describes as "the 'knowledge' of knowing" (1989:71).[1] Here the reader may hearken back to chapter 2 of this present volume, on "Theology and Faith," as Hall here attempts to describe "the different ways in which 'knowing' applies both to life and Christian belief" (ibid.). For Hall, there are three levels at which knowing functions: "knowledge," or the possession of information; "acknowledgment," that is, the place at which knowledge gains personal significance; and "trust," wherein one makes choices regarding acknowledged information. In keeping with his theme of contextualization, these choices are based on personal relationship, and thus cannot be regarded as normative. Such understanding then becomes the basis on which one can come to understand the concepts of reason and revelation.

Source: Hall 1989:369–88.

How Do You Know?

Whenever Christians make statements about the biblical God, or even statements which, while they may not concern the divine person directly, assume belief in transcendent meaning, they can expect to elicit the question, How do you know? When Christian preachers announce the reality of God's love, God's willingness to forgive, the judgment of God against social evils, the meaningfulness of the historical process, and so on, they must assume today that there are people in every pew who are asking them, silently but insistently, How do you know? Even the well-dressed and polite congregations of our middle-class churches; even old ladies and gentlemen who are not usually cast in the role of skeptic—all may be asking, How is it possible to know this? Really to *know*? And the one who is in the pulpit is also asking this question, in all probability—perhaps without admitting it.

It is better for us to ask this question explicitly and consciously. In fact, we shall be well acquainted with our socioreligious context only insofar as we have made this question in some genuine sense our own. For this question, which is much more than an intellectual question only, is one form of *the* question to which as disciples of the Christ in our time and place we must endeavor to find the answer—to use Tillich's methodological metaphor.

It is of course not the only form of the question by which contemporary *Homo sapiens* is addressed; and it is misleading when theologians take up the epistemological question as if it were the exclusive interest of twentieth-century persons in search of faith. In one sense, the questions presupposed by the main doctrinal areas of Christian theology are far more important: Is it permitted any longer to assume the possibility of transcendence (Theology)? Is the human creature in any appreciable way unique, special (anthropology)? Is salvation possible in a world that is no longer able to distinguish between "is" and "ought," existence and essence (Christology/soteriology)? Is the historical process—are our own personal histories—in any sense purposeful (eschatology)? Yet all such questions presuppose a preliminary consideration of the epistemological question. For, especially in a society which has severely limited the things that human beings may be credited with knowing, the claims of Christian faith can be entertained seriously only if they are accompanied by strong evidence that their advocates have opened themselves existentially to the rigors of the epistemological question. The discipline to which we are called is perhaps more demanding at this point, given our particular historical-geographic context, than at any other.

This is not to say that Christians are obligated to demonstrate to their world, on its own terms, the *legitimacy* of their mode of knowing. So far as many of our contemporaries are concerned, such a demonstration is in any case unthinkable. To take on the world as it presents itself to our technological society, and to seek to convince it that "God-talk" is quite permissible and meaningful, is to abandon oneself to an indefinite engagement with epistemological discourse of the sort which is never able to advance beyond the how of knowing to the what. Just that has become the fate of much Anglo-Saxon theology in our time. It lives in a methodological cul-de-sac.

What is required of us, then, is not that we prove to all concerned our "right" to pursue this "arcane science" (Bonhoeffer); on the contrary, it is that we give evidence of recognizing at depth that such a right, if it ever existed, does not exist today. It was taken away from the church by the modern world, which decided that Christians had badly abused precisely this right and that from now on they would have to *earn* whatever noetic rights they wished to have. Part of the earning of such rights has to do with our attitude towards the quest for truth. The world will listen to us only if it senses that we know that our knowing is in fact a risking, trusting, hoping, imagining, envisioning—in short, a reaching out into mystery, and not without difficulty, and not without doubt.

At the same time, it is not required of Christians today that we bow in abject humility before what the dominant systems and methods honored by our society recognize as legitimacy in the realm of knowledge. There is for us also at this point a discontinuity to be encountered, a *skandalon*. We cannot submit the subject matter of our knowing to the tribunal of the technological society—and we should not! The gap between that world's knowing and ours must be made quite plain. All the false scandals connected with the church's reputation for knowing must be cleared away so that the authentic scandal may become present in all of its boldness. The true offense of the faith so far as its epistemological aspect is concerned has nothing to with the quantity of data Christians have been traditionally credited with knowing. It has to do with the *quality* of their knowing, that is to say, with the nature of what is known, and the mode of knowing it. Suffice it here to say—in an anticipatory way—that this "what" is not properly designated "it" but only "Thou"; and this *first principle of our knowing* sets us at once in conflict with a society which has made it less and less possible for human beings even to say "thou" to one another, let alone to address an "Eternal Thou" (Buber).[2]

By the same token, the pursuit of this mode of knowing will not find Christians alone and friendless in such a world. For the very reductionism present in the dominant rational systems by which the technocratic society is regulated has produced in the last analysis its own internal protest. In a manner that was not true even for the great teachers of the faith to whom we have made reference in the preceding chapter, there is in our present context a recognition on the part of many sensitive persons in all disciplines that the reduction of knowing to quantitative and functional terms has robbed our culture of spirit and meaning, making of it a "one-dimensional" society.[3] Eschewing all wisdom but that which could, as it was thought, give *Homo sapiens* supremacy over nature and history, our species has arrived at a point where, as we have seen, its vaunted mastery could destroy what it set out to control. Many of the most thoughtful minds of our civilization have in consequence been driven to ask after an alternative form of thinking and being that seems to have been lost in the rush for facts and power. Is it not possible, then, that we shall find allies all along the way in our search to describe anew, for the postmodern era, the sort of knowing that is linked with trusting and with mystery? May we not also hope, in that case, to discover common ground and the prospect of a profitable exchange with those who are "not of this fold"?

LEVELS OF KNOWING

We may begin this search by making a distinction that is by no means peculiar to Christianity, but is nevertheless basic to Christian epistemology. It is common experience that there are different levels or dimensions or categories of knowing. I do not mean by this a merely quantitative distinction—knowing more and knowing less. What I refer to, rather, is a frequently experienced need to categorize human cognition according to types or qualities. There are distinct levels of knowing, that is to say, in the sense that one kind of knowledge is markedly different from another. To know a fact of mathematics (that six and six are twelve) implies a kind of knowing quite dissimilar to what is intended when someone says to his mortal enemy, "I know *you*, sir!" or when the apostle Peter assures Jesus, "Lord, you *know* that I love you" (John 21:15f.). When a woman explains to her husband, "We've overspent the budget again this month," and he replies, "I know," a very different sort of knowledge is implied from what may be alluded to two minutes later in the same exchange, when the husband, shedding his customary nonchalance, gives expression to his frustration over money and work and perhaps life itself, and his wife, in sympathy, responds, "I know, I know." In the same sequence, using the same terminology, qualitatively distinct messages are conveyed. We understand one another when this happens. No one has to spell it out. It is quite unnecessary to explain that one "I know" means, "Yes, I understand this deplorable fact: the budget is overspent," while the other conveys the comforting reassurance of compassion, love, and conjugal trust. These nuances of meaning, so very important in everyday life, are communicated from one person to another.

It should not surprise us, in that case, that similar distinctions also apply to the language of faith and theology. If it seems to be part of human experience in general that knowing occurs at varying levels, then one could expect this to be the case also where religious belief is concerned.

Is it possible to classify the different levels of knowing which apply to Christian faith and theology? Classification is difficult even in areas where quite precise distinctions can be noted and described. There is usually an arbitrary element in such distinctions. All the same, it may help to establish differentiations that can aid our perception of the reality which ultimately evades classification and description if we recognize three *types* of knowing which seem to apply to our subject matter. For convenience, and without committing ourselves in any rigid way to the nomenclature itself, we may designate these: knowledge, acknowledgment, and trust.

KNOWLEDGE

We begin by positing the kind of knowing which is the possession of information—data. Some conventions of our society would warrant our calling this level of knowing simply, "knowledge." A person is said to be knowledgeable when she has a good grasp of the data associated with a particular discipline or profession. Much of our time in childhood and youth is spent in the acquisition of this kind of knowledge—too much of our time, according to some critics of North American educational systems! Yet without the knowledge that fire burns and heavier things fall and energy can be transferred and things are valued according to their supply and demand, it would be impossible to live in the world. Moreover, the contemporary world seems to demand more and more of this type of knowledge for anyone who wants to avoid being victimized by forces in the society which will certainly govern our lives more effectively if we do *not* know such things.

There is a tendency among some Christians, particularly mainline Protestants in North America, to minimize or even to denigrate altogether this level of knowing. Such a criticism comes from the side of persons who believe, with some justification but little understanding of the subtlety of the relation between faith and knowledge, that the *essential* thing in Christian belief has very little to do with the intellect but much with the heart, or the hands: feeling and doing. There is a history of anti-intellectualism within the general history of the Christian movement, and it has in many ways found a fertile soil in the New World, where piety and activism have too often been more highly valued than *thinking* the faith.[4] But in fact Christian belief also assumes the necessity of knowing in this preliminary sense. The same sort of knowing that is implied when someone recites the mathematical datum six plus six equals twelve is part of what Christian theology has to treat in its epistemology.

Indeed, this type of knowing in Christianity plays an important role in the whole process of the movement of anyone towards belief. There is simply a great deal to be known in the sense of the acquisition of information; and there is a way in which this kind of knowing must *come first*. In a way, everything else depends upon it.

It is for this reason that Christianity from the outset has been a *teaching* religion, as was and is its parental faith of Judaism. The disciple community is a teaching community; its discipline is inextricably linked with the fact that it both learns continuously and communicates what it tries to comprehend. More is always involved in learning and teaching, certainly, than the mere imbibing and imparting of information. But information—and therefore knowledge in the sense in which we are presently using the term—is all the same an important aspect of this discipline. This applies rather obviously to Christian education. It applies as well to Christian *preaching*, which is always *partly* the communication of information (though when it is nothing more than that it does not deserve to be called preaching). Christianity *must* be taught, and Christians *must* teach. This is built into belief. It is inherent in belief not only because of that "necessity" which, as we have seen previously, is "laid upon" those who hear, and whose hearing itself creates the need to share what is heard. It is inherent also on account of the sheer fact that Christianity is a *historical* faith. That is, it is based upon event—upon a whole series of historical events with one especially clarifying (*kairos*) event at the center.

Part of the reason why the Protestant reformers from Wycliffe and Hus onwards stressed Bible knowledge as requisite for every Christian believer lies exactly in this recognition that such a faith requires continuous nurture through the recollection of its own foundational events. When recitation of and reflection upon these events gives place to more immediate, personal, and experientially based "spirituality," as this has happened in circles of liberal Christianity during the [twentieth] century, there is a very real danger that Christianity as such will be dissolved. And, as George Lindbeck insists, the dissolution of Christianity has implications for the whole civilization that has been formed, in large measure, by the Christian story.

> If the Bible has shaped the imagination of the West to anywhere near the degree that Northrop Frye, for example, has argued, then the West's continuing imaginative vitality and creativity may well depend on the existence of groups for whom the Hebrew and Christian Scriptures are not simply classics among others, but the canonical literature par excellence, and who are also in close contact with the wider culture.[5]

Historical occurrences are not known automatically. We are not born with historical knowledge, though we may in some way be born with a thirst for historical knowledge—for remembering. But the knowledge of events has to be acquired. The character of these foundational events—what happened, what the original participants and observers said about what happened, what was said *by* the central figures of these occurrences, especially by Jesus—all of this has to be transmitted from one person to another, one generation to another; for it is not something transhistorical, an eternal truth of which everyone may become aware quite naturally in the course of her or his life. It is historical, part of the past; it is not still occurring—not, at least, so far as the *foundational* events are concerned. "It is finished." And even if these events were still occurring—even if they were somehow recurrent events (as in a parabolic, mythic, and liturgical sense they are)—there would still be the need for transmitting information. For as the Newer Testament makes quite plain, the events as such do not communicate the thing that has to be communicated. The events have to be *interpreted*. They must be "borne witness to"—fulfilled, as it were, by words, by thought.

It is not that the events are inadequate; it is that *we* are inadequate. We do not see what is there to be seen, or hear what is there to be heard. So the God of the Scriptures does not simply "act." To name this God the acting God, and to discuss "God's mighty acts" is misleading—particularly in an activistic culture like our own. For the God of the Bible also *speaks*—is also *Deus loquens*. God's acting is inseparable from God's speaking. God's acting *is* God's speaking. God speaks through the mouth of the prophets, the law-givers, the evangelists, for "Surely the Lord God does nothing, without revealing his secret to his servants the prophets" (Amos 3:7). Thus Jesus, God's Word enacted, must not only *be* and *do*, but he must also interpret his being and his doing. He must disclose information. Indeed, he must be known *first* as "Teacher," "Rabbi."

This information is not by itself effective. It depends upon the being and the doing to which it points. And more: it depends upon a movement which no teacher, not even the rabbi Jesus, can cause to occur—what we may think of, poetically, as the movement from brain to heart. The object of the information that the disciple community receives and imparts is that it should make possible some such movement as this, but it cannot do this by itself. This movement is the subject of the next two phases of our discussion about the levels of knowing. All the same, so far as Christian belief is concerned, the kind of knowledge that is implied in this first distinction has a decisive chronological priority. What Lindbeck calls "experiential-expressive" religion may seem, for a time, more exciting and more personally fulfilling than what is offered by a disciple community that requires of its membership, older and younger, an ongoing and disciplined exposure to historical narrative and interpretation; but without this basic *knowledge*, there is in the long run nothing whatsoever to ensure the cohesion of the disciple community *or* the uniqueness of its service to the larger human community. Knowledge in this first sense is thus indispensable, and a vital aspect of the discipline to which the disciple community in our particular context is called today must involve the most serious pedagogical efforts to inculcate precisely such knowledge in those who remain within the churches of the "postliberal age."

Let us not, however, underestimate the difficulties of such a mandate! On the one hand, it leads to the temptation (which in North American Christianity today must be regarded as a very great *temptation*) to ignore all the warnings of the scientific mind and the experience of modernity as a whole, and to "return" to a defensive and positivistic biblicism. On the other hand, those who are able to resist *that* temptation are faced with another, namely, to be debilitated by the skepticism of both modern and postmodern secularity concerning all claims to knowledge of this sort. For already in the initial stages of our epistemological quest we encounter the skepticism and—not infrequently—the scorn of our world. Already the aggressive "How do you know?" of our fact-driven society accosts us. For history, too, has been forced into the role of "objectivity." And what concrete evidence do we have for these historical data which describe the foundational events of our religious tradition and must be given chronological priority in our knowing? What can be proved about the history of the people of Israel? More, no doubt, than can be proved about Jesus "the Christ"! Can we even "get back to the historical Jesus"? Albert Schweitzer demonstrated the pitfalls of such a quest already in the early decades of [the twentieth] century.[6] We intend to base our faith on events, and yet we cannot show beyond the shadow of a doubt that these events ever actually occurred! We say that "Jesus Christ and him crucified" is the cornerstone of our belief; but before we even come to the *meaning* of such a statement we are confronted by the fact that we cannot be absolutely certain that such a thing took place.

This demonstrates, among other things, the inadequacy of factual knowledge as the foundation of belief. No one is saved by knowledge—a truth which won the battle (if it was indeed won!) against the Gnosticism of the early Christian centuries. The historical data which form the substantive basis of our faith can by no means be dispensed with, yet they do not of themselves give the possibility of faith. Even if they were not limited; even if the data *could* be demonstrated in a more objective manner—even then this would be unsatisfactory as a basis for belief. The disciples of Jesus who actually spoke and walked with him had, presumably, more knowledge of this sort than could be acquired today even by the most astute and patient scholars. Observing as they could in an immediate way—not only hearing his words but seeing his facial expressions as he uttered them; not only watching in a spectator manner but participating in the events of his life—they could surely gain more information about this central figure of our belief than if many books had been written (see John 21:25) and much evidence preserved. Yet with all their firsthand knowledge not one of them "believed"! The belief with which, later, they approached the recollection of these foundational events was certainly not independent of the immediate experience of their life with Jesus in the flesh—just as *our* belief, if we manifest such, is never independent of their *testimony* to that experience (*sola Scriptura*). Yet between the fact-knowledge they had from their firsthand experience (and we from their testimony) and the post-Pentecostal state of belief or trust there is no comparison. The latter state, this *believing* knowledge, depends upon the former; but it is qualitatively different from fact-knowledge. Something had to happen to "the facts" of their raw experience before they could become foundational for belief. Similarly, something has to happen in the life of the one who has acquired biblical and doctrinal knowledge (*gnosis*) before it can become the conceptual ground of our trust in God.

ACKNOWLEDGMENT

In order to understand a little better the mystery of the movement from *gnosis* to *pistis*, fact to faith, we may posit a second type of knowing which differs from both. This second type is suggested by the fact that *some* of the data people come to acquire becomes significant for them. Not all information that we pick up is immediately significant. Most of it, indeed, remains in the limbo of semi-consciousness or half-remembered things. At two or three years of age, a child may be taught that five plus five is ten, and the proud parents stand and beam while the toddler recites this ineluctable datum of human experience. But the information is not really significant to the child, beyond the obvious fact that it gains a certain amount of prestige and self-satisfaction from reciting it (something which can be observed about many persons well beyond the state of childhood).

A few months later, however, the child stands before a candy counter with a nickel in one pocket and five pennies in another; and in the case before it there is a particularly enticing red candy which may be acquired for ten cents. Now the information that five plus five is ten becomes highly significant information. Now the child *knows* this! Did it not also know this mathematical datum before? Yes, but the child's present state of knowing, as it stands in rapt attention before a desirable object, is very different from rote knowledge.

We have a whole vocabulary for describing the difference in question. We say, for example, that the child has "assimilated" the mathematical information, or that this information has been "absorbed into" its experience. What has occurred between the acquisition of the knowledge concerning the sum total of five and five, and this new state of mind, is that the individual has acted upon the information he or she had received. Before, it was merely something there. The child did take it in, to be sure—did memorize it; so that it was never *totally* uninvolved with respect to this bit of knowledge. But now, in circumstances which have rendered this information existentially significant to the child, it does something to the information. It makes it its own, responds to it, *acknowledges* it.

In the foregoing, I referred to the mystery of the movement from fact to faith. It is possible to see something of this mystery already at this second stage, before we even reach the state of faith or trust. For there is a kind of mystery between knowing and acknowledging something. It could not be said with precision how the child got from the one state to the other. Or let us say that even if, in some instances of this kind, it were possible to describe at least the external circumstances which accompanied this movement, it would hardly be possible to describe these in such a way that they could then be taken up as a prescription, a method for turning data into *significant* data. To be sure, educators are always trying to do just that; because what all good educators desire is to move their charges from the state of knowledge to the state of acknowledgment. Thus they are forever attempting, methodologically, to analyze the mystery of this process and to turn it into a foolproof technique. But the fact remains that it is an area full of great unpredictability. Certain useful things can be learned which will no doubt aid the process, or remove obstacles to its occurring. But still it happens that what for one person comes to be highly significant information remains, for another, who may have been exposed to the very same occurrences and educational procedures, mere data.

This distinction is also very important in Christian theology. Between the data-knowledge first described and the believing-knowledge to which we shall turn next, there is this intermediate state. It is a point in Christian experience which may cover a very long period of time or a very short one. Some of the scriptural and other data which one has received becomes *significant* information. Suddenly, or quite gradually, one realizes that some aspect of Christian teaching is meaningful to oneself. It may have become so inconspicuously—like Kierkegaard's "thoughts which wound from behind"—or on the other hand it may have occurred as a flash of insight. In any case, what was before mere information, eliciting no special interest, has become important, useful, or clarifying information. One is no longer neutral with respect to it. One has acted vis-à-vis this data—in some manner one has accepted it.

Two observations should be made at this point. First, remembering the dimension of mystery, we need to recognize the difficulty of explaining precisely why certain information, which was formerly *only* information, became significant. Obviously it always has something to do with personal experience. Something happened to one, some new constellation of events and attitudes, and in the process what was previously mere fact became relevant fact. It helped to explain something. It became a window through which one could catch a glimpse of meaning not grasped previously. A question was answered, or made more tantalizing. Yet it would be unconvincing to show an absolute correspondence between the experience and the new appreciation for this aspect of Christian teaching. Always in the face of such explanations one has to ask to what extent the Christian teaching itself, perhaps at an unconscious level, shaped the experience.

The second observation is that, applied to Christian experience, this second type of knowing seems never to occur in an all-embracing way. That is, it does not happen that the *whole body* of Christian doctrine becomes significant. What is acknowledged is rather this or that aspect of Christian teaching. It may be something central in theology, such as the doctrine of justification by grace through faith; or it may be rather peripheral or at least less basic—for example, some part of Jesus' Sermon on the Mount. Often the acknowledgment of a particular idea or dogma *opens one to the possibility* that there may be more to the rest of Christian teaching than one had anticipated.

Yet the *acknowledgment* of some particular dogma or precept of the faith does not necessarily lead to belief. Many of the people who have always been on the fringes of the Christian church have been persons who could certainly acknowledge some aspects of Christianity, but who did not and do not believe in the sense of faith commitment as such. As for those for whom the acknowledgment of some aspects of the faith does become a stage on the way to belief, it is probably true that what they acknowledged was, or came to be, one of the more important, central teachings of the faith—the forgiveness of sin, the sufficiency of divine grace, faith "not works," the suffering love of God in the face of human suffering. There are, however, many possibilities here, and the programming or classifying of this cognitional movement should not overlook the enormous variety of the ways in which people are brought to discipleship.

This needs to be recognized, for there is a danger, well documented in Christian history, that *patterns* are too easily established. Augustine's or

Luther's or Wesley's faith pilgrimage becomes normative for whole segments of the church. It is assumed that one will always move, let us say, from the studied contemplation of Paul's argument in his epistle to the Romans to the acknowledgment of the "justification by grace through faith" concept to the experience of salvation. Especially in the Protestant traditions, authoritative patterns of this sort are established on account of conventions stemming from strong, foundational personalities; and these patterns become the basis of programs of Christian education, preaching, church membership, and so on.

The truth is, surely, that the Christian tradition is exceedingly rich in ideas and responses, and that there is really no predicting what aspect of this tradition will grasp an individual, or why some acknowledge this aspect while others fasten upon quite another dimension of the tradition. Catholicism has understood this much better than the Protestant denominations, and this is one reason why the Catholic church has been able, despite great internal variety, to remain more or less "one body." In North America especially, what "Protestantism" seems to mean to large numbers of Protestants has more to do with such typologies of religious experience than with the broader traditions of the faith, including those testified to in the Bible itself. In fact, it is difficult for persons in our context to experience more immediate and open exposure to Scripture and tradition in the broader sense, because their approach to these almost invariably is guided by certain communally predetermined assumptions about them. Those individuals, therefore, who are predisposed to affirm such assumptions—or are particularly in need, perhaps, of personal acceptance by their confessional community—move without great difficulty to the stage of "acknowledgment." But, as we have noticed heretofore, an increasingly large number of persons reared in Christian homes and parishes on this continent find it impossible to emulate or even to sympathize with the basic belief patterns and acknowledged "values" of their congregations, and consequently discover no entrée into the faith as such.

What this means for theology both at the theoretical and practical levels is that, beyond the need for a more disciplined and serious introduction to the basic data of the faith (at the "knowledge" level), there is in our context an equally important need to free rudimentary Christian teaching from denominational and sectarian strictures, so that the *breadth* preserved in Scripture and tradition may become accessible to more persons within and on the periphery of Christian communities. At present, this breadth is still restricted to those who are training for careers within the churches—and to minorities even within this classification. Yet without some acquaintance with the great variety of dogma, symbols, and perspectives that constitute the whole tradition of Jerusalem, the points at which what we are calling acknowledgment can occur are limited and sometimes gravely limited. Human experience and human need are always nuanced; and this nuancing must be met, if its curiosity is to be aroused, by a tradition which is capable of many shades of meaning and interpretation.

TRUST

In human experience there is also a kind of knowing which is different from either the acquisition of data or the assimilation and acknowledgment of this data. If we had only these two categories, we would not know what to do with a whole dimension of our experience of knowing.

This would be particularly true of the kind of knowing that we engage in vis-à-vis other human beings. When I say that I know my friend, I obviously mean something quite different from either the possession of knowledge or the acknowledgment of certain ideas or truths. I mean that there exists between myself and this other person a certain *relationship*. It is this relationship as such that I have in mind when I say that I know this other human being. It is not the details of her history or the characteristics of her physical or mental make-up that I intend. Nor is it just that some of these characteristics have become significant for me. Rather, when I say, "I know her," I am alluding to a knowledge which quite transcends both the information I possess about this other human being and those aspects of that information which have gained some special meaning for me. The relationship did not occur merely as a result of the information I possessed about her, or even as a consequence of the fact that some of that information became important or meaningful. There was a time when I could say that I knew a good deal *about* this person, but I could not say, "I know her"—not, at any rate, if I were being accurate in my use of language. There was also a time when I could say that aspects of this person's character interested me in certain ways, i.e., when some of the data I learned about her corresponded with traits or questions or needs within myself. But even then I could not say that I knew her. Between the state of acknowledgment and the more personal sort of knowing, knowing which implies depth of relationship, there is once again a gap. The overcoming of this gap does not occur automatically. It is not a matter of simple evolution—occasionally it is almost revolutionary! There are many persons whom I somehow "acknowledge" (i.e., the data I possess about them is significant to me), but who do not exist for me as persons of whom I can honestly say, "I know him"; "I know them." Something has to happen, some new dimension has to be introduced, if I am to pass from the state of acknowledging someone to the state of knowing him or her in this third, interior sense.

What has to happen? What does in fact happen? It is extremely hard to describe it. Art can describe it better than discursive thought. But perhaps we may notice some things about this transition, without being too superficial.

For one thing, this third kind of knowing seems to occur in one as a matter of *decision*. I decide—but it would be better to say that *I find myself deciding*—that this other one has some kind of claim on me and, correspondingly, that I have some kind of responsibility for this other. We may call this "decision," not so much in the sense that it is deliberately, consciously willed; and not in order to distinguish it sharply from a sense of compulsion or destiny (because in fact in very much of the knowing that occurs at this level there is a strong sense of "having to"; indeed it would be hard to imagine the deepest form of such knowing, love, as if it could ever be totally free from the sense of destiny or compulsion). But I use the word "decision," rather, to mean that whatever occurs when a person moves over into this kind of personal knowledge of someone else, it is something which involves not only *rational* activity but the activity of the whole self. This means in a specific sense the activity of what we call the *will*. The "Will you?" and "I will" of traditional marriage ceremonies is a formal acknowledgment of this very distinction. Willing, in this sense, is a summing-up of the whole person, inclusive of thinking and inclusive of feeling, but transcending both. The knowing that is implied here is not just the summation of all that I know about this other one, and it is not just the recognition that some of the things I know are matters which touch me. It is the knowing of an encounter between persons who indeed know that they will *never* know each other fully in the fact-knowledge sense, and will *never* acknowledge in one another fully everything that really is significant about the other, but who nevertheless determine to commit themselves to one another.

The discontinuity between the three types of knowing is most conspicuous at this point. I seriously doubt that this third kind of knowing can occur apart from the first and second types—reports of love at first sight and the like notwithstanding! But neither the data that I receive in the first kind of knowing, nor the *significant* data of the second type are sufficient to *produce* the third. There is a hiatus between the second and third types of knowing. The overcoming of this hiatus cannot be engineered. Often, people try to manipulate others into this third form of knowing, but it cannot be done. This is the stuff out of which human pathos and tragedy are made. But the bridging of the gap, which even at the strictly human and "natural" level can hardly be described apart from recourse to transcendental language, is finally what makes life worth living.

In a real sense, we have already entered the theological application of this third type of human knowing; but now we must do so explicitly. With Christian faith and theology, as in human experience generally, it must be seen that there is no easy transition from the state I have called acknowledgment to this third state, which now we may describe as the state of belief, trust, or commitment. There are countless persons for whom much of Christianity "makes sense." What Christians believe is not something neutral for such persons—is not mere data. They may even live by certain Christian precepts and ideals. Yet they would not call themselves Christian believers, for they sense, rightly, that between their acknowledgment of Christian truths and the "I believe in . . ." of the Christian confession there is a certain leap of faith. They realize that belief involves a fundamental *trust*—a commitment of the *self*, not merely of the mind. Like those who look at human love from outside the experience of it, they know that while belief *involves* rational reflection upon data and ideas, it *is* infinitely more than this.

It is the recognition of the suprarational element in belief that has caused one stream within the Christian tradition to conclude that in the last analysis belief is *irrational*. Christian spiritualism, from Montanism to present-day charismatic movements, manifests a tendency to eliminate rationality from belief, or even to court the irrational. This is wrong, but it is based upon something right, namely, the insistence, over against all Christian intellectualism and the *kind* of orthodoxy which assumes that the holding of correct dogma is primary, that "believing" is and must be a form of knowing which transcends rationality and all the data accessible to reason. My point here, however, is that such a form of knowing is by no means exclusive to Christianity. It is true that in Christian faith this knowing is applied to an "object" that is different from other objects—that is, the Christian claims that this knowing applies not only to his wife, his friend, his neighbor, but . . . to God. But at least in terms of the *kind* of knowing, as distinguished from the object or content of the knowing, what Christian faith says is not in essence different from what is experienced universally by human beings. At the deepest level, what one means as a Christian when one affirms that one "knows" ("believes in") God is not different from what any human being means who says that she "knows" a friend, child, partner. . . . The *reasonableness* of belief in God is a question to which we must turn [elsewhere]. But it will make that a more meaningful discussion if we can agree, at the end of the present section, that "knowing" in the experience and terminology of Christian theology is as such continuous with knowing in human experience and language generally—also in this third sense. Christian knowing, in short, is not of another order, as if in the Christian the ordinary faculties and potentialities of "the thinking animal" had been replaced by something else! What—or rather who—is known may be considered unusual, indeed unbelievable, in an age of religious unbelief; but the mode of knowing itself is *entirely human.*

CONCLUSIONS

Three observations follow from the foregoing discussion: (*a*) The first is related to Christian apologetics. We have noted that our present context is one which manifests a conspicuous plurality of religious and quasi-religious alternatives. It is very important in our dialogue with those who do not belong to the Christian disciple community that we always seek to distinguish the level on which the discussion is taking place. The vast majority of encounters between alleged belief and alleged unbelief or alternative belief involve persons speaking at cross-purposes, because they are assuming different types of knowing. It can almost be taken for granted that most of those who attack Christian belief are arguing on the basis of the second type: acknowledgment. They think—often with reason—that Christians are persons who acknowledge certain data as having significance, as being literally true. They themselves want to say that it is not significant, not true. Such discussions can be worthwhile *if* the Christian understands that the objections to the faith are being expressed at that level. Too often, however, Christians do not understand this, and immediately seek to defend themselves as if they were offering an *apologia* for belief as such, rather than attempting to explain some of the concepts with which Christian belief may, to a greater or lesser extent, be bound up.

(*b*) Second, the distinction between knowing, acknowledging, and trusting has important practical implications for life within the disciple community itself. One of these is that we should not assume, either about ourselves or others, that *belief* must always mean the *acknowledgment* of all the data that comes to us in the tradition. There are persons who may be described as authentic believers, who nevertheless *acknowledge* very little of the traditional data. Some of them do not even *know* this data in the first, "knowledge" sense of knowing. Others know it but do not find it significant, though they may be open to learning its significance for themselves. In the cases of many Christians who have not been formally educated in theology, whole vast areas of doctrine are like foreign lands, unvisited and undreamed of. How many laypersons—how many clergy!—have given themselves studiously to the study of the evolution of trinitarian theology, to the concept of perichoresis, to comprehension of the *Filioque* clause, to serious consideration, even, of the nature of the authority of Scripture?

Again, there are persons of great learning who find much of what has been preserved in the tradition to be inessential. *Belief (fiducia)*, in both instances, can be entirely sincere and authentic. And the reverse is also true: there are persons who both know and acknowledge very much in the tradition, and are sometimes men and women of influence and authority in the churches, who nevertheless do not "know" in the third sense that we have described, i.e., they do not trust. The knowledge and acknowledgment of *much* does not guarantee belief, nor does the knowledge and acknowledgment of *little* signify disbelief.

(*c*) Third, however, the second observation poses a problem in practical Christianity: If belief cannot be easily correlated with knowledge and acknowledgment; if people often truly believe who do not know or acknowledge very much with respect to the traditions, doctrine, and dogmas of the faith, then why should Christians exert themselves to understand this tradition and communicate it to others? This, as we have seen, is a rather pertinent question in the North American context, where the effort of understanding what is believed is rarely undertaken with enthusiasm.

While this question is frequently a spurious one or the product of intellectual sloth, it can also be quite serious. It comes close to the heart of the basic paradox of knowing in Christianity. For it contains the recognition that in the last analysis it is not possible for human beings by their efforts either to know the "Thou" of biblical faith or to communicate God's presence and "word" to others. It implies that God, if God is to be known in the third, interior sense of knowing, must engage in an act of self-communication—must *reveal* God's self.

Yet the statement of Paul remains true:

> How are men to call upon him in whom they have not believed? And how are they to believe in him of whom they have never heard? And how are they to hear without a preacher? And how can men preach unless they are sent? . . . So faith comes from what is heard, and what is heard comes by the preaching of Christ. (Rom. 10:14-17)

Trust in God, as I have maintained throughout this discussion, does not lie on a continuous line with knowledge and acknowledgment. There is a gap between knowing and acknowledging the data that belongs to the Christian faith. There is an even greater discontinuity between acknowledgment and trust. There is also, however, an element of continuity between these levels of knowing. At least it must be said that trust does not occur apart from the hearing of information. Something has to happen to this information before it can be anything more than what the writer of Job called "the hearing of the ears." What has to happen—to state this in the language of our doctrinal tradition—is that the Holy Spirit must translate what is heard externally into the kind of "language" requisite to its internal reception—*Testimonium spiritus sancti internum*. We have seen that there are analogies to this process in every human relationship. The point just here, however, is that this transformation by the Spirit, this miracle of communication, presupposes the attempt of the human being with his or her various faculties to comprehend and share the Christian message. Belief does not occur without this very human activity. It does not come straight out of the blue, the consequence of a direct encounter with deity. It is mediated.

Precisely here, the *method* to which Christian theology is bound reflects most transparently the character of the theological content of this tradition. Unlike the gods of power and miraculous feats of whom the long story of humankind is filled, the God of covenant love will not bypass the processes of history and nature. God will not circumvent the human, including human rationality, volition, and discourse, in God's self-communication. This is not because the biblical God is *bound* to what is temporal, historical, natural, rational, human. Clearly, the whole tradition of Jerusalem envisages a sovereign Lord *who would be able, were it the divine intention, to communicate directly to each and every human being without any human mediation.* But it is just as apparent from the tradition that this God does not will to do this. Even if such a form of communication sometimes occurs with respect to specific biblical figures, the Bible does not regard it as *normative*. The normative mode—so normative, in fact, as to render direct epiphany or miraculous appearance highly suspect, and never wholly distinguishable from the demonic!—is the indirect, the mediated revelation. God confines God's self to the structures of creation, to what is historical, natural, human, finite. God will not be known apart from the poor testimony of "the preacher"—the teacher, the curious and passionate individual seeker after truth, the neighbor who, according to Reformation doctrine, is priest to neighbor.

> When God wants to speak and deal with us, he does not avail himself of an angel but of parents, of the pastor, or of my neighbor.

This puzzles and blinds me so that I fail to recognize God, who is conversing with me through the person of the pastor or father. This prompts the Lord Christ to say in the text [Jesus' encounter with the woman at the well—John 4]: "If you knew the gift of God, who it was that is saying to you, 'Give me a drink,' then I would not be obliged to run after you and beg for a drink."[7]

The point of this is not the exaltation of "the preacher," i.e., the witnessing community, the *medium* of divine communication, but the preservation of a kind of knowledge of God which permits the human knower to retain his or her integrity and dignity. The trouble with religious systems which rely upon direct supernatural epiphany is that in the process of the divine revelation, the human partner is effectively overcome—taken by storm. "Divinity can crush a man" (Luther). The God whose power subjects itself to, and is a function of, the divine love will not overwhelm our humanity. While, therefore, God can be known only through God's own grace, God's approach to us is in the humble form of the ordinary: ordinary events, ordinary creatures, ordinary people, ordinary thought and discourse.

Notes

1. Hall is quoting Paul Tillich, Systematic Theology, vol. 1 (Chicago: University of Chicago Press, 1951), 71.

2. The first great disutopic novel of the [twentieth] century, Yevgeny Zamyatin's *We* (trans. Mirra Ginsburg [New York: Viking, 1972]), depicts the mass culture in just such terms. When the protagonist wishes to find a language appropriate to love ("I wanted to say 'thou'"), he cannot do so in a society that can only say "we."

3. See Herbert Marcuse, *One-Dimensional Man: Studies in the Ideology of Advanced Industrial Society* (Boston: Beacon, 1964).

4. Martin E. Marty reminds us of Alexis de Tocqueville's telling insight on the subject: "'The majority [in America] draws a formidable circle around thought. Within its limits, one is free: but woe to him who dares to break out of it.' Religion, [de Tocqueville] saw, was a major element in the formation of this circle. He believed there was no country in the world where the Christian religion retained a greater influence over the souls of men than in America" (*Righteous Empire: The Protestant Experience in America* [New York: Harper Torchbooks, 1970], 90).

5. George Lindbeck, *The Nature of Doctrine* (Philadelphia: Westminster, 1984), 127.

6. Albert Schweitzer, *The Quest of the Historical Jesus*, trans. W. Montgomery (London: A. & C. Black, 1910).

7. Martin Luther, quoted by John M. Todd in *Luther: A Life* (New York: Crossroad, 1982), 351.

6

. . . But How?

In 1998, Hall produced what is probably the most unusual and conceptual book in his oeuvre, Why Christian? For Those on the Edge of Faith. To quote Hall, "The book takes the form of dialogues between an aging professor of theology (myself!) and a university undergraduate. The dialogues at the beginning of each chapter pose the question to which the rest of the chapter—the little 'essays' this wonderfully conscientious professor prepares for his student—tries to respond" (1998b:vii). The student is a composite figure, he says, but not far removed from the many students who have come to him over the years "living on the edges, between faith and doubt" (ibid.). The book, then, is an exercise in Christian apologetics, a genre that Hall had earlier critiqued as "questionable" in its "tendency to accommodate the Christian message to the 'felt needs' of the world." (1989:338). In the book's afterword, he notes that an apologetics often either reduces the faith to "religious simplism" or is "so keen to be au courant that it ends by reflecting rather than critiquing its culture." Hall resists both tendencies here, creating an engaging, thoughtful volume that displays both his subtle humor and passion for "doubting faith." (1998b:176). The selection offered below follows well from the previous chapter on knowing, as we see Hall engaging in what might be called "applied epistemology," as his imagined student struggles to move from knowledge to acknowledgment and trust.

Source: Hall 1998b:63–82.

You arrived a little early today. The frown on your forehead suggested to me that you had come to a certain impasse in your thoughts about Christianity. Your words soon confirmed that impression. I knew that we were in for a long session.

"I'm grateful to you for taking the trouble to write such a lengthy and careful statement about salvation," you began; "In fact, it's very generous of you to treat my questions so seriously. I didn't realize this when we began to have these chats, but I know now we're thinking about really complicated things. So I don't want you

to feel that I expect you to give me the kinds of answers I'd get, maybe, if I were talking to someone about mathematics, or physics, or even history. One has to talk around questions like these—and probably over a long period of time. In another sense, though, just talking around them is already a way of beginning to come to terms with them—emphasis on beginning, of course, I mean, the fact that we can do this—can actually communicate with one another about these questions—is itself . . . well, it's something, don't you think?"

I did. "I often wonder, in fact," I said, "whether the only 'answers' that matter, where these kinds of questions are concerned, are the ones that people are sometimes able to glimpse as they reflect on them together."

"That's an interesting thought," you replied. "I'll remember that. . . . Anyway, I wanted to say that to you—to thank you, I mean—because . . . well, to be frank, there's something that has been bothering me. I'm almost afraid that if I bring it up it will make you think you are wasting your time with me."

Now I was really curious. What could this subject be that had made you so hesitant to introduce it? Were you about to become very personal, confess something—perhaps, despite your protestations of having no feelings of guilt, blurt out some guilty secret? It had happened to me before. So I tried to look as nonjudgmental as I could.

"Let me put it this way," you began. "I can follow nearly everything you say, both in our discussions and in your little essays afterward. I understand it, nearly always, even when it doesn't quite mesh with my own assumptions and experiences. But that's where it stops—with 'understanding.' I mean, I follow the argument, usually. I can see the sense in it. Your 'reasons' do, most of them, explain a lot . . ."

Here I felt I might interrupt briefly. I said: "You know this word understanding *is a fascinating word. Literally, it means to 'stand under.' Like standing under something you can see in part, but not being able to see the whole of it. It means that* real understanding *is never—well, it's never 'understanding' in the way we usually use that word. There's always a large element of unknownness in it, because the thing you are trying to understand is bigger than you are."*

"That's just it!" you exclaimed. "I can understand enough of all this to know that I don't understand it! I can't grasp hold of it. I can't get inside it. I feel like an outsider most of the time, in fact. I can see why you would want to think in the way that you do, usually, but even when I try hard to make your reasoning my own, it just doesn't come off.

"For instance," you went on, "when you wrote about Jesus as being like a friend who stands on my own ground, where I am, unlike the friends who talk down to me

from their heights—well, I like that idea, of course. Who wouldn't be grateful for such a friend? But for the life of me I can't feel that Jesus is anywhere near me, let alone right 'down here' with me!

"Do you see what I mean? Jesus is back there in history, nearly two thousand years back. Christians talk about him all the time as if he were just next door, or even closer! I don't know how they can do this. At the same time, I can see that this—this sense of his presence, or whatever—is vital to them. To you, too. Without that, your 'reasons,' I think, would lack any foundation in experience. Obviously you aren't one of these people who go around sensing unseen 'presences' all over the place. You seem to have your feet on the ground. But what did you mean, in your last piece, when you spoke about the 'spirit of Jesus'? How do late-twentieth-century people like us, products of the age of science, acquire enough of a sense of mystery to make us open to such 'spirit' talk without cutting us off altogether from our own world and its assumptions?"

My mind was racing. Where to start, what to say? In your great and typical honesty you had once again dragged another kind of spirit—the Spirit of the Age, the Age of Fact and Verifiability and Know-How—into my quiet study, and awakened once again, in me, the sleeping giant of doubt. I could only hope that this giant might in turn be challenged by something greater, however fragile my grasp of it. For many reasons, not all of them intellectual, I found myself remembering the words of an ancient Christian hymn: "Come, Holy Spirit."

SECULARISM, SPIRITUALITY, AND THE HOLY SPIRIT

What you are asking about (forgive me, I was almost tempted to say what you are asking *for*) is what Christian tradition refers to as "the Holy Spirit." That's what your "How?" is all about. In fact, in an odd sort of way your question, even down to some of the language you use, is reminiscent of many of the conversations between Jesus and his disciples that are recorded in the Gospels. These disciples too, ordinary people not given to flights of fantasy or mystical visions, are constantly baffled by the things that Jesus says and does. They understand, yet they also do not understand. His parables—those seemingly simple, illustrative stories—obviously intrigue them, but frequently they miss their point altogether. Sometimes they grasp bits and pieces of his teachings, and are moved by some of the things that he says and does; nevertheless, they give expression again and again to a typical frustration: they know, it would seem, that they are missing something, and that this something is not just incidental, but is the key to everything else.

Perhaps because it was written later than the other Gospels, John's Gospel confronts this problem in a quite explicit way. Midway through his account (John 13–16), this author introduces a scene that rather epitomizes the frustration of the disciples in their wanderings with their teacher. All along, the poor fellows must have wondered where these meanderings were taking them, and now the impulsive Peter puts the question to Jesus directly and even bluntly: "Lord, *where are you going?*"

I find it a lovely thing to see this question right there in the middle of the story. We romanticize the apostles if we imagine that they simply followed Jesus unquestioningly. Many of his followers, we know, left him. The Twelve stayed on—"To whom else would we go?" they asked. But always there was this gnawing doubt about the aim of the whole enterprise: "Lord, precisely where are you taking us?"

Jesus replies, enigmatically enough, that they "cannot follow where he is going." This aggravates their uncertainty even more, for they hear the answer (as the author of John obviously intended it) as a reference to Jesus' approaching death. Does not this death, which is predictable enough given his deteriorating relations with both secular and religious authorities, spell the end of everything for them? And in that case, what purpose has been served by their following him—and at such cost to themselves and their families?

Then Jesus, sensing their confusion and feelings of abandonment, introduces our theme: the promise of the divine spirit: "I will not leave you orphaned; I am coming to you. . . . the Advocate, the Holy Spirit, whom the Father will send in my name, will teach you everything, and remind you of all that I have said to you." And later he adds: "I still have many things to say to you, but you cannot bear them now. When the Spirit of truth comes, he will guide you into all the truth; for he will not speak on his own, but will speak whatever he hears."

★ ★ ★

The assumption here, and indeed throughout the Newer Testament, is that the life and mission of Jesus, while in a certain sense it will be completed with his death (he himself on the cross announces that "It is finished"), in another way only begins at that ending. The termination that is Jesus' crucifixion is understood by the Newer Testament as what in Latin is called a *terminus a quo*—not an end to which (*ad quem*) everything moves, but an end from which (*a quo*) something now takes place—something new. In their wanderings with their unofficial "Rabbi," the disciples are already being prepared for that new possibility, though they don't rightly know it. Even their confusion and frustration seem to be necessary to what is to happen later. They must taste the experience of being baffled and bumbling, empty of answers, before they can gain a depth of (yes) *understanding* that surpasses their present mixture of knowing and not-knowing. Right up until the coming of the Holy Spirit, described in Acts 2, these close followers of Jesus, the very "inner circle" of his disciples, feel like "outsiders"—that was your word, and it is just the right one. Though they are on the inside, so far as physical proximity to Jesus is concerned, they know they are still outsiders. Some vital connection is missing.

What is this missing "ingredient," according to the Scriptures? What is it that can only be supplied by the Spirit of God—that even Jesus himself, while physically present among them, cannot give them? To answer that, we must use several biblical and theological concepts:

- *metanoia*: a change of heart and direction, an about-face, repentance, conversion; external change is not enough; the change that is necessary, if the outsiders are to become insiders, is an internal change, a changed spirit;
- *enlightenment*: the gift of inward illumination, the experience of truly comprehending what before could only be heard "with the hearing of the ears," to use a biblical expression; this is what Jesus meant by saying that the Spirit would lead his disciples into truth, truth that they could not "bear" just now;
- *faith*: far from merely imparting knowledge, it is the work of the divine Spirit to awaken in them a response of trust in the God who has been made known to them through Jesus;
- *calling*: the effect of the change (*metanoia*) that comes over them, deepening their understanding and evoking their faith, is to give them a new and bold sense of their vocation, their mission; they are not changed, enlightened, and enabled to trust God just for their own *salus* (salvation); they are sent out into the world by this personal experience—because, as I said before, it is the world that God wants to redeem, not just individual persons, and not just "the church." This is why the very first act of the disciples following the Pentecost experience (that is, the coming of the Holy Spirit), is public preaching of the "Good News."

Now, in all of this we encounter a dimension of Christian faith so important that one would have to say that, without it, there would have been no such thing as Christianity, and we wouldn't have been discussing any of this. For, while Jesus (as we've already observed) is at the very center of this faith, he alone, as a historical figure, could not have brought about the response that was needed to inaugurate and sustain an enduring community of faith.

* * *

In other words, it is not really adequate or right to think of Jesus only as the historic "founder" of Christianity as he is sometimes designated—as if, like the founder of a philosophic school or political movement, he had got the movement going, and then it became self-perpetuating. That Jesus was the "founder" of Christianity may of course be said, but it is not a sufficient explanation of the Christian faith, and for reasons closely related to the problem with which you introduced this discussion. There must be some sense, on the part of such a community, that their "founder" is still present with them, guiding, enabling, judging, sustaining them.

What ordinary founders of movements can do, Jesus also did, and much more thoroughly than most founding personalities: that is, through his teaching, his healings, his relationships, and above all the conduct of his own life and death, he established the model of "the Way" that he intended his followers to go. They would subsequently have constantly to refer themselves and their teachings and behavior in the world to that model, to test the authenticity of their own life and work.

But there is something that founders cannot do, though they all attempt it—something that Jesus also, as founder of the Christian "Way," could not do so long as he intended (as he clearly did) to remain within the bounds of strictly human possibilities and not resort to suprahuman or divine power. I mean that founders, including Jesus, are not able to bring about profound internal transformations within the secret and innermost spirits of their followers. While with their persuasive teachings and charismatic personalities founding figures like Socrates or Karl Marx may come very close to effecting deep personal convictions in their immediate circle of disciples, they cannot transform the inner selves of the persons who surround and succeed them; and with the founders' deaths and the swift passage of the years the remembrance of their presence ceases to have even the degree of influence they had in their lifetimes. Soon, as we know from the history of both the Socratic and the Marxist schools of thought, among many others, there occur serious divisions in the once quite-united movements, brought on by new interpretations and new leaders; and soon, too, the lively discourse of the founder is reduced to doctrines and systems and slogans to which allegiance is demanded, often in a way that would have shocked the founders themselves.

The transforming truth to which Jesus wanted to introduce his disciples, the truth he names in the passage quoted above, truth that both convicts and liberates—such truth could not and cannot be reduced to dogmas, propositions, and systems that can be written down, memorized, and regurgitated. When this happens, it is no longer the lively, life-altering truth that was originally intended. Truth, if it is gripping enough to deserve that high name, always transcends "truths." Such truth must always emerge out of its unpossessible, living source, and it can only be received by human beings who themselves are made ready and willing to hear and be changed by it.

The truth into which Jesus intends his disciples to be "led" by the "Comforter" whom he promises to send, is just this living truth, which, in order to achieve a foothold in the lives of those who hear it, must radically alter those lives. For theirs (and ours!) are lives that manifest an abiding resistance to truth. Truth makes all human beings uncomfortable; it calls us into question; it makes demands of us that are beyond our ordinary capacities, not to speak of our habitual intentions and preferences. As the historical Jesus (according to John) told his original disciples, the way of truth to which he wished to initiate them could not be borne by them "just yet." First their innermost selves—their minds, hearts, souls, spirits—must be made ready to receive it. And that would be the work of "the Comforter," the divine Spirit.

* * *

What we are encountering in this whole discussion is a dimension of Christian experience that has been hard for many modern Westerners to grasp. One meets this dimension everywhere in Christian tradition, and indeed (in different ways) in all religious traditions, but it becomes unavoidable and central in Christian teaching concerning the Holy Spirit. What shall we call this dimension? We could call it the "transcendental" dimension, meaning that it goes beyond or transcends what we as modern Western people consider ordinary experience of the world. Or we could call it the mystical dimension, because it assumes the possibility of encountering mysteries not accessible to the usual processes of knowing, and of experiencing relationship with presences invisible to sensory perception. Or we could call it, simply, the spiritual dimension, referring by this to a communion of the human spirit with a center of consciousness, being and willing that is not present to us in an obvious, material form, though it is altogether real.

I say that this dimension, without which Christianity (and most if not all other religious faiths) would not exist, has been very hard for modern Westerners to grasp or to take seriously. Of course, it doesn't help matters that so much of the most vocal "spiritualism" we have observed in and around our very secular environment, much of it avowedly "Christian," has been so unacceptable to sane and sober minds. Often it has appeared simply bizarre, or even ridiculous. But even more subdued and nonostentatious forms of spirituality seem foreign to the secular mentality. Perhaps enlightened, tolerant persons are willing to listen to ancient or even contemporary "mystics" as if they were poets or dreamers; but the general effect of two or more centuries of sensory-based (empirical) rationality has made most of us skeptical of any religious or even quasi-religious thought that assumes the reality of presences or influences or relationships that cannot be explained by reference to data that is subject to "scientific" (that is, empirical and controlled) investigation.

Even if "the modern mind" admits that there is much that we do not understand, and in that sense admits of "mystery," such a mind is likely to consider the unknown simply as that which *still remains to be known*, rather than as being permanently beyond our usual means of measurement. While possessors of such a mentality are usually tolerant of those who claim to have knowledge of God or to be in communion with the risen, living Christ through the mediation of the Holy Spirit and so forth, they harbor a strong suspicion of all such claims. Such claims are so completely inconsistent with the fact-oriented world of our daily experience as a people that when they are not regarded with open skepticism they are usually politely relegated to the realm of "religion"—a realm which may or may not be respected, depending on differing social circumstances.

You yourself were giving expression to this secular bias of the modern Western mind when you said that while you could "understand," at a certain degree of comprehension, what I said and wrote about Jesus and his centrality to Christian faith, you could not grasp what Christians mean when they speak of Jesus as one who is present to them here and now. In what I have said just now about the Holy Spirit, I hope that I have at least pointed to what Christians mean when they speak of the presence of the God made particular and concrete for them through Jesus, and so of Jesus' own presence to them. But I know perfectly well that this explanation, so far as it goes, will not have cleared up the difficulty you feel. In fact, in a way this discussion of the Holy Spirit may even have heightened that difficulty for you. For while, within the framework of modern secularity, it is certainly possible to speak about the influence of the historical Jesus, when it comes to belief in the work of the Holy Spirit the standards of knowledge accepted by the modern world seem to have been completely cast aside.

I do not think, to be honest, that I am ever going to produce any arguments—*as* arguments—that will overcome for you this difficulty (I mean this sense of your being "an outsider"). In fact, as I have already observed, the only thing that will alter your attitude to all of this is an inner transformation that neither I nor any other human being can cause to happen within you. You, too, could become the subject of a *metanoia*, though that is not mine to arrange. Nevertheless, if we continue to reflect on this subject at the level of "reasons"—reasons that cannot pretend to be proofs and do not wish to be thought so—it may be possible to clear the way for the divine Spirit to struggle with your spirit, as has happened with others before you—myself included. Who knows, perhaps the "understanding" that you already feel is the beginning of deeper kind of "standing under."

* * *

With that end in mind, let's think a little about something quite interesting that has been happening lately in this fact-obsessed Western world of ours. As you are certainly aware, during the past decade or so, a word has entered the common speech of people in our part of the world that, I can assure you, no one forty or fifty years ago would have thought to hear from us except in the realm of "religion"; and even there it was not frequently used. The word is *spirituality*. Now one hears this word everywhere, often in the most unlikely places. Sometimes it is linked with another catchword of the age, *values*: "There are spiritual values," an aspiring politician announces, "that must not be set aside in our fast-moving society." Even businesses and advertisers know how to employ this language—usually, to be sure, for crass economic purposes; but then, they wouldn't use the term at all unless they knew it had some appeal for their "target group." Whole movements have sprung up, some of them admittedly religious, but others wishing to stay clear of the turmoil and in-fighting of conventional religions, and some (like much "New Age" spirituality) pretending to be "postreligious." People discover that nature is in fact brimful of spirit, that rocks and trees and brooks—yes, even the planet itself as in the Gaia theory promulgated first by James Lovelock—may be said to possess life and spirit. Suddenly there is an unheard-of interest in the spirituality of the indigenous peoples of this continent, and in Celtic spirituality, and other premodern approaches to the mystery of life.

In fact, many would link this search for transcendence and the new openness to mystery with postmodernism—a term that is still so variously defined as to its positive meaning that the only agreement about what it *is* is that it is *not* modernity, it is *post*modern.

What is going on here? It is quite astonishing, if you've lived long enough to witness the enormous change it represents. Less than four decades ago, when I was just beginning my professional career as a theologian, all the "with-it" people (as we presumptuously dubbed ourselves then) in our liberal and moderate Protestant circles were reading and praising books written by Christian thinkers who wanted to celebrate secularity. We all thought it a marvelous thing that the Christian faith did not regard this world as "sacred," or steeped in such mystery that it must always elude our grasp. We realized, with a kind of relief, that as Christians we could accept and rejoice in the secularity of the world, seeing it as a "system" that was in some real way self-contained and self-perpetuating. We could take hold of our human responsibilities within this system—yes, certainly, our God expected us to "take charge" within the sphere of nature. Moreover, far from feeling that Christianity had been bypassed by secularism, we should recognize (so we felt) that it was precisely Christianity that gave birth to secularism; for the Christian doctrine of creation meant that the world is separate from God, and not to be endowed with any kind of divinity itself.

And now, in so short a time, all of this has come to seem very premature and questionable. Why? The reason, I think, is that secularism went too far. Like most worldviews—most "isms"—secularism has certain built-in weaknesses and dangers, and the more it presses unchallenged toward its own full expression the more obvious the weaknesses and dangers are seen to be. For one thing, the tendency of secularism to dispel mystery and see everything as being ultimately fathomable and even controllable—this has to be regarded, finally, as both a weakness and a danger. Because everything just *isn't* understandable, and it certainly is not all subject to human control; and when people start behaving as if there were "no limits" to either their knowledge or their mastery, the results can be horrific. Nobody can, or ever will, tell us from a strictly scientific point of view why there is something and not nothing. Neither will human beings generally come to the point of calmly accepting suffering and death just because they are "natural."

Moreover, there seems to be a persistent need in us to have and to nurture some sense of mystery. So many of our experiences—including the most decisive and dramatic of them, like falling in love, or mourning someone's passing, or being filled with inexpressible joy before some natural occurrence or work of art—are so steeped in mystery that, without it, they would be robbed of everything that gives them meaning.

Secularism also, it should be remembered, went hand in hand with a certain economic and technological boom, following on the public euphoria that occurred in the aftermath of World War II. It is easy, and perhaps even predictable, in such periods of security and optimism, for people to think that the world is going their way, and that they themselves are beings of unusual accomplishment, for whom no task is impossible. But, in the meantime, a great many events and occurrences—the advent of nuclearism, Vietnam, the crisis of nature, the failure of so many of our institutions including governments, economic slumps, joblessness, and other things we've already touched on here and there—have conspired to make us, as a people, far less confident of our own abilities as masters in a world that is no longer so "user-friendly," [and] the secular bravado of three or four decades ago has practically disappeared among us. I don't, of course, mean that secularism has come to an end. It is still a mighty factor in the global situation at large. But its heyday in North America has, I think, passed—and in certain parts of Europe, too. We went far enough along the secular way to find out its costs and its disappointments. For many of us, it is a god that failed, an illusion; as an "ism," it has lost its great appeal.

* * *

And that has left us open, in new ways, to . . . spirituality. One can notice a kind of pendulum swing here, can't one? If one goes far enough toward a materialistic worldview like secularism, one discovers the limits and false promises of that system—quite possibly one was personally hurt by the system's unacknowledged dangers, as so many in the former Marxist lands were. So it is somehow natural that one starts to swing back to the other side of the spectrum—which is some antimaterialistic outlook, some kind of spiritualism. One wants to correct things, at least to restore some balance. It's a matter of survival!—and not only personal, but social survival.

What should Christians think about this new openness to the realm of "spirit"? Well, in my opinion they should be both open to it and (what shall I say?) vigilant, watchful. Let me explain why—as briefly as I can:

First, Christians should be open to the new spirituality because it really is a corrective to so much that has influenced—and conspicuously harmed!—the modern world. Materialism of every kind, whether ideological communism or unrestrained capitalism is simply one-sided, false, and humanly demeaning. Certainly we are "matter" and we live in a material environment; but if in our thinking everything is reduced to matter then very bad things soon begin to occur. Nature is "thingified," and we think we can do with it whatever we want. The result is pollution, the disappearance of species, the depletion of the ozone layer, global warming, and so on. Human beings too are turned into objects—after all, we're just part of matter. The personhood of persons no longer counts for anything. People become statistics, digits within a vast quantifiable whole. Finally the human spirit rebels against this reduction of itself; and Christians should see that rebellion as being "of God"!

What I am saying to you in this is that the fact-conscious, hard-data, and in that limited sense, "scientific" world that is suspicious of being labeled "spiritual," is being profoundly challenged in our time. And the challenge is coming, not only from religiously committed people like me, but from every aspect of human consciousness, *including* much of the best science, which has never been as materialistic as secular ideologies make it out to be. You yourself, let me remind you, borrowed rather too heavily on the materialist-secularist point of view when you spoke so passionately about how absurd spiritual ideas like the continuing presence of Jesus are to the modern, scientific mentality. I am just reminding you (I think you already know it!) that this so-called modern, scientific mentality "ain't what it used to be." For it was all too uncritically bound up with that ideological secularism that was ready to use science for its own purposes, but was in fact very selective in its choice of the "science" it used.

In saying this, I don't want you to hear that I now believe it is perfectly easy and straightforward to believe in "spirit"—whether that means the Holy Spirit or the human spirit, or for that matter spirit as a dimension of nature itself. It is neither simple nor natural to do so. Christian faith, like every other thinking system of meaning, continues to struggle with the prospect that matter may be all there is—that what we see (feel, touch, taste, and smell!) is what we get! But at least you should realize that Christians are not alone today in confessing that there are realities, forces, or dimensions that cannot be analyzed by the usual processes of scientific investigation, though some far-seeing scientists themselves sense them; that these realities are nonetheless very real; and that their recognition on the part of human beings is vital not only to our understanding but to our very survival as a civilization.

Isn't the very fact that there is something and not nothing, when (and if!) you come to think of it, rather astonishing? Closer to home, is not your own being, including the mystery of your birth, the wondrous way in which all your "parts" form a more or less integrated "whole"—including also the ongoing drama and unpredictability of your development, your relationships, your loves, your hopes and fears—isn't all of this a wonder so saturated with mystery that the thought of a presence called "Holy Spirit" may not be such an immense leap for you as may at first appear? Especially when, all around you today there are countless others, just as intelligent and often even more hard-nosed than you, who have found they must abandon their earlier, strictly one-dimensional points of view and realize that life is more than it appears, on the surface, to be?

But wait!—I am not saying this in order to push you into a belief for which you are not ready. That would be a foolish and even a wicked thing for me, or any other believing Christian, to attempt—though many do so. Only the Spirit of God is permitted to wrestle with your spirit in that way, because your personhood may not be violated or your freedom abused. Only the divine Spirit, the Spirit by whom we were created, can enter into such a destiny-filled dialogue with the human spirit honorably—that is, without oppressing, humiliating, or crushing our spirits. All that I have wanted to do here is to raise some questions about the kinds of presuppositions you (and many others, of course) bring to the hearing of any Christian testimony to divine presence, transcendence, and mystery. Some of those presuppositions are themselves questionable, and they may be functioning in your life as false and unnecessary blocks to your hearing of that testimony. We seem to be living at a time when the world itself, through costly trial and error, has rediscovered its own spiritual needs—or started to. Your social environment is no longer *monolithically* secular, no longer by definition hostile to transcendence.

* * *

But now to this quite positive assessment of the new spirituality of our society, I have to add a caveat—a small note of warning. Christians have to be a little skeptical also about *this* trend. The line between "spirituality" and "spiritualism" is a very fine one; and an ideology (an "ism") of the *spirit* is just as questionable as an ideology of matter or any other "ism."

Listen, in the name of spirituality, all kinds of monstrous things have occurred in history ancient and modern. Nothing in the modern world has been so "spiritual" as the mass rallies of Hitler's Nazis at Nuremberg and elsewhere. Those meetings were full of ecstatic, wildly enthusiastic people, wholly "turned on" by a highly spiritualized worldview, one celebrating the exalted spirit of the Aryan race and its allegedly redemptive mission in the world.

We have seen tragic displays of "spirituality" in North America, too, with innocent and naïve and tragically misled people giving themselves over to absurd theories and orgies of true belief and senseless self-sacrifice. Just because something announces itself as "spirituality" does not mean that Christians should rejoice in it! To the contrary, they should probably exercise greater critical vigilance in the presence of spiritualizers than in any other context. After all, biblically speaking, the greatest spirit of all—great in a way that deluded human beings always recognize greatness—is the one the Bible calls Satan, "the Father of Lies" (John 8:44), as distinct, remember, from the "truth" into which, Jesus says, the divine Spirit will lead his followers. Demonic spirits are always the more impressive ones—they are those who bring on the real fireworks! *God's* Spirit, on the contrary, is a "still small voice" (1 Kings 19:12), a quiet influence—perhaps no more impressive than the words of a simple person, even a child (Matt. 21:16), or the faces of the poor and sick and needy. God's Spirit, in the biblical understanding, does not come on strong. If we are in the end overpowered by it, it is only because we want to be—because we, like Jacob at the brook, while wrestling with that Spirit are really longing to be blessed by it (Gen. 32:22-32).

So, while the new spirituality can provide a necessary criticism of modernity's simplistic trust of technical rationality; while it can offer something like a new framework of credibility for Christian and other religious faith, it must not be seen as an obvious or unquestionably trustworthy friend of Christian belief. It remains true—what the same author of John's Gospel wrote in his first letter—that the spirits must be "tested" (1 John 4:1-6). Not all spirits are "of God," he says; in fact, he implies that most are not! So one must check them out. They will be known for what they are by the kinds of things that they entice their adherents to do, say, think, and believe. Spirits that manifest themselves in unusual displays of a suprahuman or seemingly godlike nature are held in high suspicion by the Bible. Jesus did not attempt to impress people and commend himself by resorting to such tactics; on the contrary, he resisted all such temptations as being "of the devil" (Matt. 4:1-11; Luke 4:1-12). And the life of Jesus, says John, is the "test" to which reputed spirits and their representatives have to be put. Some Christians will disagree with me here and point to the miracles of Jesus; but the miracles are really about something else—in fact, they are about that same "healing" and "wholeness" that we discussed last time: they are parables and exemplifications of salvation.

When it comes to spirits and spiritualism, what serious Christians should remember is not so much the miracles of Jesus as his many conversations with people, his way of being with them. He did not *command* belief in them; where possible, he evoked faith, but he did not cause them to believe because of fantastic displays of power. Jesus was willing to trust language; he did people the great honor of discoursing with them reasonably; he did not want to thrust change upon them, but to help it to happen within them through the ordinary processes of thought, the deepening and renewing of the mind. Jesus did not violate their understanding, however limited and frustrating it might be, by overpowering it through mystic spiritual means—that would have been to turn the miraculous into pure magic. If their understanding were to be awakened to the truly transcendent and mysterious, if they were to know themselves—as the disciples came to know themselves—to be "standing under" something infinitely greater than they could ever understand, this would have to happen from within, not as something imposed from without.

And that is why Paul, who doesn't altogether rule out external signs of the Holy Spirit's presence such as *glossolalia* or "speaking in tongues," nevertheless warns his churches against such practices. He would rather, he writes, say "five words" that make sense than to babble on in some unheard-of jibberish that might impress sensation-seeking or perhaps neurotic people, but would do nothing for genuine faith—unless it were then clearly interpreted (1 Cor. 14:18-19).

* * *

And so we are back at "reasons." As I said before, I doubt if faith ever comes to anyone as a result of argumentation, reasoning, proving this and that. It is indeed a gift of the Spirit if I believe, or, to speak more accurately, if my native *unbelief* is perennially challenged by its opposite. Faith is not just my doing—not just the conclusions of my mind. If it were simply a human possibility, I'd certainly try to argue you into it!—because I do think it would make all the difference for you.

I can't do that. But what I can do, or try to do, is to help you to look more closely at your own options as someone who lives in our kind of world. For a couple of centuries and more, ours has been a fact-befuddled world that advertises itself as "scientific" and "rational" and (of course!) "practical." Over against that "secular" worldview a new concern for "spirit" has arisen, and faith can relate positively to that concern at many points. But Christian faith is not an "ism"—it is no more a spiritualism than it is a materialism. Faith keeps its own counsel, follows its own drumbeat. If against secularism and rationalism it calls for more spirit, against spiritualism it calls for greater faithfulness to this world and to the ordinary processes of human thinking. The pendulum of human historical preferences is always swinging. It goes from one extreme to another, and in the process lives are affected—many, alas, are literally lost, for ideologies are never harmless! Christianity is not just a matter of keeping one's balance in the midst of all this—no, it is not just a matter of balance and "the middle way." But there is, I think, a kind of sanity about it, when it is well understood, which in the name of the "abundant life" that is the goal of its Lord and spirit, resists all those "isms" that promise great things but in the end, and with great regularity, rob humanity of its birthright.

PART II

The Crucified God and the Suffering Christ: Theology in the Context of the Cross

7

Theology and Doctrinal Traditions

As noted above in the introduction to chapter 2, "Theology and Faith," in part 2 of Thinking the Faith, Hall examines the discipline of theology, and how that relates to seven elements: faith, the Bible, doctrinal traditions, experience, prayer, the church, and the world. Here, by way of looking at specific theological topics with an eye toward contextuality, we return to that section to consider how theology interacts with tradition. As before, Hall takes a somewhat apophatic approach by considering this issue over against two common alternatives: modernism and traditionalism, which some might characterize as the tension between the liberal and orthodox impulses. Considering the role of the theologian in navigating this polarity, Hall advocates especially for an ethic of responsibility (see also below, chapter 15).

Source: Hall 1989:263–72.

THE DYNAMIC CHARACTER OF TRADITION

A third basic element in the discipline of Christian theology is tradition. It would be better to say tradition*s*, because, as we have already had occasion to notice, the past articulations of Christian belief with which the disciple community lives are not sufficiently unified or congruent to constitute a single entity. There is in fact great variety in the doctrinal self-expressions of the church's past, just as there is variety in its present.

Moreover, far from being a fixed or static thing, the debates and councils and decisions and counterdecisions which constitute this vast theological heritage continue to engage one another in the ongoing dialogue of the church. Of course, I do not mean that documents like the formula of Chalcedon or historically important works like the *Sentences* of Peter Lombard are themselves altered. Nevertheless, the church's assessment of such products of the past struggles of Christians to understand what they believed is in a constant state of flux, so that sometimes quite radical alterations in the significance of traditions for faith and theology can be noticed by the student of church history. A particular tradition which may have been important for one age is replaced, in the next epoch, by a different—not infrequently by a radically different—tradition. A Christian thinker taken up by this era and made, as one may say, almost the patron saint of the theologians, is dropped by the next. An obscure scholar of the distant past suddenly becomes particularly authoritative for the present disciple community, or some segment thereof.

Dramatic shifts in the evaluation and meaning of doctrinal traditions occur, especially, in periods of radical transition in church and society.[1] Indeed, part of what is meant by a term like "radical transition" is precisely this diversification in the search for authorities within the abundant traditions of the faith. At the time of the Reformation, for example, there was a sudden resurgence of interest in Augustine, who, during the High Middle Ages, had been caused to retire into the background on account of the high scholastic preference for Aristotelian categories rather than the Platonic views of the Bishop of Hippo.

. . . [O]ur own age is also an age of radical transition. It is not surprising, therefore, that this dynamic character of the role of tradition in theology is again conspicuous. Charismatics have found new meaning in ancient movements like Montanism and the spiritualistic "sects" of the sixteenth century—movements generally rejected heretofore. Liberationists are critical of the substitutionary atonement theology which has dominated Western Christendom and turn to accounts of the work of Christ which accentuate his victory over oppressive powers. Political theology manifests a special interest in minority movements of the past which were denounced more on account of their radical views about the nature of human community than their theologies: the so-called left wing of the Reformation is approached in most progressive seminaries and graduate schools of theology today in a way completely different from the largely unsympathetic treatment that it received in such institutions three decades ago. All who are conscious of the end of the Constantinian era have a newly emergent concern for *pre*-Constantinian forms of the church, and look upon post-Constantinian developments in theology differently because of their awareness of the consequences for doctrine of the sociopolitical status of the church in the situation of establishment. Perhaps most conspicuously of all, especially in the North American context, feminists have returned to the history of the church and its doctrinal traditions with a whole new perspective on what was transpiring in that long past. They pose for the disciple community at large awkward and provocative, but very basic questions about the influences of sexism and patriarchy upon the thought of the church as well as its deeds. And they discover "new" authorities, many of them women (e.g., Julian of Norwich, Hildegard of Bingen), who were obscured or purposely ignored because of the masculine domination of the tradition.

All of this demonstrates the flexible and lively nature of the role of tradition in theological work.[2] It tells us, besides, something about the reason for this dynamism. Theology always requires a past—roots! A Christian theology lacking any past would be an anomaly. For Christianity is, as we have already noted, a historical faith, and no theologian of this faith, even the most charismatic, can be content to spin theology out of his or her own entelechy. At the same time, theology that is sensitive to its context cannot be satisfied with any and every past articulation of belief. It will not simply accept what is "there," i.e., the particular traditions(s) which ecclesial convention has for the time being baptized. It needs a past which can be truly foundational for what it feels must be said and done here and now. This need is built into the theological discipline as such; it is not imported to it by restless persons who are not content with the *assumed* traditions. The rejection of regnant traditions and the search for new ones has been a feature of Christian theology throughout the ages. What is happening all around us today in this regard is simply a heightened application of a very ancient (and honorable) practice of this discipline—the quest for relevant and supportive traditions.[3]

Contra Modernism and Traditionalism

The word *tradition* comes from the Latin *tradere*, "to hand over," "to deliver." We have noted that the Christian faith is a historical faith. It is this, not only in the sense that its origins are inextricably bound up with historical events, moments of high revelatory significance (*kairoi*) . . . ; it is also historical in the sense that we receive from the past generations of Christians certain interpretations, concepts, dogmas, formulas, and the like, with which we must somehow come to terms.[4] We cannot take lightly these counsels that are delivered to us from our forebears. For one thing, whether we like it or not, we are ourselves always in some measure products of these traditions. There is no Christian alive, regardless of her or his specific intellectual background or ecclesial allegiance, whose belief has not been influenced by thousands of Christian thinkers of the past. Even persons who imagine that they can go straight from the present to the Scriptures (of whom there are a great many in North America) bring to their reading of the Scriptures countless presuppositions that they have gleaned, consciously or unconsciously, from the centuries of evolving Christian tradition.

We have spoken in an introductory way about the dynamic character of the role of tradition in theology, but we are left with a number of questions: How ought theology to be informed by tradition? What responsibility does the disciple community have towards what is "handed over" by previous generations of Christians, including aspects of the tradition which it cannot or will not itself appropriate? What attitude towards tradition should the theological community adopt?

As was the case in our discussion of the two previous elements (faith and Scriptures), so with tradition it may be that the most instructive method of responding to such questions would be to formulate our answer over against two alternatives which present themselves to us in our North American religious context—what we may name (without being too committed to the nomenclature as such) modernism/individualism and traditionalism.

(a) *Modernism* or, as one might say more accurately, the modernistic dimension within most forms of theological liberalism, seeks to minimize—and, in extreme expressions, to eliminate—the regulative role of tradition in theology. In the name of what is—or seems—relevant to the present, the modernist spirit feels quite free to dispense with whatever it receives from the past that does not relate in any obvious way to present spiritual needs. This approach generally assumes that *most* of what has been handed over from the long Christian past is in fact irrelevant to the present, and that much of it constitutes a downright impediment to the Christian apologetic.

It is, in other words, the present situation with its most conspicuous ("felt") needs that constitutes for the modernist the touchstone of authenticity. But this concern, laudable in itself, can be problematic—to the point of a betrayal of itself—when it is not accompanied by a perspective that is gained from a dynamic relation to the past. The case of early twentieth-century modernism exemplifies the point:

A time came when modernist forms of Christian liberalism, having so thoroughly identified themselves with the modern project, had nothing to say to the society that had bought into that project. With the year 1914 and following, the present to which modernism attached so much importance began to cast up questions and experiences which the architects of modernity had assumed no longer belonged to advancing history. Like its secular counterparts, religious modernism was so certain that the world was progressing towards the realization of the good that it could only be chagrined and embarrassed by the "primitive" and "medieval" associations of historic Christianity. In the name of adapting the Christian message to the times, the modernists discarded whole segments of tradition which did not, in their estimation, measure up to the enlightened standards of the new era. But in the end many who were influenced by this trend realized that they had thrown out the baby with the bathwater. For when the world began to show signs of growing darker instead of lighter, there were no categories left in the modernist vocabulary to name such phenomena as were once designated sin and the demonic and spiritual death and transcendent evil, etc. To comprehend their world, the successors of modernism had to return to earlier, "orthodox" language (hence "neo-orthodoxy"[5]), and to take up traditions which the generations of their teachers had consigned to the dark ages.[6]

The modernist mentality has nevertheless persisted in North America, despite the fact that many or even most of those who have been exposed to the formal study of theology in the past half-century have learned from their teachers to distrust it. For modernism on this continent has been able to depend on a powerful ally not found to the same extent in the European situation—individualism. The truth is, tradition has never appealed to the North American spirit, especially to the middle classes, even though (as we shall see in a moment) this same phenomenon begets a traditionalistic reaction. As [Robert] Bellah and his associates report in *Habits of the Heart*, "the very freedom, openness, and pluralism of American religious life makes [the traditional pattern of Jewish and Christian religion] hard for Americans to understand. For one thing, the traditional pattern assumes a certain priority of the religious community over the individual."[7] What comes naturally to most North Americans who have "found themselves" associates of the more established denominations of Christendom is not adherence to inherited dogma and ritual, but a sense of the rectitude or self-determination in matters of belief. Before the tribunal of the self, the most sacred and time-honored teachings of religious communities are nothing but matters of taste and opinion. Every young clergyperson, straight from seminary classrooms, where he or she has been inspired by some fresh introduction to the beauties of some great tradition, knows how powerless such messages are in the face of the omniscient souls of self-directed parishioners. Moreover, the same spirit frequently invades the theological communities themselves, which on this continent easily move from one consuming cause to another. Nothing is immune to the winnowing of individual preference—a preference containing, of course, a generous portion of peer and group pressure, and therefore readily giving way to faddism. "God himself becomes a discardable item, as for some 'death of God' theologians of the 1960s, even among those who continue to think of themselves as Christians."[8]

(b) *Traditionalism*: There is an opposite response to tradition that is equally questionable. I am referring to the tendency to conceive of the real task of theology as preserving intact, without blemish from the side of the world, the corpus of Christian teaching handed over by the past. In practice, of course, this always means the preservation of *some particular doctrinal tradition*, although the selectivity (not to say arbitrariness) involved in this procedure is seldom acknowledged by those who engage in it.

Modernism at least concerned itself with the present and future, and from the standpoint of a theology committed to contextuality this must be judged commendable. Its weakness was that it misconstrued appropriateness to the present, identifying pertinence with acceptability. Contextual theology does not seek to be acceptable; its goal is to be appropriate. Appropriateness may well mean confrontation and opposition to the major trends of its social context, and support for this opposition may well come from the tradition. But the contextualist regards the tradition as a resource for addressing the present, not as an end in itself. Traditionalism, on the contrary, is not primarily interested in speaking to the realities of its present historical moment; rather, it aims to preserve ideas and practices whose definitive articulations were given in the past. It would not be accurate to say that traditionalism is *dis*interested in the present—this is to caricature the traditionalist; but its primary intention is to cause persons and institutions in the present to accept as true the traditions to which it has given its loyalty. It will certainly be ready to *interpret* these traditions, and many of those whom I would include in this category are willing to devote great energy to the task of demonstrating the applicability of their traditions to the present. But traditionalism rejects (what is essential to contextuality in theology) the notion that the context provides the mold—"the question" (Tillich)—which theology must allow to shape its articulation of the faith. For the traditionalist, where a *consistent* traditionalism can be assumed, both the form and the content of Christian teaching are provided by the tradition.[9]

What is really happening in traditionalism is the same thing that happens with biblicism, only now the subject matter is not the Bible but some fondly held doctrinal orthodoxy. What is not recognized or taken seriously in this way of responding to the tradition is that the traditions which are thus fondled and preserved are themselves *historical* expressions, ergo contextual expressions, of Christian belief—ideas and systems thoroughly influenced by the particularities of their times and places. So that what is frequently transpiring in this type of attitude towards tradition (as in biblicism) is that the worldview of another epoch, or another clime, is being substituted for original reflection upon the present context. Such usage is almost by definition repressive. It functions, that is to say, as an ideational *alternative* to the actual present, a sanctuary from the always unknown land that is Now and Here.

It is enormously tempting for *all* religion to perform in this way, because it is far more comfortable to live with the questions of the past, and the Christian responses to them, than to be open to the unresolved, and even unknown, or only half-understood anxieties of the present. Much of the renewed interest that can be found today in past expressions of Christian belief comes from this (entirely understandable) need to escape from a particularly anomalous and agonizing present. It is the religious equivalent of the current vogue in Victorian antiquity. On the one hand the *problématique* of the age drives faith to search for a "usable past"; on the other, the same *problématique* tempts faith to take refuge in the past. It is always in practice difficult to distinguish the one motive from the other.

Developing a Dialectic of Dependence and Independence

These reflections on two questionable attitudes towards tradition help us to formulate a positive response concerning the relation between theology and doctrinal traditions. Over against the impulse to free ourselves from the past, it must be said that the discipline to which Christ's disciples are called necessitates a greater attentiveness to the past—indeed, a new alertness to the past as a whole, since it is for faith the unfolding story of God's good creation, but a concentrated and cultivated awareness of the Christian theological past in particular, since it is faith's mode of communication with the faithful of the ages. The community of faith needs this past, and it belongs to the gift of grace that the disciple community is given access to it. Because it has such access by grace, as *God's* gift, it is less tempted to regard the past as an oppressive authority to which it must do obeisance. Only God, the giver of the gift, is ultimately authoritative; therefore God's gift of a tradition can be received in a spirit of gratitude, as a support and a source of courage.

At the same time, this gift of tradition has a humbling effect on those who receive it. It causes them to realize that they stand along the moving edge of a lengthy process. They did not invent the gospel. They have come upon the scene, late in time. Today as we approach the year 2000 we think of two millennia of Christian tradition, not to mention the even longer Judaic past into which we have been "grafted" (Rom. 11:17f.). We are inheritors of a precious depository of thought. We do not begin *de novo*. It would be nothing short of crass arrogance and ignorance for us to imagine that we had nothing to learn from this treasury of meditation. If we are wise enough and humble enough, we shall realize our dependence upon this foundation. There is hardly an idea in our minds which does not have a hoary history! To acknowledge this, to admit our dependence, is not a mark of weakness but of maturity. The need to flee from the past belongs to adolescence. Perhaps it is a necessary stage, also within the disciple community. But as a permanent response to the past it is just as immature as adolescent rebellion carried into adulthood.

On the other hand, there is an equally immature type of dependence upon the past. Against the traditionalist impulse which is found, in some measure, in nearly everyone, it must be said that the process depicted within the Christian tradition itself, rightly understood, is an unfinished one. To fix the end, or the apogee, of this process at any point in the past is not only questionable ontology and eschatology (and an affront to the Holy Spirit!); it is also a failure to notice the most obvious thing about that past, namely, that *each generation has to do it all again, has to think the faith all over again.* Faith itself cannot be transferred from one generation to another, nor does time stand still. Therefore each new cohort of the disciple community has once more to expose itself to the basics, to think the faith for itself, under the conditions of its total environment. . . . [H]umanity's story of itself is never quite the same today as it was yesterday; those therefore who intend to bear witness to God's story of humanity must submit to a discipline which demands of them the most *original* thought, no matter how ancient the antecedents of this thought.

To be dependent upon the past after the manner of doctrinal traditionalism is to confuse profession with confession, preservation with conservation, doctrine with theology. On the other hand, to boast of independence from the past is to equate the liberty of the Spirit with arbitrariness. Between these two attitudes lies a third, which knows how to be grateful for and responsible towards the authority of the tradition without using it as a refuge from intellectual and spiritual struggle. Anyone who has subjected herself or himself to the task of seeking to know, deeply, any of the great thinkers of the Christian past will realize how inconceivable it is for her or his generation to dispense with such testimony. But neither Augustine nor Aquinas, Calvin nor Luther, Barth nor Niebuhr can tell us what we have to understand, as Christians today, as we face nuclear war and continental famine and racial strife and sexual tensions whose precise character none of these persons could have anticipated. From them, as from the Scriptures, we can receive inspiration and courage without which our own thought is impoverished, trivial, and literally impossible. But in the end it is we ourselves who must do theology.

Notes

1. James Gustafson writes that "theologians tend to hold the tradition and what is received with a greater degree of reverence and respect than do scientific investigators. . . ." Nevertheless, the history of theology is marked by "radical changes" in the reception of biblical and postbiblical traditions. "Abandoning and discarding are part of theological development. . . . Selection of what is to be retrieved or sustained is relative to knowledge and understanding present in the culture that pertains to matters of concern to theology." Such development can be seen both in great issues of belief, such as the readiness of the reformers to "discard a great deal of the philosophical apparatus of the tradition they inherited" and in more explicit issues such as ethical teachings of the church. Gustafson cites homosexuality, "long judged to be a mortal sin against nature," but "now interpreted by some Roman Catholic moral theologians as an excusable act in those instances in which the agent cannot be held accountable for the conditions which disposed him or her to act in this way" (*Ethics from a Theocentric Perspective* [Chicago: University of Chicago Press, 1981], 140f.).

2. In the conclusion of his insightful book on the subject of tradition, Brian Gerrish writes: "What the theologian receives from the past as 'tradition' is not a fixed, external authority, but the constantly changing expression of the church's interior life. In other words, tradition . . . , while no substitute for thought, is the occasion for thought; and precisely because it is something mobile. It requires to be transmitted, not passively or mechanically, but by a conscious, creative act" (*Tradition and the Modern World: Reformed Theology in the Nineteenth Century* [Chicago: University of Chicago Press, 1978], 181).

3. See Edward Farley, *Ecclesial Man: A Social Phenomenology of Faith and Reality* (Philadelphia: Fortress Press, 1975), 232.

4. In this sense, George Lindbeck is right when he castigates the condescending attitude towards tradition on the part of many Protestants and Catholics who view Christian faith in what he names the "experiential-expressive" manner: "The very words 'doctrine' and 'dogma' have the smell of the ghetto about them, and to take them seriously is, it seems, to cut oneself off from the larger world. One way to escape from this dilemma is to argue that the (from the modern perspective) absurd doctrines of the past never were important in themselves, but were only expressive symbolizations of deep experiences and orientations that ought not to be articulated in other and more contemporary ways" (*The Nature of Doctrine* [Philadelphia: Westminster, 1984], 77). (I feel constrained to demur, however, when Prof. Lindbeck proposes that my colleague, Gregory Baum, is "a Roman Catholic example" of this approach [ibid., 89]. Prof. Baum lives with the tradition in an earnest and responsible way, and while he shares with most of us the conviction that the past must not be allowed to dominate the church or determine its manner of confessing the faith, he is a very long way from the kind of "religious privatism and subjectivism" that Lindbeck [rightly] laments.)

5. It has largely been forgotten by history that Karl Barth and others were embarrassed by their association with "orthodoxy," and that (therefore) the term "neo-orthodox" is hardly one that accurately describes what they felt they were doing. To Eduard Thurneysen on February 1, 1924, the young Barth writes: "To me the shadow of the orthodoxy in which we necessarily stand for the moment presents the most painful problem of the situation. I was overjoyed in Bern at the citation of Overbeck which I had introduced at one point and which saved me from an all too unconditional approval by Hadorn. Also Hormann had to concede that 'our' position is not simply a return to 'conscience-enslaving' orthodoxy. In this connection the liberal resistance concerns me far less than the fact that one necessarily finds himself in a certain remoteness in relation to the humanists and the socialists, i.e. in relation to the ethical problem that is certainly pressing enough" (*Revolutionary Theology in the Making: Barth-Thurneysen Correspondence 1914–1925*, trans. James D. Smart [Richmond: John Knox, 1964], 165).

6. This happened in Europe long before it happened on this continent. . . . It is said that when the European student of theology, Dietrich Bonhoeffer, as a graduate student at Union

Theological Seminary, New York, in the early 1930s, invoked the names of Luther and Calvin, his classmates were astonished that he would turn to such outmoded authorities.

7. Robert Bellah et al., *Habits of the Heart* (Berkeley: University of California Press, 1985), 227f.

8. Lindbeck, *The Nature of Doctrine*, 77.

9. In his article, "Answering Pilate: Truth and the Postliberal Church" (*The Christian Century*, January 28, 1987, pp. 82ff.), William H. Willimon accuses Paul Tillich of "setting the agenda" for subsequent theologians by being too concerned about the "cultured despisers" of his day. This is a superficial—if common—accusation. As an apologist, in the long line of Christian apologists, Tillich naturally wished to be in dialogue with his epoch, and especially with those whom he regarded as its primary representatives and spokespersons. But the same Tillich, who sought ongoing converse with the present ("the situation"), maintained throughout his lifetime an active dialogue with the Christian theological tradition—in fact, during most of his years at Union Theological Seminary he taught the history of Christian thought as well as systematic theology. Possibly more than any other teacher of theology on this continent, this man, trained in the rigorous scholastic traditions of pre–World War I Germany, valued *the whole* (Catholic and Protestant) past of the church, and taught his students to develop a sympathetic and listening attitude towards even those aspects of the tradition with which neither he nor they could immediately identify.

8

Theology of the Cross as Contextual Theology

In 2003, Hall published The Cross in Our Context: Jesus and the Suffering World, which originated in a series of ten lectures at Trinity Lutheran Seminary in Columbus, Ohio. As he writes in the book's introduction, "I have planned this brief volume to address . . . the traditional concerns of Christian theological reflection, in each case asking how that particular aspect of doctrine is affected by reading from the perspective of the theologia crucis [theology of the cross]" (2003:7). The book, however, also follows closely the major themes of his trilogy Christian Theology in a North American Context, though it is not a condensation of that epic work.

The theology of the cross is the theological motif that Hall most often engages and with which he is most often identified. As he writes below, it may be understood "as faith's continuous commentary on the incarnating of God's suffering love for the world" (2003:42), which in turn moves one to ongoing, ever-deepening engagement with that world. He sets it over against the "theologia gloriae" (theology of glory), which he understands as triumphalism or religious ideology. As Luther wrote, "A theologian of glory calls evil good and good evil. A theologian of the cross calls the thing what it actually is" (2003:20). In explicating the theology of the cross, Hall often cites Jürgen Moltmann, who says that the theology is the "key signature" of the whole faith even though it was "never much loved," and thus may be seen as a "thin tradition" (2003:6–7). Following on the previous chapter on theology and tradition, then, this excerpt helps place this theological motif within the larger contextual perspective of Hall's project.

Source: Hall 2003:35–52.

THIS EARTH IS THE LORD'S

The cross of Jesus Christ is at the same time a historical reality and a symbol. Like all symbols its meaning transcends all possible explanations of its meaning. As the history of atonement theologies attests, the symbol of the crucified savior is able to absorb many differing interpretations, not all of them mutually compatible. Despite the obvious dangers it courts, this openness must be maintained, for without it the symbol is restricted in its universality and loses, in fact, its symbolic status.

One dimension of the significance of the cross remains steadfast, however, and is the presupposition of all possible interpretations of this event: namely, faith's assumption that the cross of the Christ marks, in a decisive and irrevocable way, the unconditional participation of God in the life of the world, the concretization of God's love for the world, the commitment of God to the fulfillment of creation's promise. "God so loved the world that he gave his only son . . ." (John 3:16).

The theology of the cross, at its most rudimentary, is nothing more nor less than a rapt, ongoing contemplation of and commentary upon this foundational claim of Christian faith. Unlike theologies of glory, which invariably tend to supersede creation in favor of a supramundane redemption, the theology of the cross is bound to this world in all of its materiality, ambiguity, and incompleteness. It will not—cannot—opt for a doctrine of redemption, however theoretically or spiritually appealing, that in effect bypasses or contradicts the biblical affirmation of creation. What God loves and is determined to save is not an abstraction and not a "savable" *part* of the whole, but the real world in its inseparableness and interrelatedness. God is as firmly committed to the life of this world as that cross was planted in the ground at Golgotha, that is, (symbolically) at the very center of death's apparent sovereignty.

The symbol thus understood—but simultaneously misunderstood—was appropriated to the uses of imperial peoples and their sovereigns for a thousand years of Christendom. In the year 1534, for example, while Martin Luther was still actively engaged in his reforming work, the French explorer Jacques Cartier sailed up the St. Lawrence River to the site of the Mohawk village of Hochelaga—the very location today of my employer, McGill University, at the heart of the city of Montréal. With some of his sailors, Cartier made his way to the top of the small mountain that dominates that city and gives it its present-day name (Mont Réal), and he caused a rude cross to be driven into the rocky soil at its summit. By this gesture the French explorer declared: "All this land now belongs to the king of France." Had the indigenous peoples (Mohawks) who were present on that occasion grasped the intent of this act and its future ramifications for their race, they would not have indulged the strange behavior of the newcomers! For unlike the God of the Scriptures, whose cross at Golgotha was the consequence and promise of suffering love (*agape*), Cartier's cross, like that of so many other wandering European conquerors, bespoke an ownership and a sovereignty from which even tolerance, to say nothing of love, was to be expunged. Even in its distortedness, however, the historic custom of claiming sovereignty through the planting of a cross preserves one dimension of the meaning of the original cross of faith: its insistence that, all appearances to the contrary, the creation is God's own handiwork and the sphere of God's benevolent dominion. The cross of Jesus Christ is God's claim to this world—the claim, however, not of a despot, yearning for greater power and glory, but of a lover yearning to love and be loved, and thus to liberate the beloved from false masters. "The earth is the Lord's and the fullness thereof" (Ps. 24:1).

Expressing the same thought in other language, the cross of Jesus Christ is the end-consequence of the divine determination to be "with us" (*Emmanuel*) unreservedly. It is the inevitable though not necessary final step in that sequence of events that has its genesis in the divine decision to "visit and redeem my people" (Luke 1:68). The when of that decision certainly cannot be pinpointed. That the Lucan writer believed the annunciation of the Virgin to stand in strict continuity with the history of Israel is clear from the references in Gabriel's address to the central figures of Israel's past, David and Jacob. There is no Marcionitic bypassing of Judaism here! The divine determination to "redeem my people" has, as we may say, a long history. That it is perhaps even inappropriate to assign that decision to time has been the rationale of all who have insisted that the incarnation was planned before the foundations of the world—though such a concept runs counter to the biblical assumption that human history is predicated on human freedom and not predetermined. In any case, the when of the divine decision is not as vital as is its character as decision. God's unconditional commitment to the world is not the consequence of destiny—is not necessary, as if by the sheer act of creation the Creator were bound to see the creation through to the realization of its full potential. God, in the biblical tradition, is with us voluntarily—through love alone. And this quality of volition, which is the origin and essence of what the biblical tradition means by *grace*, must be borne in mind in all dimensions of theological reflection, particularly when that reflection has to do with the *suffering* that such a commitment entails—and it always entails suffering, whether it applies to Jesus Christ or to his disciples. Given the conditions of historical existence, genuine world commitment entails "affliction" (Simone Weil). The commitment as such, however, is an act of great freedom—and perhaps the only truly great freedom. It is not necessary; nevertheless, if there is love—if one is moved by love of the world, the commitment and its consequence, the suffering, are inevitable. God, declares the entire Bible, has made Godself vulnerable to love for the world. The incarnation, declares the New Testament, is the (inevitable though not necessary) consequence of that love.

CROSS, INCARNATION, AND CONTEXT

The theology of the cross is incarnational theology at its most unalloyed and all-embracing. Characteristically, the incarnation of the divine Word is associated in Christian doctrine and liturgy with the *birth* of the Christ. But we—creatures human and extrahuman—are not only born; we live, and we die. Our being, as the nontheist Martin Heidegger so accurately if starkly stated it, is "being-toward-death." A Creator who through loving and liberating participation in the creaturely condition would redeem it "must" (once the decision has been taken) follow the creature through to that nonbeing "toward" which all creaturely being moves—that end, let us already note,[1] which does not come only at the end of life but is deeply embedded in human consciousness all the way through. The Christmas story is beautiful because it affirms and celebrates the great good and eternal worth of all creation—of all that is embodied, of all that is involved in its embodiment. But if the Christian narrative were to end with Christmas it would not yet reach us in the reality of our being. The divine love that is ready to suffer birth in human form "must" follow through, if it is really love for creatures, for *us*. It "must" suffer life, not only birth; it "must" suffer death, too.

In a moment I shall take up the discussion of that *must*, which I have carefully placed in quotation marks in the foregoing. But first I would like to comment briefly on the subject of incarnational theology, in order to underline the point being made here. Am I mistaken, or do I detect in much of the theology that calls itself "incarnational" a hidden—or perhaps not so hidden—reluctance to dwell on the *cross* of Jesus Christ? Or, if not that, a tendency to find in the fact of incarnation as such a sufficient basis of the gospel? I should not quarrel with the assumption that the incarnation in itself, as the divine participation in creaturely existence, is already reason for the greatest wonder and rejoicing. If the human condition were no more problematic than that we are flesh, one might even concede that such participation on the part of our Maker is enough to constitute "good news." But our *problématique*, to speak at least for the human, is by no means just our enfleshment, our mortality, our finitude—and indeed the tradition of Jerusalem, as distinct from that of Athens, does not regard *that* as the source of our trouble, the thing from which we need saving! A theology of incarnation that does not go on to become a theology of the cross "heals the wounds of my people lightly." If we are speaking about God's assumption of our human condition (and what else could incarnation mean?), then we are speaking not only about Christmas but also about Good Friday.

The Friday event must be seen as the culmination of the movement of the Creator toward the creation. Here the decision to be God-with-us is brought to its final test. Gethsemane, that "cross before the cross," displays in the most dramatic and poignant terms the excruciating pain that such a final step entails: pain for the man who is our representative and priest; pain for the God whom he also represents. For this purpose, he says, he has been sent. It has been known to him throughout his short ministry of teaching and healing. It has been the destiny that he sensed long before hostility toward him had reached its frenzied height. "The Son of Man must suffer, be rejected . . ." This "must" of the predictions of the passion, this *necessitas*, has been throughout his wanderings the pressing terminus of his earthly sojourn. But again we should note: it is only necessity so long as the free decision of God to seek such solidarity with humankind is affirmed. That is why what Jesus of Nazareth struggles with at Gethsemane, that second Garden of Temptation, is not simply whether he will or will not submit to the execution that his human enemies have been planning for him, but whether he will or will not reaffirm the divine decision to be Emmanuel. Death as such, even the violent and truly horrible death of crucifixion, is not the primary issue here. Many have chosen, actually chosen, an honorable if torturous death in place of a life of compromise and quietude. The fundamental question of the Representative, the High Priest as the biblical writers dare to call him, is whether as God's deputy he will take this final step toward the world, or, to state the other side of the matter, whether as *our* deputy he will say yes to our creaturely condition, including the mortality that this implies. From neither side, neither the divine nor the human, can that step be taken easily, lightly, or as a matter of course. It is at least as hard for God, as God is conceived in this tradition, to identify Godself with creation fallen and distorted as it is for us, humankind, to say yes to our creaturehood (and each of us knows in his or her heart, in all the specificity of our personal histories, how hard that is!). The crucifixion, which is no glorious thing, as event, is nonetheless celebratory as symbol; that is, in our Good Friday remembrance of it, Christians celebrate the victorious decision of the Christ to traverse this final sad portion of the Via Dolorosa, to take this final step toward the world God loves. For all the pain of it, it is also a triumph over pain—the pain, namely, of the decision that has preceded it, the decision to go *that far.* When this is understood, the victory of the Christ is not reserved for Easter Sunday; it is already fully present at Golgotha. The third day, along with the other post-resurrection events (ascension, reign, and promised return), can only confirm, reveal, and illumine the scope and meaning of what has already occurred in the cross: namely, the fulfillment of the divine determination to follow the course toward which the divine pathos has been pressing and to participate unconditionally in the creaturely condition, to the end that it may be healed *from within.*[2]

I have commented on the passion narrative in this much detail because this kind of meditation on the central event of the Christian story is the presupposition of the main point that must be made in this chapter, namely, that what today we are calling the contextualization of the faith has its genesis and its foundation in an incarnational theology of the cross. The movement of God toward this world, understood in the light of the cross of Jesus Christ, is a movement into which all who profess this faith are drawn. Though the journey of the Creator toward creation has already, in the Christ, achieved its goal (yes, already), it is also a process, a becoming, a hope, a "not yet." That is not because God's loving solidarity with the world in Christ is less than it could be. No, as Christ's final word from his cross announces, "It is finished": nothing greater by way of divine compassion and solidarity could be achieved or imagined. But life goes on, the world goes on, history goes on. Eschatologically it may be said that the *end,* meaning the *telos* or "inner aim" of creation's redemption, has already been introduced into time in the middle of things (*in media res*), but time, *chronos,* has not come to an end. In a way, for faith, it has only begun, or begun *again* (as we might say, borrowing the thought from Elie Wiesel).[3] This new beginning is the beginning of the church, the community of Christ's discipleship. The movement of the divine toward the world becomes now the necessity (the "must") under which all of us live who through the divine Spirit have found in the crucified and risen one new life and a new beginning. We, whose movement in one way and another had always been *away* from the world, whether into our own private little worlds or to some theoretic superworld of our own devising—we, through our "baptism into *his* death" (Rom. 6:1f.), are being directed toward the world where *his* life is being lived, hidden among the lives of those especially whom the world as such seems to have denied fullness of life (Matt. 25:31ff.).[4]

Discipleship of Jesus Christ is nothing more nor less than being sent with increasing insistence "into all the world"—or, in other words, embracing our freedom to manifest something like a new nonchalance about self and a new attention to the other. This movement toward the world, which is the gift and command of the crucified one, is the basis and motivation of the whole process of contextualization. For the world toward which we are sent is not a fixed and unchanging condition; it is rather a constant flux. It is in fact "the world" only as specific sets of circumstances, particular events and conditions, explicit combinations of people, races, ethnic groupings, extrahuman creatures, and processes, and the interactions of all these. It is the world—namely, God's beloved world—only as history, constantly unfolding, forever moving from one possibility to another, one problem to another. To name as "world" anything other than this ongoingness is to substitute for the specific reality toward which the love of God is directed a construct, an idea, an abstraction. The theology of the cross as faith's continuous commentary on the incarnating of God's suffering love for the world can only prove itself such by extending itself further and further into the actual. A theology of the cross that contented itself with a theoretical-theological contemplation of the cross of Christ, however spiritually satisfying that might be to those involved, would fall far short of the inner aim of this whole tradition. For that aim is not the meaning of Christ's cross in itself and as such, but its meaning for and application to the here and now. By definition, the theology of the cross is an *applied theology*. How *in this world of the here and the now* are we to perceive the presence of the crucified one, and how shall we translate that presence into words, and deeds—or sighs too deep for either? That is the question to which adherence to this theological tradition drives.

THE TIME AND PLACE DIMENSIONS OF CONTEXTUALITY

If, then, we speak of *contexts* today, and do so intentionally and on the basis of serious theological reflection (and not just because contextuality has become a cliché), it is because we have begun to recognize at long last that the beloved world in its actuality, as distinct from the mere idea of the world, manifests an astonishing variety and diversity. It differs not only from time to time but also from place to place. The world today is not the world of the Nicene theologians or of the Reformers (the biblical view of history is not cyclical, but linear); "there is a time, and there is a time" (Ecclesiastes 3). But it is also true that the world as it comes to us *here* in this place (North America, for instance) is not the same world as the one experienced *there* (in Africa, perhaps, or Indonesia).

The time dimension that is one of the two primary aspects of contextual thinking has long been part of the discourse of Christian theology, at least in the more sophisticated circles of academic theology. Historical consciousness has been with us in the West throughout the modern period, and so responsible Christian thought since the eighteenth century has recognized—in a way that was not true of earlier epochs—that theological thought has constantly to be done with an eye to what time it is, and to be ready to adjust itself to historical change. It must do so not for the frivolous reason of seeming au courant, up to date, or immediately "relevant"; to the contrary, it does so in order to maintain, so far as possible, the continuity of evangelical significance that discipleship strives for throughout the ages. Even to say "the same thing," you cannot simply "say the same thing"; because language is also historically conditioned, as anyone knows who reads Beowulf, or even Shakespeare—or, more to the point, the King James Version of the Bible. For instance, if today we tried to commend the Reformation dogma of the peculiar and unique authority of Scripture (*sola Scriptura*) by asking people to accept the idea of the Bible's direct dictation by the divine Spirit, not only would we go against the grain of every contemporary assumption about historical documents, but we would also put in the way of faith a barrier, a "false scandal," that would inhibit our contemporaries from appreciating what the Reformers and even the biblical authors themselves actually understood about the nature of Scripture's inspiration. Making sense of the concept of the holiness of Scripture in our time must mean assuming and teaching historical-critical method not as an end in itself, we hope, but as a means to better understanding on the part at least of Christians, as to why this collection of writings is sacred and authoritative. (I realize, of course, that there is an impressive following—especially in the United States—for a biblicism that deliberately refuses historical-critical method, but this has to do with another problem that comes into the present discussion only tangentially.)

While the time dimension of contextual theological thinking has to some appreciable degree affected the Christian community for the past century and more, the other main component of contextuality has been much slower in making itself felt. I refer to what may be called "the sense of place." By this I mean not only location, though that is certainly paramount, but also state or condition, as in the phrase "knowing one's place" or "the place of something or someone" (for example of government in moral questions, or of children in family decision making). A *context* can be a certain geographic area, or a certain shared condition (gender, race, ethnicity, economic status, war). It is only lately, and at that only partially, that the discourse of the churches has begun to recognize that *place*—not only *time*—conditions the manner in which the Christian message is to be articulated and can be received. There is still, moreover, a conspicuous resistance to this aspect of theological contextuality usually on the grounds of its capitulation to relativity, or allowing the world, as one says, to set the Christian agenda.

But if the Christian message is intended for this world, if it is to be rendered in language and act that are in any genuine manner "address" (that is, being-spoken-to), then the specificity of contexts must be allowed to play a vital role in the theological reflection that serious Christian obedience and wisdom presuppose. Both Christian ethics and pastoral theology have recognized the veracity of this in a way that systematic theology has not. In ethics, unless one is given to a moral absolutism that makes itself ridiculous in our vastly changed and changing society, ethical principles and moral precepts that were binding upon past ages, such as the limitation of full human rights (for example, the right to vote) to male property owners, must be reconsidered in the light of more recent thinking and behavior on the part of both religious and secular segments of society. Ethical relativity is not introduced just as soon as this happens; for very often, if not always, the expanding or rethinking of the assumption of what is truly human must be seen, simultaneously, as an unfolding and flowering of the Christian faith itself; indeed, such expansion is very often inspired by Christian initiative. Similarly, in pastoral theology contextual thinking, by whatever name, has long—perhaps always—been practiced; for every sensitive pastor knows that what is pertinent to the life of one parishioner, say a person in mourning, is hardly the appropriate "word from the Lord" to another—such as the parent of a newborn infant. Preaching, too, when it has been worthy of the name, knows how to distinguish contexts: the comfort made mandatory by great catastrophe, such as the terrorists' attack on New York and Washington, is not appropriate, surely, as a perennial message and becomes quite inappropriate when, perhaps on the grounds of such consolation, congregations become smug about their own seeming innocence and victimization.

Systematic or dogmatic theology has been slow to learn the lesson of contextuality, especially its place-component, and one cannot avoid the conclusion that a (if not the) predominant reason for this lies in the character of the enterprise as such. The very adjectives *systematic* and *dogmatic* (or even the less blatant *constructive*) betray a predilection to permanency. It so easily happens that a (right and good) desire to "see the thing whole," to integrate, to describe connections, to honor the unity of truth, and so on becomes, in its execution, an exercise in finality. Who can devote his or her life to the contemplation of the wondrous indivisibility of God's truth and avoid, in the process, crossing that invisible line between theology and ideology that we discussed in the preceding chapter? Truly great theology (if that combination of words is not already idolatrous!) anticipates this danger at every turn, and builds into the enterprise a corrective principle. For St. Thomas that principle lies in the distinction between faith and reason, and it was dramatically accentuated for this saint of the intellect by his mystical experience, which caused him to question his whole endeavor as a schoolman and tempted him to regard his systematic work as "straw." For Calvin the distinction is expressed by the ontic distance between the Word of God and all human words and work, including that of theology. Barth followed Calvin in this. For Tillich, who in my view chose the better path, the thing that prevents the theological answer from assuming the status of the absolute is the human question, which is never silenced, and the situation, which keeps changing. Yet every one of these systems, and most of the others that could be mentioned, have functioned for the church as *theologia eterna*, their disclaimers notwithstanding. The extent to which this represents the hubris of the theologians or, on the other hand, the insecurity of the churches is a matter for discussion. But, wherever the blame may be placed, it remains that systematic theology (which on account of its holistic character tends to be the most influential of the theological disciplines in the churches) has manifested a perennial reluctance to open itself to the great *variety* of worldly contexts and has again and again resisted criticism from the perspectives of those whose worlds were virtually ignored or excluded in the great systems of Christian thought.

This is not a mere academic concern, for the excluded ones have not just been individuals or tiny minorities but whole populations, whole races, whole economic and other groupings. We have argued here that the theology of the cross drives to greater and greater contextual specificity and concreteness, for it is the ultimate incarnational theology, a theology that insists upon encountering the real world and not an ideational construct called "world" or "cosmos." And when, knowingly or unknowingly, theology identifies as the world or the human condition some particular *part* of the world, or some specific segment of human experience (for example, the experience of white middle classes in the United States toward the middle of the twentieth century), it not only severely limits the faith but courts the danger of turning the lively address we call gospel into a fixed and sterile formula—a frozen waterfall.

The history of Christian theology in North America amply demonstrates this point. Partly because we began as European colonies, partly because most of our founding denominations were based in Europe and continued, in some sense, to adhere to European authority structures, but also partly because we, as a people, lacked sufficient confidence in our own capacity for intellectual originality, European theological systems have dominated our Christian self-understanding. While we have produced a few theologians who dared something like "original thought" (one may think especially of Jonathan Edwards and Reinhold Niebuhr), we have been on the whole extraordinarily dependent upon European theological thought. To this day, despite the fact that the past thirty or forty years have seen the emergence of many sophisticated and insightful Christian scholars in the United States and Canada, theologies that are "made in Germany" or perhaps even in Britain, France, or Italy are given a certain weight that our indigenous scholarship cannot assume. Particularly in the case of Germanic theological work, there has been a kind of hidden assumption—at least among the teaching theologians on this continent—that it surpasses anything locally grown. (The problem is not limited to this continent. The Japanese speak of "the German captivity of theology." But as a largely European colony, we are especially prone to such behavior.) This is not to disparage theology done in Germany. It often bears an unusual stamp of authenticity and depth, which is not unrelated to the torturous history out of which it has emerged. The "contradictions" (Thomas Mann) in German history and culture represent, in my view, a heightened and sometimes a hysterical form of the duplicitous character of Western civilization as a whole. Out of the chaos of conflicting influences and characteristics that constitutes German history, great art and great thought have been born.

But it remains, all the same, that the Germanic context is not our context, and when North Americans rely as heavily as they do upon the insights of the wise who live and work within that quite different *hic et nunc*, they substitute for genuine theological struggle the bogus professionalism of applying to one context the questions and answers derived from the struggles of persons and communities in other contexts. There is nothing to be said against learning from others—indeed, today such learning must incorporate the theological work of the whole ecumenical church. But entering into the specificity of one's own time and place is the *conditio sine qua non* of real theological work. Without that *participatory* act and identity, theology inevitably lapses into mere doctrine. The world that the disciples of the crucified one are obliged to take seriously is first of all that world that is their own. To refrain from seeking to plumb the depths of one's own context is in all likelihood a sign of one's reluctance to enter the real world at all. While there is always a danger of becoming stuck in one's own, this usually occurs only where the penetration of the here and now is too shallow. If, with the prompting of the Holy Spirit, Christians delve deeply enough into the crust of their own society and culture, they will discover, sooner or later, that it will be necessary also to widen their horizons to include that greater world of which their own is a small part. For—today especially, in this "global village" (Marshall McLuhan)—no one worldly context is ultimately isolatable. But this leads to yet another aspect of our reflections on the theology of the cross as contextual theology.

THE THEOLOGY OF THE CROSS AND THE CRISIS OF PLANETARY JUSTICE

If we let a line four inches long stand for the whole human population of our planet, the populations of Europe and North American taken together account for approximately one-half inch of the four. Yet that half-inch, in economic and cultural (pop-cultural) terms, dominates all the rest. As Dorothee Soelle writes in her [2001] book *The Silent Cry: Mysticism and Resistance,*

> The fragmentation of the world into center and periphery is generally known. There is life that is said to be productive and worth living, and there is life that is economically useless. Twenty percent of humankind have the right to use, to exploit, and to throw away, while eighty percent are superfluous, the losers. . . . Living in the center of the fragmented world means there is nothing you cannot think of that cannot be produced and bought, accessed and possessed. . . . Far, far away from us, in some Third or Fourth World, there is a marginal sphere, the periphery.[5]

What such observations ought to tell us (and Soelle's is only one of countless such observations) is that any *deep and honest* analysis of our own context today must lead to a probing, a self-assessment, a judgment for which few churchfolk, not to mention citizens at large, are the least prepared. As is well known, the biblical (Greek) word for judgment is *krisis*. It is not short of a *krisis*, that is to say, a *crisis*, when members of the possessing, largely northern peoples of the earth confront openly, unguardedly, the data that pertains undeniably to their context, taken in its greater, planetary context. Our conventional theological assumptions, which as we have seen manifest an almost consistent triumphalism, simply will not suffice to take in the naked negativity—not to say condemnation—that this planetary crisis conjures up.

In consequence, we usually and regularly repress or suppress any truly relentless pursuit of truth where our own cultural analysis is concerned. If, traditionally, contextual theological thought has been rare in North America for the colonialist and other reasons adduced earlier, it is discouraged today by the heavy burden of guilt that such analysis is likely to inflict upon us. Rather than question the rectitude of our way of life, we will ignore incontrovertible economic, environmental, geopolitical, and other statistics, minimize the extent of our consumption and waste and its effects upon the biosphere, and consign to exaggeration and scare-mongering all those who demand of us a rigorous accounting and a change of lifestyle. As the aftermath of September 11, 2001, demonstrates, among other things, we are rather relieved when it becomes possible again to blame some other enemy for earth's malaise; for then we no longer have to face that subtle enemy that lives within our own corporate self.

Such a critique by no means implies that everything about our way of life is wrong or wicked. It does mean, however, that neither cultivated ignorance of what *is* wrong and wicked about that way, nor flag-waving defense of that way, can be tolerated—at least by Christians! For Christians are committed to a love of the world—that is to say, a love that, though it must certainly begin with the honest ownership of one's own specific context, cannot allow that specificity to become a myopic concern for one's own.

The contextualization of Christian theology on the part of all the possessing peoples of the planet today represents, in fact, a particularly excruciating task. In some ways, as a Christian in this so-called First World, I envy my fellow Christians in contexts less affluent, less developed (so-called), less technologically and economically smug; for I know that it is hard for the rich to enter the kingdom of heaven—or even to stand on the doorstep thereof and contemplate the glory that belongs to *that* sphere, so different from the glory of the kingdoms of this world. To contextualize the faith where *we* live—to follow the incarnate and crucified one into *this* world—is to submit oneself to truly daunting questions, literally to "the judgment [*krisis*] that begins with the household of faith" (1 Pet. 4:17). And all the more so because it is precisely *this* world, this sphere of the imperial peoples of the West, that rejoices still in the nomenclature *Christian*.

What shall we say about this Christian world of ours—this remnant of sixteen centuries of Christendom? What shall we think, as those who still want to claim this identity in some meaningful way, when, official protestations notwithstanding, our nations have allowed themselves to draw (in an albeit surreptitious way) upon the symbols and imagery of the Christian religion in their confrontation with the largely Muslim East? And what shall we say to one another in the churches when it is brought home to us again and again, by the ecologically vigilant, that it is in fact our religion that has given Western *Homo sapiens* the license to assault the earth and lay waste to its precious resources along with thousands of its species and natural processes? Is it *Christianity* that has taught us to love consumption and overabundance and waste? Is there some link between our trust in God and our astonishing prosperity, our being "First," our superpower-dom? Many avowed Christians think so, and they can count upon a whole hoary tradition of so-called Deuteronomic and puritan ethics to back up their argument. But can we, who have at least some niggling consciousness of the victims that have been created by our abundance, continue to draw upon that argument? Can we, who have had to face the racism, classism, sexism, homophobia, and other once-hidden realities of our "Christian" culture, still avoid the *krisis* that "begins with the household of God" (1 Pet. 4:17)?

To engage in contextual theological thought as an American or a Canadian today, in short, is to encounter questions for which our polite and decent Protestantism has not prepared us. I have argued here that the theology of the cross is by definition a contextualizing theology: if we pursue it in spirit and in truth, it will lead us more and more deeply into the world—the real world, not the world as a religious construct. If this theology has never been "much loved" (Moltmann), it is probably least loved *today* by the possessing peoples of this planet, for it wants them to become truthful about their own worldly condition, and about the manner in which that condition affects all other creatures and cultures. In such circumstances, it would be understandable if a theological seminary or a thoughtful congregation of the church were to settle for a theology of the cross that remained at the level of theology—a theology that did not drive to gospel or to ethic. But such a theology of the cross would not be, in fact, a theology of the cross. A purely professional theology of the cross is a contradiction in terms, an oxymoron. We need the vantage point of such a theology even to open ourselves, in our kind of context, to the questions that are there. Without some intellectual and psychic assurance that God, very God, participates with us in this submission to reality; that God, very God, is both the source of the *krisis* and the source of the courage we need to submit ourselves to the *krisis*—without this, we could not even begin, as First World people in this out-of-joint world today, to listen to the questions that must be asked of us, that are asked of us.

But beyond that listening, we are asked to think and speak and act in such a way as disciples of the crucified one that there may be, in the midst of this world that is "First," some insistent witness to the fact that, in the economy of God, "the first may be last." That, instead of assuming we have done our work as Christians and North Americans when we have urged the dispossessed to aspire more diligently to our level of alleged development, we have begun to act upon the belief that we ourselves must undergo something like *un*development.[6] For, as a Canadian scientist has calculated with as much scientific accuracy as can be applied to such an equation, if all the peoples of earth were to demand of its total resources what we North Americans ask of it, it would require "four or five more Earths *right now* to supply that demand."[7] In short, what is being asked of us all—Christians and everyone else in our sphere—is a radical reorientation of our so-called values and of what we think is necessary to a good life.

But of Christians more is asked: we are asked whether we can rethink not only our manner of life but our faith itself. If it is *not*, after all, Christianity that has brought about the great instabilities of the creation, if it is *not* Christianity that has taught us how to pillage the earth and wage warfare against all who question or threaten our way of life and accept as given the inequality of classes and races and genders—if all that is not to be laid at the feet of the Christian faith but represents a misinterpretation and distortion of this faith, then *what precisely is Christianity, and to what would it lead, humanly speaking, if it were really "tried"* (G. K. Chesterton)?[8]

Notes

1. See Hall 2003: ch. 10, for elaboration of this point.

2. Luther understood this intuitively, and therefore he would not separate cross and resurrection. The resurrection is not the undoing of the failure of the cross; it is the unveiling of its "success"—that is, of its intentionality, and of the *interiority* of the victory it already achieves. That victory can only be grasped in its fullness if it is premised on the reality of the divine freedom: it might not have happened that way at all! God is not obliged to embrace the fallen creation. Jesus Christ *could have said no to the cross*, that is, to human and worldly solidarity. (That, for instance, is the presupposition of the reference to "legions of angels" that might appear in defense of the arrested Nazarene—well, and of the entire narrative.) The drinking of the "cup of destiny," which is both divine reaffirmation of the decision to love and human affirmation of creaturehood, is already the victory that faith apprehends and celebrates. Not the vindication of God's glory (which does not need vindicating), but the realization of God's compassion: that is the victory. And not the deification and immortalization of the human (which could only be capitulation to religious hubris) but the joyful acceptance of our creaturehood: that is the victory.

3. Elie Wiesel writes that the great gift God gave to humankind was not the gift of beginning—only God can begin—but God gave to human beings what is perhaps an even greater gift, the capacity to "begin again" (*Messengers of God*, trans. Marion Wiesel [New York: Pocket Books, 1977], 42).

4. See Hall 1987.

5. Dorothee Soelle, *The Silent Cry: Mysticism and Resistance*, trans. Barbara and Martin Rumscheidt (Minneapolis: Fortress Press, 2001), 179.

6. See in this connection Sallie McFague's *Life Abundant: Rethinking Theology and Economy for a Planet in Peril* (Minneapolis: Fortress Press, 2001). Note especially her "Manifesto to North American Middle-Class Christians," 205–10.

7. See David Suzuki and Holly Dressel, *From Naked Ape to Superspecies: A Personal Perspective on Humanity and the Global Eco-Crisis* (Toronto: Stoddart, 1999), 42.

8. "The Christian ideal has not been tried and found wanting. It has been found difficult; and left untried" (G. K. Chesterton, *What's Wrong with the World?* [London: Cassell, 1910], 22).

9

Reasons for the Ideological Triumph of the Positive

In part 1 of Professing the Faith, "Theology: The Christian Doctrine of God," Hall explores Christian thought regarding the Deity in historical, critical, and constructive perspectives (see chapter 4 above, "The Sisyphus Syndrome," for an explanation of these categories). In the critical section ("Questioning the Father Almighty"), from which this excerpt is taken, Hall asks the reader to consider this hypothesis: "The Christian doctrine of God has tended to accentuate the aspects of transcendence and power, as befits a patriarchally conceived deity in the service of empire; but in doing so it has severely jeopardized the essence of God testified to in Holy Scripture, and has risked confirming belief in God to contexts amenable to 'positive religion'" (1993:92). Relative to the previous chapter on the theologia crucis, we can see here how the theologia gloriae has taken precedence in the North American context, and our theologies have become captive to the demands of establishment religion—Christendom. (Readers should also note that Hall capitalizes the word Theology when he is referring to the Christian doctrine of God, but lowercases it when he is referring to the general discipline.)

Source: Hall 1993:101–8.

Summarizing the discussion thus far, we may suggest that: (1) in its zeal to present the knowledge of God as a triumph over ignorance and doubt, historic Christendom forfeited the language of *faith*; (2) in its zeal to present the being of God as a triumph over nonbeing, historic Christendom forfeited the language of *suffering love*; (3) in its zeal to present the work of God as a triumph over evil, death, and sin, historic Christendom forfeited the language of *hope*. Or, to speak less absolutely, if in each case the language or mode of reflection was not altogether forfeited, neither was it adequately explored and exploited. And, given the centrality of these three categories in biblical thought (and not only in 1 Corinthians 13), one must certainly ask why they were not exploited.

Three types of reasons may be given in response—one from the standpoint of psychic and "religious" considerations; one on the basis of philosophic influences in the life of the early church; and one relating to the political functioning of the Christian profession concerning deity. The first reason belongs to the human condition existentially and can be discerned under all historical conditions. The second reason, like the third, is more expressly historical.

HUMAN NEED FOR SYMBOLIC FULFILLMENT

We are asking why Christianity in its Theology developed a picture of God in which, at every point, the positive decisively triumphs. To begin with we do not have to go farther than our own conscious and unconscious human experience for an answer. There is that within us which wants and even needs the positive to triumph and which, precisely because the positive does not obviously triumph in the realities of our daily experience, creates images of triumph that bolster within us the will to affirm life despite its negations and ambiguities—the courage to "go on." Such images may be secular, this-worldly ones, and in recent Western history this has indeed been their characteristic form (for example, the belief that medical and other sciences will overcome all illnesses and threats to life). But historically they have usually been otherworldly, supernatural, and in the usual sense "religious" conceptions of reality. The divine reality is held over against the realities of earthly experience, and the resolution and victory that are absent from mundane experience are affirmed by belief as nonetheless real—as ultimate reality.

"God" thus becomes the symbol of a wholeness, unity, power, majesty, simplicity, righteousness, and wisdom that we lack and for which we long. No god is ever exempt from this human longing for fulfillment, and even human figures or historical events that become the vehicles of this overpowering psychic need for completion tend to lose their creaturely qualities or are frankly apotheosized. Later we may speak of the fate of Jesus in Christendom in just these terms. Every hero from Moses to Lenin has suffered the loss of purely human qualities because humanity demands of its gods and of its substitutes for gods that only the positive should triumph. It would be remarkable indeed if the Christian God had not been subjected to this same psychic-religious need, especially after Christianity had become the religion of a whole civilization; then—at least then—its God had to stand for all that the gods usually stand for.

But the need of which we are speaking predates the Establishment [of Christianity] and is present in every historical situation. That the godhead should function as a fulfillment symbol is already well known to biblical literature. Indeed one could say that such a deity is the great option with which biblical theology struggles beginning to end. This deity is present not only in the alternative "pagan" religions with which Israel and the new church do battle. The deity who conquers every negating reality is the ever-present alternative God of Israel and of the church. This is the god for whom Israel longs in its wandering in the wilderness; the god whose promptings, despite the prophetic protest, lead to the establishment of the kingship as the earthly model and mirror of heavenly power; the god for whom the heroic warrior, David, comes to stand; the magnificent god whose house Solomon builds; the god whom Satan quotes before Jesus in the wilderness, whom Peter represents on the Mount of the Transfiguration, whom the disciples serve when they vie for prestige in "your kingdom" (Matt. 20:20f.), and so on.

And precisely this is the god by whom Jesus is deserted on Calvary. For prophetic religion, whether of the Hebrew Scriptures or of the faithful church, resists this god steadfastly. Why? Because this god can only produce a people that settles down, secure in the knowledge of the power of its deity, basking in the wake of divine triumph; a people, therefore, that shuts its eyes to the reality of evil, injustice, death, bondage, and sin—especially its own sin; a people that no longer struggles with evil, no longer searches for truth and justice, no longer hungers and thirsts for righteousness, no longer feels an evangelical responsibility for the world.

The God of the prophets and of the crucified one will not have such a people. The God of Pentecost does not aim to achieve a ready-made triumph for the disciple community. That is not the meaning of prevenient grace. God's aim is rather to achieve a victory with the covenant partner—that is, to instill in human beings the courage to be in the face of that which negates being. For, unlike the "Almighty Father" of Christendom tradition (and of so many of this world's religions and quasi-religions), the holy and loving God of biblical tradition does not function to protect "his children" from life, giving them the consequences of a victory in which they have not participated as combatants; rather, God aims to bring the "children" to maturity, to lead them through suffering and trial to the glad acceptance of their creaturehood and the responsible use of their freedom. Certainly, this is a matter of grace, not of works—of permission, not only of command: without God's own gracious participation in the structures of negation, human beings do not find the will or the courage to enter that struggle. For it is truly not a struggle with flesh and blood but with powers and principalities (Eph. 6:12; Col. 1:16), and with human beings this is impossible (Luke 18:27). Responding faith enters the darkness because it believes the darkness to be inhabited. It believes that even at the darkest hour it will be given light enough. But this is very different from a religion whose God is said to have banished the darkness.

The trouble with "the Father Almighty" is that "he" necessarily belittles those to whose need "he" stoops. The child remains the child; he or she does not become the "friend" of whom Jesus spoke (John 15:15). The Father God does it all for the child and, precisely like the children of overprotective human parents, Christian "children" have too often remained at the level of the child, waiting for the Father's power to effect its miracles and victories, down to the last little need. Meanwhile, the God of the tradition of Jerusalem calls for friends, for covenant partners, for laborers in the vineyard, for stewards.

There can be no doubt that the fulfillment symbol of a deity who has triumphed for us over every negating element is psychically appealing from one standpoint, that of our dependency syndrome. As Feuerbach and, following him, Freud, Marx, and Nietzsche have variously shown, such a theism is deeply rooted in the psychological and social needs of the human creature. But far from condoning these needs and simply supplying what they demand, biblical faith in its prophetic expressions calls for a trust that will enter more consciously and deeply into the negations that are there—into "the rupture of creation";[1] a trust that will find its courage, not by embracing a theological ideology in which all the negations have been negated already, but through believing that the struggle with them is an integral part of their overcoming.

TRANSCENDENCE: ATHENS AND JERUSALEM

The triumphant deity of Christendom is thus not to be traced solely to historical factors but also to that deep religious longing for fulfillment that will always use whatever is at hand to satisfy its demands. Yet, without the historical influences to which we now move, this longing would surely not have been sufficient to turn the *koinonia* from the wilderness God, the "Abba" of that One who had no place to lay his head, to the settled, opulent monarch of the evolving Christian religion. After all, Israel resisted (though with difficulty) capitulation to that deity for centuries, and in spite of the fact that Israel did manage, at times, to become a settled people. Something had to be added to the religious needs of the human psyche to give us the "Father Almighty" of Christendom. Observing the proper chronology, we may say that the first dimension of this external historical influence comes from the traditions of Greek and Hellenistic religion and philosophy. There can be no doubt that the intellectual and spiritual climate into which early Christianity moved brought the faith ever closer toward a Theology that embraced a "high" account of the divine transcendence. We may mark negative as well as positive reasons for this. On the negative side, serious Christianity did not want to—and as the offspring of Hebraic monotheism, could not—identify itself with popular religions of the polytheistic variety. Positively speaking, it did want—and could in some sense legitimately attempt—to enter into dialogue with the higher philosophic traditions of the Hellenic world: Stoicism, and the Platonic and Aristotelian remnants that, later on, became even more important in their Islamic, Judaic, and Christian revivals.

In these philosophic traditions, the deity is characterized above all by transcendence—partly as a result of the philosophic struggle against popular Hellenistic religions and superstitions of the ancient world. As the career of Arius and most of the Alexandrian school illustrates, the most difficult aspect of Judaic-Christianity for this mentality was its habit of associating the deity too familiarly with creaturehood.

Israel too, of course, believed in God's transcendence: "My thoughts are not your thoughts, nor my ways your ways" (Isa. 55:8). But Israel articulated God's otherness, not in spatial, antimaterial terms, but temporally and ethically. God is the Eternal—the creator of time, not time's captive. God brings to pass what God will bring to pass and makes human wrath the vehicle of divine purposes (Ps. 76:10). God breaks the strict cause-and-effect sequence of historical events, causing *chronos* to bear kairotic meaning, meaning that time has not itself begotten. God is the "high and lofty one who inhabits eternity" and as such communes with the humble and meek (Isa. 57:15). Therefore God's transcendence is to be seen in dialectical tension with God's critical involvement in time. God's love qualifies God's unapproachable majesty: qualifies it, but also serves it. For the wonder of God in Hebraic and biblically Christian profession is precisely that in being *totaliter aliter* (wholly other), God *is* love. In accepting what is not acceptable, in justifying what is not justifiable, in loving what is not lovable, God is different, wholly different.

The philosophic forms in which the tradition of Jerusalem had to be articulated as, with the Christian mission to the Gentiles, it entered into the sphere of Greco-Roman culture, could not endure the vulnerability of such a God. The open-endedness of the working out of God's love and justice; inevitable proximity of divine and human being (a proximity as much Judaic as Christian); above all, the agapaic suffering that could not be avoided by such a divine orientation and presence: all this was foreign to the spirit of high philosophic thought about deity. The tradition of Athens is very great, but it cannot bear the idea of a suffering God.[2] In the meeting of Athens and Jerusalem nothing was more at issue than this. And despite the relative victory of soteriology in Western Christendom, the Greek traditions of philosophic Theology have exercised a lasting influence upon empirical Christianity's conception of deity. In most of its historic manifestations, Christianity has never overcome the transcendentalization of its Theology through the encounter with the tradition of Athens. Even in the 1960s, a Christian bishop could startle Christendom by announcing that God is not "up there and out there."[3] Apparently even liberal Protestantism, which seemed to stress the divine immanence to the exclusion, sometimes, of God's transcendence, did not prepare us for this kind of critique.

In fact, while theological liberalism, especially in the North American context, modified classical Theology by sentimentalizing "the Fatherhood of God," it can hardly be said to have entered a serious critique of the power/transcendence principle. The "Father Almighty" may indeed, under the aegis of liberalism, have become (as I put it earlier) "the Grandfather All-Merciful," but there was at least as much power behind the ubiquitous and unquestioning love of this benevolent deity as there was in the more traditional Theologies of the Classical and Reformation periods. Liberalism was no fight against the entrenched triumphalism of Christendom's Theology. Indeed, it would be more accurate to see the liberal revisions of conventional theism as a strategic updating of Theological triumphalism; for neither the Thomistic Final Cause nor the Calvinistic Sovereign God could claim any longer the respect of enlightened modernity. A God of inspiring and uncritical love could command more influence in the world of progressive ideals than could the exacting and distant judge of human perversity known to our Puritan forebears. Ironically, the liberal insistence upon the divine immanence functioned—for a time—to reinstate a waning emphasis upon the transcendent power of God. It was a variation on a very old theme. For all its sentimentality, it was at base a novel and temporarily effective application of the *theologia gloriae*.[4]

THE POLITICAL CO-OPTATION OF THE CHRISTIAN DOCTRINE OF GOD

The all-powerful Father God of Christendom was not created, however, by psychic needs and philosophic associations only. There was a third influence and it seems to me to have been the decisive one. Without it, the prophetic protest against the God of transcendent power could have endured throughout the history of the church as it endured (and endures) throughout the history of Israel. Psychic needs and philosophic conceptions, strong as they may be in molding our views of reality, do not altogether preclude criticism coming from alternative visions and traditions. When, however, these more nebulous spiritual and intellectual influences are accompanied by sociopolitical structures that sustain similar or compatible aims, the prospect of consistent protest is more difficult to mount.

This is precisely what the Establishment of Christianity meant and means.[5] A religion designed to serve the purposes of empire cannot present the spectacle of a God whose kenotic long-suffering detracts from "his" majesty. A less-than-absolute deity; a deity torn between impartial judgment and unwarranted mercy; a deity who "stoops to our weakness" and actually becomes weak for our sake; such is not the blueprint for a god designed for empire, any empire. If the aims of those who, like Arius, were deeply influenced by Greek philosophic Theology were to preserve the Christian God from a compromising participation in mundane materiality, the struggle of Constantine and his theological servants was to exploit the power potential of the Christian God and minimize everything reminiscent of divine vulnerability and self-emptying. An empire founded on military might, carefully layered structures of authority, the subordination of inferiors, and the unity of political intention and order—such an empire simply could not take as its primary religious cultus a faith whose deity struggles with the paradoxes of love and justice, forgives the gravest of offenders, punishes inordinate human pride and ambition, questions every authority structure, and listens to the pleas of the lowest citizens while putting down the mighty from their seats.

So much of what happened in the early decisions of the church is attributable to the religio-political needs of empire—particularly in the areas of trinitarian and christological thought—that one is tempted to wonder whether Christianity is not permanently and irrevocably shaped by this influence. The struggle to maintain the divine transcendence in Eastern Christianity served not only the philosophic and psychic needs discussed above but also this sheer political need; for under the conditions of establishment heavenly governance mirrors and is mirrored by earthly governance. The insistence upon the unity of the divine being that dominated Western Theological preferences even at the risk of courting forbidden Sabellian Monarchianism also clearly serves an imperium requiring allegiance to a single emperor/monarch. In the christological discussions . . . , the most difficult thing for the church to preserve was the real humanity of Jesus, and in fact it did so only in a formulary sort of way. What prevailed, for all intents and purposes, was a docetism that either through straightforward divinization or by making Christ's "humanity" the *perfection* of humanity removed the Christ effectively from the actualities of "finitude in anxious self-awareness" (Tillich).

Let us not forget: What Constantine heard, according to the legend was that, in this "sign" he would "conquer" (*in hoc signo vinces*). It was a conquering, heroic God that his counselors in the church gave him; and those who objected in the name of the crucified one (particularly the school of Antioch) were rejected.

The political co-optation of Christian Theology did not end with the Roman Empire. It has been present in all the empires with which, in subsequent history, Christianity has commingled. . . . [I]t is an unmistakable motif in the religious history of the American empire. The young airmen who bombed Vietnamese and Iraqi towns and cities after training sessions that were closed with prayer were invoking the same God that Constantine's soldiers were ordered to invoke prior to the battle of the Milvian Bridge.

Power—and precisely power understood in the usual sense—is of the essence of divinity shaped by empire. The purposes of the imperial god are sure and this god's power is absolute. It does not matter greatly what specific mores he upholds or what language he uses, whether it is the language of unrepentant fascism or of liberal, militarily maintained democracy. The chief thing is that this god is unambiguously supportive of the established earthly powers that honor him, fully in accord with the aims of the imperium, and unassailed by self-criticism. He is always "the Father Almighty," even when he is grandfatherly, and he triumphs over every enemy, no matter who, in that historical moment, the enemy happens to be.

But the great enemy of this god is the God of prophetic faith, who is always conceived critically precisely over against this deification of the power principle.

Notes

1. Wendy Farley, *Tragic Vision and Divine Compassion: A Contemporary Theodicy* (Louisville: Westminster John Knox, 1990), ch. 2.

2. "Greek epistemology was based on the principle of analogy: We come to know something through its resemblance to something already known. If the deity is pictured in terms of power or intelligence or wisdom, then one can hardly recognize God on the cross of Jesus because it displays no trace of power or wisdom. The principle of dialectical knowledge, of coming to know things through their seeming contrary, was not developed by Greek philosophy. That is in marked contrast to the gospel scene of the last judgment, where it turns out that the Son of Man was concealed in the oppressed and needy and persecuted. Greek epistemology could not take account of the surprise needed to recognize God on the cross. . . . It did not envision suffering

as a source of knowledge" (Jon Sobrino, *Christology at the Crossroads: A Latin American Approach*, trans. John Drury [Maryknoll, NY: Orbis, 1978], 373).

3. J. A. T. Robinson, *Honest to God* (London: SCM, 1963).

4. This ironic aspect of liberalism's Theology is more conspicuous in the art to which it gave rise than in its doctrine. For example, Lloyd C. Douglas's *Magnificent Obsession*, first published in 1932 (Toronto: Thomas Allen), presents the Christian God, supremely exemplified in Jesus, as the "Great Personality" whose resources may be tapped for the enhancement of our own personalities. It is in fact a very entrepreneurial concept of the deity, and it is not accidental that the protagonist and all the major characters of the novel belong to upper-middle-class American society and would hardly be attracted to presentations of the divine power along the lines of earlier forms of Christian triumphalism. They are not, after all, feudal lords and ladies but New World business and professional people. Their conception of "victorious living" requires, accordingly, a deity who reflects their own brand of ambition, success, and happiness and can help them to acquire and maintain the same. Divine transcendence, conceived in the mode of the *theologia gloriae*, only "works" if it accommodates itself to the existing values of its clientele, elevating those values to the level of the eternal.

5. See Jürgen Moltmann, *The Way of Jesus Christ: Christology in Messianic Dimensions*, trans. Margaret Kohl (London: SCM, 1990), 31, 104, 135, 313.

10

The Crucified God

Contra the previous chapter, which shows how the theology of glory has infiltrated our understandings of God, and kept the church in thrall to Christendom, this excerpt from The Cross in Our Context examines at length how it is that the suffering God may be recognized in the crucified Christ. In so doing, Hall also shows how the theology of the cross presupposes trinitarian theology and suggests that disestablishment of the churches can make room for the reemergence of the theologia crucis.

Source: Hall 2003:75–90.

WHICH GOD?

In theology, as in most other human pursuits, it is not really possible to separate form from content, but [here] our focus shifts quite definitely from questions of method to questions of substance. *What* precisely do Christians believe? What do they believe about God, to begin with? More particularly, what conception of God emerges when we attempt to discern God through the lens of this tradition, *theologia crucis?*

In order to set the tone for the response I shall give to that question, I want to refer to an incident that seems to me one of the most illuminating moments in all of Christian history: the appearance of Francis of Assisi, the poor man of God, before the greatest ecclesiastic and political potentate of the day, the supreme pontiff, Innocent III. The event occurred early in the thirteenth century, and it was later depicted by the famous Florentine monk-artist, Giotto.

In Giotto's painting one has in visible form the contrast between *theologia crucis* and *theologia gloriae*. The truly innocent one, little Giovanni (Francis) Bernardone, the rich merchant's son, now clad in a plain brown robe, stands with a small band of similarly robed men, all of them in an attitude of evident awe, before the great Innocent—who is far from innocent in any conceivable sense of that term. Unlike Luther, Francis did not write about the theology of the cross, but perhaps he exemplified it more faithfully than anyone, including Luther.

So well, in fact, did the saint of Assisi intuit both the anthropology and the Theology[1] of this tradition that, given the power and pomp of Christendom in that age, his vision and style of discipleship were probably doomed from the start. For in his anthropology he exemplified the sheer creaturehood of humans (that is to say, the *shared* creaturehood of our species) and thus presented an offense to the high anthropology of classical culture as well as that of the emerging Renaissance; in his Theology he assumed an unhierarchic solidarity of the Creator with the creature, and was thus an offense to the high Theology of scholasticism that was the transcendent basis of the patriarchal establishment.

In his well-known series on *Civilization*, Sir Kenneth Clark writes about the fate of Francis and his vision of the Christian life in a way that must give pause to anyone with a modicum of historical imagination. Commenting on the great basilica that Francis's followers began to build shortly after his death, Clark writes:

> A strange memorial to the little poor man, whose favourite saying was "Foxes have holes and birds of the air have nests: but the Son of Man hath not where to lay his head" [Luke 9:58, KJV]. But of course, St. Francis's cult of poverty could not survive him—it did not even last his lifetime. It was officially rejected by the Church; for the Church had already become part of the international banking system that originated in thirteenth-century Italy. Those of Francis's disciples, called *fraticelli*, who clung to his doctrine of poverty were denounced as heretics and burnt at the stake. And for seven hundred years capitalism has continued to grow to its present monstrous proportions. It may seem that St. Francis has had no influence at all, because even those humane reformers of the nineteenth century who sometimes invoked him did not wish to exalt or sanctify poverty but to abolish it.[2]

It is easy enough to claim belief in God. But the question that must always be put to all such claims is, simply, *Which God?* What is your image of this God in whom you claim belief? What kind of company does your God keep? What does your God ask of you—if anything? And the real challenge, where belief in God is concerned, surely, is whether such belief can be held without presupposing or leading to a subtle yet entirely effective *dis*belief in the ultimate worth and meaning of life, creaturely life. So much religion is rooted in an implicit despair of creaturehood. God appears as the transcendent *alternative* to the ephemeral and transitory—as a *Deus ex machina* who rescues us from the impossibility of our finitude, or who dresses up creation as a kind of dress rehearsal for the glory that it cannot now contain (Innocent's papal court). Feuerbach's thesis that God is a projection, in reverse, of our own sense of failure and inadequacy as creatures cannot be written off. We are finite, we project an Infinite; we are mortal, we project an Immortal; we are mutable, we project an Immutable; and so on. We turn to "God"—a god made not in our own image but in antithesis to our self-conception—to escape the psychic fearfulness of our actuality. Both Freud and Marx—and still more profoundly Nietzsche—built upon this thesis, and Christians would do well not to dismiss it, because in the end it is doctrinally purifying.

And our Christian doctrine of God badly needs purification! For there has been an ambiguity running throughout the length and breadth of it from the beginning. This ambiguity is already recognized by the Scriptures of the two Testaments, and perhaps there is finally no way of escaping it. Perhaps we just have to live with it. But it is one thing to live with it consciously, knowingly, and another to be uncomprehendingly at its mercy.

The ambiguity is this: Where deity is concerned, is our foundational assumption that of *power* or that of *love?* In homely terms, when we think "God," do we think the last word in sheer might, authority, supremacy, potency? Or do we think compassion, mercy, identification, grace, benevolence—*agape?* This, of course, is too simplistically stated, and I shall qualify it later. But for didactic purposes let it stand for the present. I am really asking for first thoughts. What does the word *God* (or its linguistic equivalents) first suggest to you? What comes nearly unbidden to your mind?

Now, if we are North Americans of a more or less Protestant blend, it may be that the thought that comes first to our minds derives from the second category, love; for we are nearly all of us products of the liberalization of Theology in the nineteenth century, even when we think we stand solidly in a more conservative doctrinal tradition. If that is the case, it is by no means without its problems; because what the Japanese theologian Kitamori called the "monism of love" in North American Christianity is indeed a highly problematic aspect of our religious context.[3] For the "love" we associate with God when we say, for instance (quoting 1 John 4:16), that "God *is* love" is frequently a dubious blend of sentimentality and pietism. If we loved our spouses or our children in the way that many of us say we love God, the unfortunate human objects of our love would quite rightly flee from us forthwith! For a love that involves no dialectic, no yes and no, no familiarity with hate, no suffering, no darkness but only light—such love is not the New Testament's *agape*. As Bonhoeffer stated the matter with his usual clarity, in the sentence "God is love" the emphasis is upon the first word. Love, as usually conceived, does not define God; God defines love.[4] And if the cross of Jesus Christ is the apex of God's definition of love, then the divine love has very little to do with the "luv" that is passed around so liberally in our contemporary context.

This quite modern way of picturing God, however, constitutes an exception to the historical norm. Perhaps it can be a useful exception, if it is not relegated to pure mawkishness; perhaps it is a corruption of the divine love articulated and depicted in the Scriptures; but it is an exception, in any case. For the dominant thought that human beings have entertained concerning God is certainly that of *power*. Even when love seems to color our *Gottesbild* (picture of God), it often turns out to be a love so perfect, so superlative, and finally so distant, that it is really being used as a synonym for power. God may be like a parent, but preferably the paternal parent, "the Father *Almighty*." (Though, let us add in all honesty, given the Freudian potency of Momism in our culture, Mothers Almighty as well are not unheard of.)

It seems inevitable, almost natural, that human beings would think of God in terms of power. Whether we follow the disturbing logic of Feuerbach and locate that natural impulse in our consciousness of our frailty as finite beings or in more positivistic terms find its genesis in sheer awe before the majesty of nature and the elements—no matter how we explain its origins, the association of deity with ultimate power and authority seems an incontrovertible fact of history. Indeed, it would be hard to entertain the idea of a Sovereign Creator, a First Cause, a Prime Mover, and so on without having recourse to the attribute of power.

What I shall want to say on this subject does not *deny* the place of power in Christian Theology, but it does, on the other hand, seriously and deeply qualify and reinterpret what the power of God must mean if it is contemplated under the aegis of the incarnation and cross of Jesus Christ.

Love Qualifies Power

One thing that we must grasp if we are to appreciate the ambiguity of our Western Christian doctrine of God in its clearest light is that, over and above the seemingly natural inclination of the human spirit to associate God with power, principally, there is a purely historical-cultural reality that renders the psychic association of deity and omnipotence doubly complex. I am referring of course to the political functioning of the Christian religion over a millennium and a half. When religion is brought into the center of political power and caused to serve as the spiritual guarantor and cultic legitimator of the powers-that-are, the natural or psychic propensity to link God with power is given a new and subtle twist. God, then, is no longer merely the transcendent force behind the ever-changing scene of existence but an eternal sovereignty reflected in and radiating from the throne of earthly might and authority. Christian monarchies as well as ecclesiastical hierarchies have had vested interests in sustaining an image of God informed by power and a concomitant hesitancy about Theologies that draw upon love, justice, compassion, and other attributes that necessarily qualify the power motif. To say as the liberationists do that "God has a preferential option for the poor" is to suggest a Theology that is bound to be threatening to the rich and powerful.

It is instructive in this connection to listen to the testimonies of those who have been victims of the God of glory and power represented by Christendom. In his [2001] book *Constantine's Sword*, James Carroll quotes a Jewish author, Leon Wieseltier, who, writing in *The New Republic*, stated: "'No, "Jesus on the cross" is not a repugnant symbol to me. But the sight of it does not warm my heart, either. It is the symbol of a great faith and a great culture *whose affiliation with power almost destroyed my family and my people.*"[5]

The implicitly polemical side of theologies that fail to affirm power as God's chief attribute is often not grasped by those who—often quite spontaneously—bring to the fore attributes that implicitly challenge the power motif. This was certainly the case with Francis and his associates. They had no idea of the extent to which their vision called in question the very thing the pope's court represented. To the contrary: when the guileless Francis—this Christian Parsifal—stood before the exalted Innocent, he and his simple followers imagined (so unsuspecting were they) that Almighty God Himself (certainly, Himself!) had deigned to bless their little enterprise, and they were so delighted in their innocence that they actually danced in the pope's august presence. They did not know the meaning of co-optation, nor did they suppose that their simplicity—their absurd dedication to "Lady Poverty"—constituted a direct affront to the age-old equation of deity and power, and specifically to the establishment of the Christian religion as the high priestly cultus of Western military supremacy and economic prowess. They were not the first victims of established Christianity's duplicity with respect to the nature of

God, but they surely represent the most dramatic historical instance of ironic misunderstanding.

One wishes that Francis could have had Luther among his theological advisors—the early Luther, before he had himself become so embarrassingly involved with his own society's developing powers, the new nationalism. The sixteenth-century German monk's counsel would no doubt have robbed Christian history of the delicious irony of this thirteenth-century encounter, but at least Francis might have gone into his much-anticipated meeting with the great pontiff understanding somewhat better than he did what was really transpiring there. He would have known that there could be no melding of Innocent's God with his own; that however amiable the encounter, the theology of glory would not be able to accommodate the theology of the cross—certainly not in such a stark form as this, at any rate! Of course, it is quite possible that Innocent himself, a brilliant man and a sincere Christian, we are told, cherished a profound personal sympathy for the vision of St. Francis.[6] He is said to have had a dream in which the rule of Francis would save the church. (Giotto painted that, too.) But Innocent was, after all, the supreme pontiff. Whatever his own feelings, he had to uphold the establishment.

And that, surely, has been the dilemma of Christendom from its inception. At its best, Christendom was never without the realization of its inherent contradiction, perhaps even its apostasy. The self-knowledge that was present in a figure like Bernard of Clairvaux and surfaced again so movingly in John XXIII has always been there, just beneath the surface of the establishment. But establishment has its own logic, and so long as the guardians of that logic are—or can seem to be—in charge, it must be obeyed, even by the sensitive.

This, however, is what makes our present experience in the Christian movement so very interesting. Because the establishment has become unraveled or unconvincing in all but a few places within the precincts of what was Christendom,[7] the question now presents itself whether the disciple community will be able to overcome somewhat its ambiguity about God and at least allow its predilection for divine power to be qualified by a more consistent recognition of the manner in which love always qualifies power, no less when it is divine love than when it is human.

Paul, in whose thought the theology of the cross first assumed a distinctly Christian form, stated the matter with utter clarity in 2 Corinthians 12. Reflecting there on his famous "thorn in the flesh" (which, fortunately,[8] he did not identify more explicitly), the apostle relates his fervent attempt to be rid of this impediment. "Three times I besought the Lord about this, that it should leave me; but he said to me, 'My grace is sufficient for you, for my power is made perfect in weakness.'" And he concludes, "when I am weak, then I am strong" (vv. 8–9).

"My power is made perfect in weakness"—a statement that Paul puts into the mouth of God because he meant it not only as comfort in the face of his personal struggle but as a description of the God he served. Paul's God does not lack power. As Jesus is reported to have said to those who came to the Mount of Olives to arrest him, God could, if God would, send a whole legion of angels to defend God's anointed one (Matt. 26:53). But then the very object of God's power, namely, to reach down into the soul of the creature and judge it, cleanse it, befriend it, would have been forfeited in an instant. Those who wield the sword perish by the sword—a motto, surely, that applies to divinity as much as to humanity. A god who rules with the sword will not survive the revenge of his victims, however long it may be in coming. If God's object is proximity to us ("I will be your God and you will be my people"), if God wills to transform us through the power of "suffering love," then no application of power in the usual sense could possibly attain this object. Love, as Paul declares in the beautiful hymn of 1 Corinthians 13, "does not insist on its own way . . . [but] bears all things, believes all things, endures all things." We hear this Scripture, usually, as the divine imperative under which we should live, and that is right. But we ought to hear it first as a description of the love that God manifests, voluntarily; for that is the presupposition of any such love that we might here and there, now and then, manage to live out. And what it makes very clear is that, wherever love is the objective and motive of the act, the act necessarily involves relinquishment of the impulse to pure power. Even in human love, when our love approaches something greater than the erotic or the filial, a certain sacrifice of self, of our natural *superbia*, is required, and most of the problems clustered around our human struggle to love come down to the immense difficulty we all have in letting go of self and the demands of self for preeminence.

Christianity makes the astonishing claim that God, who is preeminent in the only unqualified sense of that word, for the sake of the creature's shalom suffered—suffers—the loss precisely of that preeminence. In the words of Reinhold Niebuhr, "The crux of the cross is its revelation of the fact that the final power of God over man is derived from the self-imposed weakness of his love."[9] Not incidentally, Niebuhr's qualifying adjective is tremendously important here: "*self-imposed* weakness." Against Nietzsche, the pastor's son who complained so bitterly about the "feminine" weakness of the Christian God and his Christ, Niebuhr recognizes here that God's apparent weakness is the sign and consequence of a strength that is greater than mere brawn: it is the strength that is demanded of those who voluntarily forfeit their strength in order to be strong for the other.

THE TRINITARIAN PRESUPPOSITION OF THE THEOLOGY OF THE CROSS

Students of the evolution of trinitarian Theology will have observed that what I am doing here involves an intentional application of the principle of divine unity in trinitarian thought or at any rate an insistence upon the unity of God's *work*, as in the dogma of coinherence or *perichoresis*.[10] That is, what we posit of the second person of the Trinity cannot be reserved for the Son only but applies in some quite definitive sense to the Father and the Spirit as well—*no matter how radical the consequence*. Otherwise, the integrity or unity of the godhead is compromised. Thus, if Christians confess that the Christ, the divine Son, "suffered,"[11] they cannot turn about and claim that suffering is impossible where God the Father is concerned. So that, for instance, when the author of Philippians declares that the Christ, though "in the form of God, did not count equality with God a thing to be grasped, but emptied himself, taking the form of a servant . . . humbled himself and became obedient unto death, even death on a cross" (2:5f.), this must be taken as an indirect statement about God in the totality of God's being, and not merely as a statement about Jesus. In other words, the "emptying" or *kenosis* of the incarnation and the cross must be understood to apply to God in God's indivisibility. If Jesus Christ is the Revealer of God and not merely a subordinate who, finally, submits to the will of his superior (the Father Almighty), then the cross must be understood to apply to God's own being and acting and not only to that of the Christ.

It was with that assumption in mind that C. S. Dinsmore at the turn of the twentieth century penned the illuminating sentence, "There was a cross in the heart of God before there was one planted on the green hill outside Jerusalem."[12] It would be impossible to read the Scriptures of Israel without concluding, long before one had reached the end of them, that there is indeed "a cross in the heart" of Israel's God. It says more than one would like to admit about the supersessionism[13] of historical Christianity that so many Christians through the ages have been able to assume that suffering love, *agape*, appeared on the scene of God's dealings with humanity only with the advent of Jesus Christ. Luther was a better student of Scripture than most when, over against a whole philosophic tradition of Theological "aseity" (entire self-sufficiency) and ontic transcendence, he dared to speak about "the crucified God."[14] Following that same kind of Theo-logic, Dietrich Bonhoeffer, more strikingly still, wrote that while "Man's religiosity makes him look in his distress to the power of God in the world . . . the Bible directs man to God's powerlessness and suffering." And he added from the depths of his own suffering, "Only the suffering God can help."[15]

Such declarations constitute an enormous polemic against both the Theology and the Christology that has dominated particularly Western Christendom. To consider first the Theology, the power principle has been so prominent, so untouchable, that it has been nearly unthinkable for orthodox Christians to associate "God the Father" with the cross of "God the Son." It appears that the theologians would rather risk undoing the doctrine of the Trinity, which in the West always accentuated the principle of divine unity, than to suggest that God the Father suffered. Early in doctrinal disputations, Christian orthodoxy had—in the so-called Patripassian controversy—rejected precisely that idea, and there are few in the history of Christian thought who were ready to demur. Calvin, though a thoroughly christocentric theologian in most respects, continued, as Barth demonstrated with force, to embrace a picture of God (the omnipotent, omniscient, immutable, holy deity) strangely uninformed by Christology—as though, when he considered godhood, the French Reformer were more beholden to pagan classicism than to the biblical thought that he revered beyond any other source. One of Barth's major contributions to Reformed theology is his insistence that all of the great attributes (or perfections) that reason and piety attribute to the divine being (omnipotence, omniscience, omnipresence, aseity, immutability, holiness, and so forth) must, in their Christian articulation, be brought under the lens of Christology. What can one profess about the omnipotence of God, for instance, if one considers it from the perspective of Golgotha?[16]

Luther, whose more random, less systematic theological reflection could take many turns, nevertheless broke conspicuously with the regnant Theological tradition and carried his christological point of departure right into the heart of God: *Deus crucifixus*. If the central fact of the Newer Testament's witness is the passion and death of Jesus, the Christ, then this fact must not become a mere addendum to an a priori theism in which God is defined by a power and glory that precludes any kind of qualification. If the crucified one is truly representative of the God by whom faith believes him to have been sent, then, however ponderous the transcendent power that reason and religion have attributed to deity, the Christian God must be seen as a suffering God.

Tillich's commentary on this subject, to which I referred earlier, bears repeating: "One of Luther's most profound insights was that God made Himself small for us in Christ. In so doing, He left us our freedom and our humanity.

He showed us His heart, so that our hearts could be won." The passage goes on to recognize that the human longing for a God of power and glory is very strong—which is of course why so much religion and so much political ideology can capitalize on it. We yearn for a God who sets everything to rights—indeed, who prevents wrong from occurring in the first place. But in such longings we overlook the fact that to have such a God we should have to relinquish our own freedom and become automatons who could only do right. And Tillich concludes that while in that case we might be happier (if happiness could still be used of creatures without freedom), we should have become beings quite different from what we are, "perhaps more like blessed animals." "Those who dream of a better life and try to avoid the cross as a way . . . have no knowledge of the mystery of God and of man."[17]

To illustrate: At the end of that fateful day, September 11, 2001, a day that bruised the spirits of us all, I was confronted by a woman—a good friend, in fact, but now quite distraught and almost belligerent. She glared at me, the representative of religion closest at hand. "Where was *God* in all of that?" she demanded. An avowedly unreligious person herself, she was apparently able, in that moment, to reach back into some previous flirtation with the God of power and might in order to find someone to blame. I refrained from saying to her that there were large numbers of people in the world—not in our immediate sphere but nonetheless fellow citizens of Earth and highly God-fearing in their own terms—who believed that God was precisely in charge of that whole plot against godless America, and who could look upon the dread event as a wonderful vindication of God's great glory and power. (Again one asks: Which God? Whose God?) I should have liked to explain to my friend the theology of divine providence that emanates from this "thin tradition" we are considering; but it would not have been heard, for her fundamental assumption about deity (and in this she is entirely representative of her age) is that the term *God*, if the term means anything at all (which it probably doesn't), must stand for unequivocal power. Ergo, why doesn't He (yes, of course, He!) use it? This is the best argument for atheism known to our race, because of course the God of power and glory never has and never will set things to right in the manner that we, with our many and conflicting views of what right and just and true and good and beautiful would mean, could be satisfied. Thus, like my friend, many disbelievers have a permanent and very effective rationale for their high disbelief, and they are strangely self-satisfied (they manifest a high degree of what the Germans call *Schadenfreude*) whenever tragic or horrendous events occur that give them an excuse to berate and humiliate others who claim belief in God.

What such persons seem not to grasp, or even entertain, is that gods who prevent evil and set everything to rights can only do so by overruling the behavior of that one creature that creates more havoc than any other: ourselves. Ironically, those who most complain of God's failure to act godlike, that is, to exercise unmitigated power, are the very ones who are most affronted by any curtailment of their own freedom. They want the world to be what they want the world to be, and the only god they can abide is one whose will coincides perfectly with their own.

If we posit a God who both wills the existence of free creatures and the preservation and redemption of the world (and I take it that neither of these intentions can be dispensed with by Christians), then we must take with great seriousness the biblical narrative of a God whose providence is a mysterious internal and intentional involvement in history; a God, therefore, who is obliged by his own love to exercise his power quietly, subtly, and, usually, responsively in relation to the always ambiguous and frequently evil deeds of the free creatures; a God who will not impose rectitude upon the world but labor to bring existing wrong into the service of the good; a God, in short, who will suffer.

I said that statements like Bonhoeffer's "Only a suffering God can help" constitute a polemic against the dominant christological as well as the dominant Theological assumptions of the Christian establishment. The elaboration of the christological aspect of that statement must await another chapter [see Hall 2003, ch. 6], but in view of the trinitarian conception of the godhead that Christians embrace, we ought at least to notice it already in this consideration of God. Western Christendom in both its Roman Catholic and its major Protestant expressions has been welded to an atonement theology that has guaranteed keeping God the Father quite distinct from the suffering Son. For in the Latin or Anselmic or satisfaction theory that the West has adopted in various forms almost without exception, the suffering of the Son is virtually at the hands of the Father, who requires satisfaction for the guilt and unholiness of the human race, for which the Christ substitutes himself. This presents a picture of God entirely different from the one that emanates from the theology of the cross. Anselm's Father God is still very much informed by the power principle. While such a God may be said to be motivated by a *desire* to forgive and love sinful humanity, this God is able to do so only indirectly through a transaction that, to say the least, calls into question the trinitarian unity of the godhead. There is in fact a tremendous gulf between the Anselmic conception of the atonement and the anguished cry of Bonhoeffer that only a suffering God can help. Anselm's *God* simply cannot suffer.[18]

A New Openness to the Suffering God?

The wide reception of the work of Bonhoeffer, as well as of Moltmann, Weil, and many others (including artists and writers like Georges Rouault, Shusaku Endo, Georges Bernanos, Flannery O'Connor, Rudi Wiebe, and many others) who in the past century have developed conceptions of a suffering God, raises an interesting question: Is there a new openness to this Theology? I believe that there is, and I also think I understand some of the reasons for it.

The first reason is quite simply that the god of power has failed. The failure of the omnipotent deity to prevent or resolve evil and human suffering could be overlooked, so to speak, so long as people could be persuaded of a heaven in which their sorrows would all be healed. But with the increasing orientation of humankind (especially but not only in the West) toward the present life and our own earthly condition, a God for whom omnipotence was claimed could not be received as credible in a world where suffering both personal and corporate seemed interminable. It is not accidental that one problem has preoccupied Christianity in the past two centuries: the problem of evil. For if the thing you most wish to say about God is that God is absolutely and ultimately powerful, then in a world newly conscious of both its potentiality and its vulnerability, you will have to explain how such an omnipotent deity can tolerate the seeming triumph of evil, wickedness, and death. If Christianity has begun at last to consider the meaning of Paul's dictum that divine power is "made perfect in weakness," it is at least partly due to the fact that the conventional religious claim concerning God's limitless power ceased to persuade after about the seventeenth century.

But the move away from the equation of God and power has also had something to do with the sidelining of the Christian religion itself. Whatever else may be said about our de facto disestablishment, the good side of it is that the remnant of Christianity that remains is no longer obliged to mirror, in its doctrine, what is acceptable to the dominant culture and the policy-making classes. If, as I have maintained, the association of God principally with power has been profoundly affected by the functioning of the Christian religion as the cultic guarantor and legitimator of earthly power structures, then the removal of Christianity from that role, wherever it is true, means that Christians are at liberty (if they will take the liberty) to explore the dynamics of their own tradition without feeling bound to make their tradition serve the extraneous purposes of a perhaps moribund civilization.

The new freedom to explore the nature and meaning of God without looking over one's shoulder to see how one's Theology is being received by kings and governments and powerful classes is one of the most exciting realities of contemporary Christian theology. In the following statement of Moltmann . . . , we have a marvelous instance of what this new freedom can mean:

> To recognize God in the crucified Christ means to grasp the Trinitarian history of God, and to understand oneself and this whole world with Auschwitz and Viet Nam, with race-hatred and hunger, as existing in the history of God. God is not dead, death is in God. God suffers by us. He suffers with us. Suffering is in God.
>
> God does not ultimately reject, nor is he ultimately rejected. Rejection is within God.
>
> When he brings his history to completion, his suffering will be transformed into joy, and thereby our suffering as well.[19]

Notes

1. I capitalize the word *Theology* when it refers explicitly to the doctrine of God; lowercase *theology* signifies the discipline of systematic (dogmatic, constructive, etc.) theology.

2. Kenneth Clark, *Civilization* (London: British Broadcasting Corporation and John Murray, 1969), 77–78.

3. In an extended conversation with me in 1989, Kitamori stressed repeatedly his conviction that North American Christians on the whole were incapable of appreciating the biblical concept of God's *suffering* love (*agape*) because our culture had so sentimentalized love, removing from it the pain that is always involved in profound relationships of love. His theology of the pain of God may be best exemplified in the novels of his compatriot Shusaku Endo, who was influenced by Kitamori. See especially Endo's *Silence*, trans. William Johnston (Tokyo: Sophia University Press, 1969). See also my essay, "Theological Reflections on Shusaku Endo's *Silence*," *Interpretation* 33, no. 3 (1979): 254–67.

4. "For the sake of clarity, this sentence ['God is love'] is to be read with the emphasis on the word God, whereas we have fallen into the habit of emphasizing the word love. *God* is love; that is to say not a human attitude, a conviction or a deed, but God Himself is love. Only he who knows God knows what love is" (Dietrich Bonhoeffer, *Ethics*, trans. Neville Horton Smith [London: SCM, 1955], 173).

5. Cited by James Carroll in his *Constantine's Sword: The Church and the Jews* (Boston: Houghton Mifflin, 2001), 15 (italics added).

6. "Innocent III was unquestionably a man of personal humility and piety, but no Pope ever had higher conceptions of the papal office and under him the papacy reached its highest actual power" (Williston Walker, *A History of the Christian Church*, rev. ed. [New York: Scribner's, 1959], 259).

7. Whether a new Christendom is being born among the churches of the Southern Hemisphere (Africa, Asia, Latin America) is a question that we shall have to tackle later; my argument here refers to the historical Christendom of the West (including parts of the Near East).

8. I say "fortunately" because Paul's point would be lost if the problem to which he alludes were narrowly defined. *Whatever* his (or our) particular "thorn," what it betokens is a lack of self-sufficiency, the knowledge of which makes the human being open to undeserved and unearnable grace.

9. Robert McAfee Brown, ed., *The Essential Reinhold Niebuhr: Selected Essays and Addresses* (New Haven: Yale University Press, 1986), 22.

10. This refers to the mutuality or interdependence of the being and acting of the three *personae* of the Trinity. Each person—Father, Son, and Spirit—reflects the others. The dogma is based on John 10:28-38 and was important in the thought of the Cappadocian fathers, Augustine, Hilary, and many others.

11. As many have pointed out, the only term in both the Apostles' and the Nicene Creeds descriptive of the *life* of Jesus as distinct from his birth, death, and resurrection is the term *suffered*.

12. C. S. Dinsmore, *Atonement in Literature and Life* (Boston: Houghton Mifflin, 1906), 232.

13. On the question of Christian supersessionism see the excellent study of R. Kendall Soulen, *The God of Israel and Christian Theology* (Minneapolis: Fortress Press, 1996).

14. As Moltmann points out, Luther gleaned this phrase from "the theology of the mysticism of the cross in the late Middle Ages" (*The Crucified God: The Cross of Christ as the Foundation and Criticism of Christian Theology*, trans. R. A. Wilson and John Bowden [London: SCM, 1973], 47). A reference in Luther himself is found in Martin Luther, *Luthers Werke: Kritische Gesamtausgabe (Schriften)*, 65 vols. (Weimar: H. Böhlau, 1883–1993), 1:614, 17.

15. Dietrich Bonhoeffer, *Letters and Papers from Prison: The Enlarged Edition*, trans. Reginald Fuller, Frank Clarke, et al. (London: SCM, 1953), 361.

16. See Barth's discussion of "The Perfections [Attributes] of God" in "The Doctrine of God," *Church Dogmatics*, 4 vols. (New York: Scribner's, 1955–57), 2:322ff.

17. Paul Tillich, *The Shaking of the Foundations* (New York: Scribner's, 1953), 148.

18. For an interesting discussion of Luther's relation to Anselm, see Bernhard Lohse, *Martin Luther's Theology: Its Historical and Systematic Development*, trans. Roy A. Harrisville (Minneapolis: Fortress Press, 1999), 223ff. Lohse argues (contra Aulén) that Luther's atonement theology cannot be identified with any one of the three dominant types of theory, yet he is inclined to distinguish Luther from the Anselmic emphasis on "satisfaction." And he notes that "the importance of the victory motif should not be ignored"—which is at least a guarded and partial acceptance of Aulén's famous hypothesis in *Christus Victor* (trans. A. G. Herbert [London: SPCK, 1953]). My own view on the subject is that, when Luther's theological perspective is understood as an (unsystematic) elaboration of the *theologia crucis*, it could not possibly give rise to the species of divine transcendence and impassivity that Anselm's soteriology assumes. While, therefore, it is entirely possible and historically explicable to find in Luther's writings reminiscences of all three major theories of atonement, the soteriology by which Luther is grasped throughout fits *none* of the extant theories in any neat manner but is uniquely his own; and this is nowhere more in evidence than in his readiness to see God ("The Father Almighty" of the creeds) under the sign of the cross.

19. Jürgen Moltmann, "The Crucified God," *Theology Today* 31 (1974): 18.

11

Redemption: Conquest from Within

Hall's first major book in the United States, Lighten Our Darkness: Towards an Indigenous Theology of the Cross (1976), is also his most concentrated consideration of what the theologia crucis means in the North American context. Ten years later, God and Human Suffering: An Exercise in the Theology of the Cross, took that theological motif and set it in relation to the perennial problem of suffering, as a matter of applied theology, or Christian praxis. As he writes in the book's introduction, "To ask about the theology of suffering is, in part, to reflect on theology as suffering. For when the Christian community takes to itself the task of comprehending and engaging the culture which is its worldly context, it is not assuming a merely intellectual investigation; it is entering into the deepest darkness of the world" (1986a:23)—words that reflect the exact aim of nearly all of Hall's theological writings. In this excerpt, Hall undertakes a critique of the traditional language of power relative to God's work in the world, suggesting that these are precisely what contribute to much of human suffering. An understanding of power filtered through the lens of the theology of the cross, however, can also re-form our understandings of God, the incarnation, and the Trinity—and, ultimately, our christological and soteriological approaches.

Source: Hall 1986a:93–121.

Redemption as "Point of Departure"

In this brief attempt at a theological overview of the theme "God and Human Suffering," we turn now to the third focus of the threefold perspective from which Christian theology considers this recurring and many-sided problem of human and religious experience: redemption. From the focus of the doctrine of creation we have argued that there is a form of suffering which is inherent in creaturely finitude, not as a flaw or a mistake of the Maker, but as a positive aspect of the being that God intends for humanity: the suffering of becoming. Then, from the focus our tradition has named "the fall," we have reminded ourselves that there is a suffering which is the consequence of humankind's distorted freedom, and which is present in our situation both as act and as condition, both as a reality for which we are humanly and personally responsible and as a tragic fact of our corporate existence and history. It is here that biblical faith places its *chief* stress with respect to the reality of human suffering—though, wisely, it does not indulge in attempts to demonstrate direct or obvious connections between empirical suffering and actual sin.

Now from the focus that our doctrinal heritage names redemption or salvation, we are to remember that the reality of human suffering (the first of our tradition's two basic affirmations in relation to this whole topic) is met by an even greater reality: the conquest of suffering by the God of "suffering love" (*agape*). There is, after all, according to the tradition of Jerusalem, an answer to suffering. But no, let us use our words judiciously from the outset: there is . . . *an Answerer!*

Before we attempt to amplify that perhaps enigmatic but all-important distinction, however, it is expedient at this point that we make a methodological observation. If it is not already clear, then at this juncture it ought to be made quite explicit that the vantage point from which Christian faith considers this entire theme is not neatly separable into three distinct aspects or foci. Rather, the three foci (creation, fall, redemption) belong to a *single perspective*, a seamless robe of belief and contemplation. Moreover, even though we have treated our subject in a sequential way, starting with the doctrine of creation (as is usual in most theology), faith as distinct from *theology* does not adhere strictly to this sequence. In fact, in a real sense the basic point of departure for faith is heavily informed by the substance of this third dimension of our threefold perspective—redemption. For it is this aspect of the total perspective upon the question of suffering, namely, the gospel's *engagement* of the reality of human suffering, that lends to faith both the courage and the wisdom that it needs in order to consider, with greater openness than would otherwise be possible, the reality of suffering as it is glimpsed through the foci of creation and fall. Suffering is real—so real that the human psyche can only bear to contemplate the depths of its reality if from the outset it is given some cause to believe that suffering is not the *ultimate* reality, nor as such the last word about existence in this world. Apart from such a prospect, who would have the stamina to expose himself or herself deeply to the fact of human suffering? Without at least the hint of a promise that meaning might be found in, alongside, or beneath such suffering as human flesh is heir to, no doubt the better course would be (what in fact so many of our contemporaries do!) to avoid so far as possible any such exposure!

It is from the perspective of redemption that Christian faith derives this necessary promise. Accordingly, we have assumed that perspective throughout these reflections. But now we must attempt to make it explicit. "Christian faith," wrote Reinhold Niebuhr, "fully appreciates the threat of meaninglessness which comes into history by the corruption of human freedom. But it does not succumb to the despairing conclusion that history is merely a chaos of competing forces."[1] Our task now is to provide what we can by way of background to this kind of faith statement. On what basis does Christian faith, while remaining entirely honest about the reality of human suffering and the "meaninglessness" that it conjures up, both admit this reality and affirm that it is nevertheless only the penultimate and not the ultimate reality?

NOT BY MIGHT

In the title of this chapter I have used the phrase "the conquest from within." I must begin these reflections on redemption and human suffering, however, by registering a warning about such language as this. Words like *conquest*—and conventional theology and liturgy abound in them!—too easily suggest the application of sheer power to any problem. To employ the word *conquest* for the gospel's approach to the problem of human suffering, and to do so without any critical commentary on such language, is to invite people to think once again (as nearly all religion has conditioned us to think) in terms of the divine attribute of omnipotence: God, whose power is infinite, takes on the sources of human suffering in much the same fashion as St. George takes on the dragon, or the forces of law and order in old-fashioned Hollywood movies take on outlaws and criminals, or an imperial host takes on a rebel army. Feminist and other types of critical theology remind us, rightly, that the church's resort to power language, as well as most of the analogies, myths, and illustrations that we employ to back it up, is very much a culturally conditioned approach to Christianity. For one thing, it is a characteristically masculine approach. As masculinity has been defined in Western civilization generally and in the New World in particular, power is of the essence! It is certainly not the only conceivable way of describing the male being—in fact it is highly reductionist; for men, like women, are capable of compassion, gentleness, meekness, humility, and identification with weak and suffering things. But every little boy in this society knows that these are not the qualities he is expected to cultivate. He knows that his calling as a man, regardless of his vocation, is to accentuate whatever he can by way of physical, intellectual, and spiritual strength, and to approach life with its challenges and problems in a spirit of self-confidence, leadership, and conquest. On this continent, where until recently that kind of spirit could find its proper outlet only in the milieu of the deed, the masculine mystique has hardly even known the courage of thought. Meditation upon complex and technically insoluble issues of human experience has been regarded for the most part as an unprofitable pursuit for "real men"—with the consequence that work requiring such meditation (especially teaching—except where prestige could be gained!) has been relegated to women; and with the further consequence that in the present sociohistorical moment, whose complexity requires unusual powers of abstract reflection and renders most technical solutions and mere deeds questionable and even dangerous, many men especially are frustrated and disorientated. After generations of the kind of problem solving which called for quick decisions and decisive deeds, executed with dispatch and sure power, an age whose great problems are in large measure due to the very delusions of mastery created by the power mentality presents enormous threats to all—female as well as male—who still want to assume that might is right.

All the same, the language and posture of power have in fact informed whole segments of the Christian tradition. As C. S. Song has put it in his provocative study *The Compassionate God*, we have been handed a "high-voltage God" and a "high-voltage theology" by our tradition. "Power has been stored up, and we must be on our guard." Ours is "a highly charged deity, a dangerous God." Our theology, accordingly, accentuates power, and itself functions powerfully in the post-Constantinian situation:

> It provides the church with theological grounds for anathema and excommunication administered to those recalcitrant souls who want to bring God away from ecclesiastical protection and let the world have a better look at God. Mission theology too has been, on the whole, a militant theology that defends God from pagan gods and draws a clear line between salvation and damnation. It is a very highly charged theology from which very few pagans could get away scot-free.[2]

The language of power is prominent in Christian doctrine as it relates to our present theme. It can be observed both in the conventional way in which the so-called problem of suffering is stated, and in at least one of the three major types of atonement theology through which evolving doctrine responded to human suffering.

Formulating the problem of suffering in its conventional statement revolves around the seeming contradiction between the divine power and the divine love. If God is *loving* and at the same time *all-powerful*, then why is there so much suffering in the world? The assumption is that the deity *could*, if the deity *would*, simply eliminate suffering. Why then does God not do so, if God is truly loving?

When the question is put in this way there is, I think, no satisfactory way of addressing it. The chance of there being a convincing response to such a formulation of the problem is at least severely limited; and the limiting factor is just this power assumption. When infinite power is posited as the primary and characteristic attribute of deity, then no one can be satisfied with an answer that is less than the abolition of suffering as such!

It is the power assumption itself that must be questioned. Behind it lies a whole preunderstanding of both God and humanity which does not belong to the tradition of Jerusalem, and which in fact may be the direct antithesis of that tradition, despite obvious linguistic parallels. The Judeo-Christian tradition does not deny the power of God, but neither does it magnify this attribute; moreover, and more to the point, it does not abstract the divine power from the divine-human *relationship*. The relationship qualifies—radically—the nature and deployment of power on God's part.

This can be appreciated at least in a rudimentary way. . . . If suffering is inextricably bound up with human freedom (not that all suffering is a direct and obvious consequence of freedom's misuse, but it is nevertheless impossibly intermingled with it) then *through power* God could eliminate suffering by eliminating freedom. But if freedom is of the very essence of the human creature, as the tradition has generally maintained and as we also insisted earlier, then the elimination of freedom would imply the virtual elimination of humanity.

A parallel to this prospect exists today within the human sphere as such. Because of the rampant freedom of individuals and societies, problems of population, pollution, distribution, violence, and the like, have multiplied in an alarming manner. Behavioral scientists like B. F. Skinner have a solution to the dilemma: condition human beings from birth to desire only what they should desire and do only what they should do! Freedom and dignity are luxuries the species can no longer afford; therefore let the power of science solve the problem by effectively eliminating freedom and dignity. *But*, reply Skinner's critics (and with reason), even if this could be accomplished it would not really solve the existing dilemma. It would only eradicate the problem by substituting something else, some other organism, for *Homo sapiens*. For without freedom and dignity there is no longer humanity.

There are, in other words, situations in which *power* simply does not work. Such situations are not foreign to any of us. Even the most macho of males (and females) experience such situations, and it may well be asked whether their resort to power and brute force is not frequently a consequence of their frustration over knowing in the depths of their souls that power does not change anything but usually only complicates existing problems. There are (if we are permitted to speak in such a way) analogies to *God's* problem of dealing with human suffering in every nook and cranny of historical existence, personal and social. Who, through power tactics, can eliminate the self-destroying habits of a son or daughter who has fallen prey to hard drugs? What nation, through power alone, can ensure world peace? We live in a world which attempts through the sheer show of military might to deter nuclear warfare—with the very real prospect *that this power play itself*, through design or accident, will trigger the very thing it is supposed to prevent! There is no *sword* that can cut away sin without killing the sinner.

Beyond that, there are connections—deep and mysterious links—between our suffering and our grandeur that render power approaches to this question abysmally simplistic. Frederick Buechner in his novel *Lion Country* poignantly discloses some of these connections. The protagonist of his story, Antonio, has a twin sister who eventually dies of myeloma, "a fatal disorder which has to do with bones." At the end of the story, Antonio makes the following observation:

> When Miriam's bones were breaking . . . if I could have pushed a button that would have stopped not her pain but the pain of her in me, I would not have pushed the button because, to put it quite simply, my pain was because I loved her, and to have wished my pain away would have been somehow to wish my love away as well. And at my best and bravest I do not want to escape the future either, even though I know that it contains what will someday be my own great and final pain. Because a distaste for dying is twin to a taste for living, and again I don't think you can tamper with one without somehow doing mischief to the other. But this is at my best and bravest. The rest of the time I am a fool and a coward just like most of the other lost persons that in the end it will take no less than Mr. Keen himself to trace.[3]

To reiterate: there are situations where power is of no avail. *They are most of the situations in which as human beings we find ourselves!* May we not also dare to say that, from the standpoint of a faith tradition which posits love, not power, as *God's* primary perfection, they are most of the situations in which God finds God's Self too? Not only has power dominated the articulation of the conventional statement of the problem of suffering; it has also functioned as the principal metaphor of at least one of the three major types of soteriological theory which evolved in the course of Christian reflection on the meaning of Christ's suffering and death. I am referring to the so-called ransom or (in Gustav Aulén's famous analysis) classical theory of atonement:[4] Christ the Victor, cloaking for the time being his divine omnipotence beneath the apparent weakness of the flesh, deceives and finally destroys the forces of evil that are responsible for human misery, and delivers the human victims from the bonds of sin, death, and the demonic.

There are, of course, times and seasons when such a theory can have something very important to say to both church and society. It can give courage to those who sit in darkness and the shadow of death, to the discouraged, the fatalized, the oppressed. Strategically, it can be the right word in certain contexts—as it is again, in forms necessarily different from its classical expression, in some types of liberation theology. But to present such a strategically relevant message as if it were an ultimately satisfactory theological response to the question contained in our theme is to overlook important and complex things about the human condition with which the redeeming God must contend.

One of these things (as we have just been reminding ourselves) is that it is virtually impossible to separate the sources of suffering from the sufferer, especially when the condition of the sufferer is understood, as it finally must be, in its total communal and historical setting. The "ransom" or "deliverance" type of atonement theology on the contrary finds the sources of suffering to be external to the condition and being of the sufferer. Classical expressions of this theology located the cause of evil in an objectifiable, transhistorical demonic power, separable from the human community or at least from the elect within it, so that the relief and deliverance from suffering could be effected by a powerful Christ figure, dealing the death-blow to Satan. The temptation for liberation theology when it takes over this ancient motif of the deliverance of the oppressed, is to identify the source of earthly suffering with equally objectifiable enemies, only now within the mundane sphere: with certain classes, with the capitalists, with the multinationals, with the industrial complex. So the gospel becomes a statement and praxis of liberation from these oppressive forces.

In raising this critique, I am by no means accusing liberation theology of actually or consistently succumbing to this temptation, nor am I in the least denying that the evils named by most expressions of this theological movement are truly evil and must be challenged and rooted out. My point is only that the *temptation* of every theology or soteriology which capitalizes on the power motif is too one-sidedly to locate the sources of evil and human suffering "out there," i.e., in some external, objectifiable, and separable entity; and thus on the one hand to exaggerate the ultimacy of those evil entities, courting in this way an unwarranted dualism, and on the other hand attributing to those who are "delivered from evil" too much innocence and goodness. If evil is located externally and the causes of suffering thus isolated, it is of course possible to develop versions of the work of the Christ in which the destroyer/oppressor is vanquished and the victim set free.

But, as Anselm of Canterbury knew (for all his own psychic and theological limitations), the causes of suffering cannot so readily be isolated from our own selves, collectively and individually. This is why Anselm, in *his* attempt to answer the question of how the Christ delivers *us* from suffering,[5] did not present his case as a struggle between God and Satan, but as a struggle between God and the human soul, whose cause was espoused by God the Son. The other principal atonement theology developed in the long history of Christian reflection upon the meaning of the cross (I refer to the theory that was given classical expression by Peter Abelard and was taken up by nineteenth-century liberal theology as the "moral influence theory") is even more adamant than Anselm concerning the location of the sources of suffering as being *within the deepest recesses of the human spirit*.[6]

Without buying into the whole story that is told in either one of these alternatives to the Classical/Ransom theory, we may nevertheless see in both the work of Anselm and of Abelard an implicit protest within the Christian tradition against overuse of the motif of divine omnipotence in the articulation of the gospel of the cross. Once faith has overcome the perhaps "natural" but nonetheless simplistic tendency towards a Manichaean separation of good and evil, it is necessary to employ concepts far more sophisticated than power to the interpretation of the redemptive event.

Power is in the long run an intensely limited mode of response for meeting the subtle questions present in our theme. The changes that need to occur if there is to be any real or profound "conquest" of suffering are mainly internal ones. I do not mean internal, in this case, to be heard as a synonym for private or personal. It is not a matter merely of altering individual souls, one by one, to make the world right. This approach, the perennially announced program of religious personalism and pietism, overlooks the corporate aspect of that "tragic dimension" to which we have drawn attention in the previous chapter. Individuals are conditioned by societal circumstances far greater than themselves; so that even to alter the condition of the individual "soul," if it is *seriously* intended and not just a matter of pious rhetoric, would drive any who attempt such a thing into the social arena. (As I was informed by one of my students who has made it her vocation to "take care of" of elderly women who are otherwise alone in the world: "If I follow one of my women carefully for one day only, I am led directly into all or most of the *social* problems of our society!") It is not only the spirits of private persons that must be reached and changed but the spirit of the collectivity, of the community—indeed of the species. A *metanoia* must be undertaken which is aimed at the anxiety that seeks security in the building of "greater barns," at the collective fear which is always busy fashioning images of the enemy (*Feindbilder*), at the false pride which sets race against race and sex against sex and generation against generation, and at the economic concupiscence which tries to find permanence and meaning in the amassing of possessions. How can power, as it is ordinarily understood, meet and transform this anxiety, this fear, this false pride, this concupiscence? Such spiritual qualities, which belong not only to individual persons but describe the spirit of our First World, can be altered only through encounter with a judgment (*krisis*) which convicts from within and an alternative which commends itself through forgiveness and love.

In stressing the *internal* or "spiritual" qualities which, in my view, the tradition of Jerusalem identifies as the core causes of the greatest human suffering, I in no way intend to minimize the evil of the external manifestations of these qualities. Who could not discover, looking about in our contemporary world of "have" and "have not" people, that the bulk of the great physical forms of suffering in this world is inextricably linked with the *institutionalization* of greed, the *legitimation* of lust and concupiscence, and the public *authorization* of a system which rewards the strong and punishes the weak? And who could not surmise, regarding such a world, that the external symptoms of its malaise must themselves be dealt with; that steps must be taken to remedy injustice and unequal distribution and the arms race and violence in our cities and pornography—the list goes on? Yet who could not also detect, given a little time for reflection, that these and similar phenomena *are* in fact symptoms, manifestations of a more deadly cancer that eats away at the collective human spirit? To despise the activists who treat the symptoms—some of whom devote their very lives to the treatment of the gross symptoms of our spiritual malaise—is a travesty of Christian wisdom and obedience. In such a time as ours we must all be activists, all giving our energies to the conquest of economic injustice, racial and sexual oppression, violence and war, and the other evident evils that bedevil our world. Civilizations, like individual organisms, can die of the symptoms of their diseases! Too many of the intellectuals and "spiritual people" among us maintain our safe distance from the world by telling ourselves that we are interested only in the root causes of our late twentieth-century dis-ease. Thus, theology, preaching, the conversion of souls, and "pastoralia" become for us fences upon which to sit, while others risk their lives and fortunes to save human bodies and the body politic.

In pleading for a deeper understanding of the spiritual causes of First World disorder and the suffering that it begets, then, I do not wish to provide a rationale for ethical passivity. Yet surely, while actively participating in God's work of saving the world from death through the symptoms of its disease, Christians must at the same time give themselves to the more complex work of seeking under God to comprehend and to change the collective spirit which begets these symptoms. It is not only the actual *practices* of the rich nations of the world that must be changed, it is the spirit which incites these practices and sustains them; it is the goals, the values, the anxieties, and bogus hopes that make such practices seem necessary or natural. It does not require any special revelation nor an explicit religious faith to know that it is the invisible, intangible, spiritual core of human society that must be altered if what is visibly and tangibly wrong in the world is to be altered significantly. Much of the secular wisdom of our time has led to that very conclusion. Faith, if we confess it, only adds to rationality at this point the courage to believe that the collective spirit can be changed—because faith believes that the God revealed in Jesus as Christ is committed to life, and without significant change in the human spirit the life of the world is sorely jeopardized.

INTIMATIONS OF AN ALTERNATIVE: THE THEOLOGY OF THE CROSS

The change for which faith hopes, which it believes possible (not necessary or inevitable, but possible), cannot be effected through power, might, majesty, dominion, and the like, but only through a *divine modus operandi* that stands all such preconceptions of God's way of working in the world on their head. Perhaps we have come to a moment in our history as a religion, we Christians, when more of us can be open to the alternative to power-orientated thinking that is present in the depths of our tradition—in the declaration that "Jesus is the Christ."

This is no doubt a very optimistic assessment of the religious situation, especially at a time when the most *vociferous* forms of Christianity on this continent are given to even greater boasts than usual! But I make the claim on two grounds especially. On the one hand many sensitive Christians in our time have already for a long time sensed the inappropriateness of the power motif in an age so gravely threatened by a surfeit of power, and are therefore open to radical alternatives. At the same time, the church itself, where it is capable of self-knowledge, recognizes that it is no longer the powerful institution that it once was; this knowledge, which is debilitating to some, is liberating to others. Perhaps, since we do not have to play the role of the powerful any longer, we may discover another way of being in the world, another way of serving, even another kind of message.

In other words, as we emerge out of the Constantinian captivity of the faith,[7] the need to think triumphalistically is replaced by new seriousness about the meaning of the event which stands at the center of our confession, the sacrificial suffering and death of the Christ. Kosuke Koyama speaks, I think, for many thinking Christians when he voices the following critique of conventional Western Christologies:

> The name, Jesus Christ, is not a magic name which transforms the broken world into an instant paradise. Has not the true dimension of the glory of this name suffered since the faith associated with this name became the state religion of the Roman Empire? Has it not been difficult to maintain the quality of the stumbling block of this name when the church became the powerful social group? How could the prestigious church proclaim the crucified Christ? The name of Jesus Christ is not a powerful name in the manner of the imperial power. It is a "foolish and weak" name (1 Cor. 1:21-25)! . . . Jesus Christ is not a quick answer. If Jesus Christ is the answer he is the answer in the way portrayed in crucifixion![8]

Koyama is here drawing upon the alternative to theological triumphalism that Luther named *theologia crucis*. Luther contrasted the "theology of the cross" with what he called "theology of glory" (*theologia gloriae*), whose essential metaphor is that of power. The theology of the cross, which, as Jürgen Moltmann has so aptly put it, "is not a single chapter in theology, but the key signature for all Christian theology,"[9] does not altogether eschew the idea of power and such related terms as triumph, victory, or (our word) conquest. But it *does* eschew—and radically so—the models of power, triumph, victory, and conquest which Christian doctrine has all too consistently employed in its endeavor to interpret the meaning of the work of God in Jesus as the Christ. The theology of the cross does not intend simply to discard the metaphor of power, but it does want to transform it; for it is an adequate way of speaking about the redemptive work of God only if it is conformed to the image of God revealed in the *crucified* One. The models by which heretofore too much Christianity has permitted its theology and its Christology to be informed have been culturally determined. They have been shaped primarily by the triumphalist societies and successive empires with which from Constantine onwards the Christian church has cohabited. As Koyama suggests, a "prestigious church," the official cult of empire, can hardly afford to be known through the symbol of a crucified man—or a crucified God! It belongs to empire ("superpower!") to establish itself and to subsist on power alone. To make the faith amenable to the imperial mentality and at the same time a fitting symbol for and reflection of imperial splendor itself, the church through the ages has permitted its message to be filtered through the sieve of worldly power and glory. What adjective do we use for God more frequently (especially in our prayers) than "Almighty"? Jesus, in our hymns and liturgies, turns out again and again to be the Victor, the Conqueror, the Warrior-prince, the Captain of souls, the Slayer of foes. The church is "like a mighty army," a powerful and glorious movement, a crusade, waging battle (mission!) against all comers. The life of faith, accordingly, is a fight, a conflict with unbelievers, a struggle against the flesh, and so on. The language of our religion has been so consistently informed by the spirit of might, winning, success, and related concepts that it is difficult to use any of the *scriptural* nomenclature of glory and triumph without conjuring up the whole ideology of empire.

For many self-professed Christians, on this continent particularly, the heritage of imperial imagery and the confusion of Christ with Caesar presents no problem. It is indeed a bonus. It can be aligned very conveniently with that same imperial mentality that at the secular level has not yet noticed the question mark that the nuclear age has written over the whole notion of empire. The "theology of glory"—possibly the most crass and decadent form of the *theologia gloriae* ever to have articulated itself in a very long history of religious triumphalism—is openly displayed as normative Christianity every day of the week! Yet, in more thoughtful quarters of the church catholic we are beginning, I believe, to realize not only that such Christian bravado gives the lie to existence, and is credible only to chauvinists and philistines, but (what is worse) that it is a betrayal of the more subtle "wisdom of the cross" (1 Corinthians 1–2). That wisdom understands that the anatomy of human suffering is infinitely more complex than triumphalism of every variety conceives it to be, and that it defies the "answers" of the powerful. The only power that can address suffering humanity is the power of love, and that is a power "made perfect in weakness" (2 Cor. 12:9).[10] The only victory that is both real and credible in face of human suffering is a victory visible to faith, not sight, a victory *sub contraria specie* ("hidden beneath its opposite"—Luther). What Reinhold Niebuhr called "the logic of the cross"[11] (for there is a logic in it; it is not merely irrational) must interpret power in terms the world calls weakness, and victory in terms the world calls failure, because the thing that this power would overcome and this victory win is delicate indeed: it is the human spirit. The root causes of our suffering in its burdensome sense being inseparable from our very selves, the conquest of them *must* be an intensely subtle one—a conquest *from within*.

The Conquest from Within

It is not easy to speak about this conquest from within. Here, I think, more than at any point in the "modest science" (Barth) of theology, the language of dogma and doctrine is shown up as paltry and inadequate. The truth of the cross, if it is to be conveyed at all through words, must finally draw upon the language of art, of story, drama, symbol, metaphor, analogy. The cross of Jesus Christ is after all not a theological statement—not a soteriology! It is an event, a deed, an enactment. One walks very close to blasphemy when one attempts to put it into words!

We, too, shall turn presently to story. But in order to keep our minds fixed on the tradition that we are rehearsing here, with its perhaps stilted but sometimes convenient signs and guideposts, I should like first to remind the reader of two doctrinal concepts (traditionally they are for Christians the *central* doctrinal concepts) which for all their awkwardness have precisely to do with this conquest from within. I refer to the concepts of the incarnation and the triunity of God. Each of them has been, and could also be for us, the subject of endless discussion and debate. I mention them here, however, only to demonstrate their connection with our theme.

It is unfortunate that the doctrine of the incarnation of the divine *Logos* was so soon and so successfully co-opted by non-Hebraic assumptions and priorities. Under the impact of a religious and philosophical worldview which distrusted matter and sought redemption in the realm of pure and disembodied spirit, the concept of the indwelling of the "mind and heart of God" (*Logos*) in historical existence was uprooted from its essentially Hebraic matrix and, in the decisive early centuries of doctrinal evolution, encumbered with the heavy, heavenly language of metaphysics and abstract mysticism. If, however, one gets behind all the mystifying terminology of the "two natures," the concept of virgin birth ontically rather than historically understood, the *homoousios/homoiousios* debate, the *theotokos* idea, and all the rest, one discovers an affirmation that is both simple (in the profoundest sense of the term!) and in striking continuity with the whole bent of Hebraic faith, namely, God *identifies with humanity*. God, who in the faith of Israel certainly transcends creation, but who in this same faith is from the outset orientated in love towards the creation, now enters into full solidarity with the creature. God, who unlike Aristotle's god will not be God in isolation but only a God who is with *us* and for *us*—who "will be your God and you shall be my people"—this same God of Abraham, Isaac, and Jacob, declares the apostolic witness, takes the final step and gives flesh to the Word (the *same* Word) that from the beginning God spoke through the Law and the Prophets. Through an impossible (certainly, impossible!) act of grace and self-sacrifice, God bridges the unbridgeable gulf between eternity and time. The One whose ways are not our ways, nor whose thoughts our thoughts, yet who is never mentioned in the Hebraic Scriptures except in conjunction with the world of human and other created beings—this earthward-yearning God of Israel becomes now "Emmanuel."

It is this movement of solidarity and identification, of full participation in the life of the world, that is fundamentally intended in the dogma of the incarnation, whatever the language may be. When this is forgotten; when religion or doctrinal rationalism develops a special interest in Jesus' *physis* (nature); when the important thing becomes believing in the divinity of Jesus (what does *believing* in Jesus' divinity mean, anyway?), then the point of Advent and Christmas is lost. For faith in the Incarnate Word (which is very different from "believing in Jesus' divinity") means confessing the unconditional and unreserved presence of God with us. Incarnation is our tradition's way of speaking about the divine *Mitsein* (being-with). It signifies the determination of the Christian community from now on only to think about God as it thinks about "us," God's creatures and God's world. It means the church's refusal to indulge in God-talk that is not at the same time world-talk. It means that theology is no longer just "theology"; it is "theo-anthropology" (Barth).

God has entered effectively and without reserve into the life of the world. That is what we mean when we repeat the Johannine statement ". . . and the Word became flesh and dwelt among us . . ." God *freely* did this, our tradition maintains: God was not under some external compulsion to enter into solidarity with the creation. Yet in another sense there is a certain *necessitas* in this movement of God toward the world. Remember the passion predictions: ". . . the Son of man must suffer . . ." "Must suffer"—not on account of external pressure, but on account of the compelling internal necessity that the apostolic tradition names God's love—*agape*. Behind the "must" of Jesus' passion there is the "must" of the divine *agape*—and it is visible all the way from Eden! The God depicted in that long and tortuous story that begins already with the wrong turning of human freedom must take the road that leads, at last, to Golgotha, because the sin and suffering by which God's beloved creatures are bound can only be engaged profoundly from within the historical process itself.

History is not by itself redemptive. Here Christianity and Judaism differ markedly from Marxism and from every variation on the theme of progress. Left to itself, our tradition strongly suspects (though it does not know this, for it has not witnessed a creation left entirely to itself!), the world would capitulate to the Nihil that it is always in some way courting. But while the tradition of Jerusalem rejects the idea that the historical process is itself redemptive, it also rejects the contrary belief (deeply embedded in Manichaean and many other religious traditions) that history is irredeemable. Between these two unacceptable alternatives, our tradition conceives of another possibility: *History has a capacity for being changed from within.*

In a very real sense, the whole story that is told in the continuity of the Testaments is an illustration and documentation of that theorem. Contrary to the logic of sin, the disobedience of the first pair does not end in shame and death; they are clothed, they are given a way into the future—with pain, but still a way. Despite the finality of his deed, the murderer Cain, marked, to be sure, by his desperation, is able to go on; and the parents, bereaved now of both their sons, are given another. At the end of possibilities in his native Ur, Abram and his family discover, through many trials and errors, another homeland. Sold by his brothers into slavery, Joseph after decades of exile and fame in a foreign country, is able to preserve his kinsfolk from extinction ("You meant evil against me; but God meant it for good," Gen. 50:20). Driven away from slavery and "flesh-pots," the children of Israel discover a route to safety . . . to the wilderness . . . to the land of promise . . . to exile . . . to return from exile . . . We could go on, but the theme is well known.

History is not fixed. It does not move *inevitably* towards either perfection or destruction, paradise or oblivion, the fulfillment of dreams or their ultimate frustration. The continuing freedom of the human creature, though marred, gives it an openness to the future. Men and women, both individually and corporately, do things, say things, leave things undone and unsaid. Their words and their deeds are sometimes good, beautiful, and true; sometimes better intended than their results cause them to appear; sometimes confused and tentative, sometimes "meant for evil," sometimes truly evil. And out of this apparently chaotic welter of acts and words and thoughts *history* comes to be; that is, faith perceives patterns of meaning and direction. To speak more accurately, it sees the miraculous! Not crass and gaudy shows of supernatural power in which the laws of nature are ignored, but true miracles of the everyday sort: the miracle of life going on; the miracle of something and not nothing; the miracle of purpose—*sub contraria specie*. The dismal portents of the present become, miraculously, portals to an undeserved future. No truth is heard in the land and prophecy feels itself utterly alone, yet seven thousand have not bowed the knee to Baal. Israel is occupied by arrogant men, and in Jerusalem a puppet king of the Jews does their bidding, but in a village a child is born in a stable. The little band is scattered, their hopes dashed by the execution of their leader as a common criminal—and "we had hoped that he was the one to redeem Israel . . ."

Our tradition names this *providentia Dei*, the providence of God. It also names it *grace*. Grace is not nature. As for nature—that is, as for what *we do*, and what is done by all creatures—it is not in itself terribly promising. Even when it is "meant for good" it can introduce questionable and even devastating results. And much of it, like the dark deed of Joseph's brothers, is not meant for good! Faith, therefore, does not account for the redeeming patterns and directions that it sees in history by pointing either to human intentions or human deeds. Faith confesses rather that God *is* able and willing, using the raw stuff of our deeds and misdeeds in much the same manner as God used the primeval chaos to create a world, to alter the course of things, to provide a way into the future. Finitude as such does not provide this way, is not "provident"; but the finite "has a capacity for the infinite" (*finitum capax infiniti*). Touched by the eternal, time gives birth to wonders of which neither ancient astrology nor modern futurology can know.

History, then, has a capacity for being changed from within; and for the Christian the incarnation is the seed of radical change, of the new. It introduces into the process of time a new future, so that the future of death and oblivion which has been bequeathed to the historical process by distorted and confused human freedom is challenged by a radical alternative: life instead of death. *Abundant* life.

The second doctrinal concept that we need to review as we consider the conquest of suffering from within is the doctrine of the Trinity. While this is not a biblical concept (the New Testament uses neither the term *Trinity* nor most of the technical language associated with the doctrine; it only leaves us with the *problem* of the Trinity, to which early Christianity had then to address itself), it is, in its best theological articulations, strictly continuous with the biblical message. For it is in the last analysis—nothing more or less than—an extension and elaboration of the same scriptural insistence that the tabernacle of God is with humanity.

Jürgen Moltmann, more sensitively than most other theologians of our time, has spelled out the linkage between the Trinity, the incarnation, and the cross. It was never the intention of the incarnation dogma in its responsible expressions to claim simply that "Jesus is God"; this in fact was identified by the early councils as a heretical view, put forward especially by the modalistic Monarchians. But it *was* the intention of incarnational theology to say that Jesus—precisely this human being (*vere homo*) in all of his earthly vulnerability—is truly God-in-our-midst (*vere Deus*), that God is not other than this, that God's nature and intention is not other than what they are declared to be in and through this One.

> When the crucified Jesus is called "the image of the invisible God," the meaning is that this is God, and God is like *this*. God is not greater than he is in this humiliation. God is not more glorious than he is in this self-surrender. God is not more powerful than he is in this helplessness. God is not more divine than he is in this humanity.[12]

The doctrine of the divine triunity, like that of the incarnation, is misconstrued as soon as it becomes interesting in itself. Had the fundamental matrix of the evolution of trinitarian theology continued to be that of the Hebraic understanding of the divine Being, the kind of metaphysical-speculative approach which did in fact color its development could not have been dominant. For Hebraic theology manifests very little, if any, interest in the interior life of the deity. Its thrust is always towards God's relatedness with creation and, though the prophetic tradition of Israel is keenly aware of the divine otherness, its manner of treating God's transcendence is entirely different from the theme of transcendence pursued in the tradition of Athens. God's *discontinuity* with creation is not understood by Judaism in physical (spatial or even temporal) terms but in terms of righteousness, that is, ethically. It is part of the divine transcendence that Yahweh wills to be *so close* to creation, to be immanent, to be "your God," in short, to love. In contrast to the human reluctance to love, and fear of proximity—transcending precisely our human attempt to be alone, autonomous, self-sufficient—the God of the Bible goes to unheard-of lengths to achieve communion with us, even union, in a covenant closer than marriage. Not God's distance but God's bridging of the distance—this is God's transcendence; in this is God *totaliter aliter.* . . . [I]t is God's weeping with us that constitutes God's being "beyond" us and beyond our expectations of God.

The Trinity, at base, is nothing more—nor less—than a doctrinal device or symbol for affirming just this good news of "the beyond in the midst of life" (Bonhoeffer). As Moltmann has stated the matter elsewhere:

> To recognize God in the crucified Christ means to grasp the Trinitarian history of God, and to understand oneself and this whole world with Auschwitz and Viet Nam, with race-hatred and hunger, as existing in the history of God. God is not dead, death is in God, God suffers by us. He suffers with us. Suffering is in God. . . . God does not ultimately reject, nor is he ultimately rejected, rejection is within God. . . . When he brings his history to completion, his suffering will be transformed into joy, and thereby our suffering as well.[13]

The theology of Bethlehem and Golgotha—that is, of the enfleshment and the cross-bearing of the divine Word—directs us from the lonely and morbid contemplation of our own real suffering to the suffering of God in solidarity with us. Because God is "with us," our suffering, though abysmally real, is given both a new perspective and a new meaning—and the prospect of transformation. Not through power but through participation; not through might but through self-emptying, "weak" love is the burden of human suffering engaged by the God of this faith tradition. *Engaged* is, I think, the right word. It implies that God meets, takes on, takes into God's *own* being, the burden of our suffering, not by a show of force which could only destroy the sinner with the sin, but by assuming a solidary responsibility for the contradictory and confused admixture that is our life. God incarnate and crucified bears with us and for us the "weight of sin" that is the root cause of our suffering, and that we cannot assume in our brokenness.

But here theology must go to art for help—a fact which is as much demonstrated by the stolidness of soteriological doctrine which does not turn to art as by the current trend to enucleate a narrative theology. There are numerous tales both in classical and in contemporary literature which can enrich our understanding of Christology and soteriology, but when it comes to the conquest from within, I know of no more profound expression of the mystery of Christ's priestly act of solidarity with suffering humanity than the one presented by the Japanese novelist Shusaku Endo in his book *Silence*.[14]

Endo's work in its entirety, including his perceptive *Life of Jesus*,[15] is a protest against the power-orientated Western "gospel" that was brought to his native land by the Jesuits in the sixteenth century in the wake of Western armies and Western trade (the Dutch). On the positive side, Endo's art is an attempt to discern an alternative to the gospel of power; and it is not incidental that in this search he has been aided by various expressions of the *theologia crucis* tradition, that "thin tradition"[16] which has functioned like an antiphon beneath the high triumph song of Christendom. Although he is a Roman Catholic,[17] Endo's greatest contemporary theological influence seems to have come from the Protestant theologian Kazoh Kitamori. Kitamori, whose constant theme is "the pain of God," has provided many oriental Christians with an entrée to the Judeo-Christian tradition that is accessible to oriental experience in a way that the Western *theologia gloriae* is not. "The pain of God," writes Kitamori, "this is the essence of God, this is the heart of God!"[18] In this vein, and (as oriental students of Endo's work have told me) in the tradition of the school of Antioch, which over against the Alexandrians stressed the humanity of Jesus, Shusaku Endo attempts in all that he writes to depict a deity whose primary attribute is "suffering love" rather than omnipotence.

> The God of love, the love of God—the words come easy. The most difficult thing is to bear witness in some tangible way to the truth of the words. In many cases love is actually powerless. Love has in itself no immediate tangible benefits. We are therefore hard put to find where the love of God can be, hidden behind tangible realities which rather suggest that God does not exist, or that he never speaks, or that he is angry.[19]

Endo's novel *Silence*[20] is set in the so-called Christian century of Japan (i.e., the mid-sixteenth to mid-seventeenth centuries c.e.) when Western missionaries in the wake of Western military and commercial invasions of that realm made a concerted effort to convert the as-yet un-united country to Christianity. A young priest, Rodrigues, leaves his native Portugal to take his Christ to the "swamp of Japan," and at the same time to trace, if possible, the fate of his revered teacher, a famous Jesuit theologian who had preceded him to the Orient and is reputed to have apostatized.

The priest Rodrigues exemplifies a genuine and high devotion to the Christ whose image dominates the popular Catholicism of the age. He spends his hours of prayer and meditation contemplating the face of his Christ: a face that is noble, serene, unearthly in its beauty, its strength of character—full of the very qualities that the young priest himself wishes, in imitation of Christ, to possess: conviction, total trust, certainty of aim, strength of spirit, the willingness to suffer and die for one's beliefs.

Yet the communication between the priest and his Christ is all one way. The Christ remains for Rodrigues a *visual* image. He does not speak. He is . . . silent. And as Rodrigues, having reached Japan, finds himself in increasingly difficult straits, the victim of a national uprising against the Christians; as he becomes in the course of time the fugitive, the hunted criminal, the enemy, and finally the prisoner and potential martyr, this divine silence is increasingly deafening.

At last, finally cornered by the anti-Christian nationalists, he is asked (as was his famous teacher) to renounce his faith. Naturally he refuses, still hoping to emulate the glorious Christ of his meditations: hoping even for martyrdom, which will surely bring him into the very presence of God! But instead of a triumphant martyrdom, Rodrigues is routinely imprisoned. In the darkness of his cell, he learns that the distracting noises which have kept him from sleep and which he believed to be the drunken snoring of his guards are really emanating from the mouths of native Japanese Christians—people who have already apostatized many times—who are hung upside down over pits of excrement, their heads half-buried, and so breathing only with the greatest difficulty and pain. They will be kept in this position, Rodrigues is told, until he renounces his Christ. The priest's still heroic, though battered, faith is being bought (as such faith has so often been bought!) at the expense of other human beings with little courage and no influence.

Under the impact of this awareness, Rodrigues is again invited to apostatize. The method is simple—it has always been simple, like the pinch of incense on the flame to honor the genius of the emperor, the method applied to the early Christians. In this case it is more interesting, though, and more direct: a metal image of the Christ, a sort of *bas relief* called a *fumie* is brought before the convict. He is instructed to put his foot upon the face of this Christ, to trample on it, to grind it ever so slightly with his toe.

The face of Christ as it appears in the *fumie* placed before Rodrigues does not at all resemble the face that the young priest has been trained in his seminary to adore and to emulate—any more, in fact, than it resembles, by now, his own haggard, hunted, prematurely aged face. The face in the *fumie* has already been trampled on many times, and it is horribly distorted from the grinding toes and the dirt of many feet. Still, the priest hesitates: to step on this face, even though it has been shaped by pagans and trampled on by the faithless, is for him to deny the whole bent of his Western piety. He recalls, however, the hanging prisoners, whose lives depend upon his decision, and it is in this agony of existential torment that suddenly, miraculously (but in that everyday sense) he hears the voice of the Christ, speaking to him out of the *fumie*: "Trample, trample, it is for this that I have come. Trample!"

The silence of God is broken. The triumphing Christ of Christendom could only function as a model—really, an impossible model of strength—by which the weak and failing priest could only be judged. Only a Christ upon whom the sufferer could cast the impossible burden of his suffering could break the silence of God. In a statement about the suffering of the Christ which could be a commentary on this saga, C. S. Song has written:

> The suffering of Jesus the messiah has removed all human barriers. It makes God available to human beings and enables them to be part of the divine mystery of salvation. The depths of God's suffering ought to be the place where all persons, despite their different backgrounds and traditions, can recognize one another as fellow pilgrims in need of God's saving power. Religious traditions tend to alienate strangers. Ecclesiastical structures become walls surrounding faithful believers. Doctrinal precision creates heretics and infidels. Even expressions of religious devotion in worship and liturgy make peoples alien to one another.
>
> Suffering, however, does not need to be transmitted by traditions; it is present here and now, as well as in the past. It needs no ecclesiastical sanction; it comes and goes without anyone's bidding. It does not have to be defended doctrinally; it is our daily experience. It cannot be worshipped and adored by fine liturgy; it is to be endured and not to be idolized. To be human is to suffer, and God knows that. That is why God suffers too. Suffering is where God and human beings meet. It is the one place where all persons—kings, priests, paupers, and prostitutes—recognize themselves as frail and transient human beings in need of God's saving love. Suffering brings us closer to God and God closer to us. Suffering, despite all

its inhumanity and cruelty, paradoxically enables humans to long for humanity, find it, treasure it, and defend it with all their might.[21]

God suffers because God would be *with us*, and suffering is our condition. Echoing Luther's last written words ("Wir sind Bettler, dass ist wahr . . ." [We are beggars, that is certain]), the Roman Catholic theologian Johannes Metz writes: "We are all beggars. We are all members of a species that is not sufficient unto itself. We are all creatures plagued by unending doubts and restless, unsatisfied hearts. Of all creatures, we are the poorest and the most incomplete. Our needs are always beyond our capacities, and we only find ourselves when we lose ourselves."[22] This being our state, God's redemptive work in our behalf is given its *modus operandi*, its way: it cannot be the way of the sword; it cannot even be the way of friendship, filial devotion (*philia*). Both of these ways are proposed by the disciples, notably by Peter; both must be rejected—and forcefully (Matt. 16:23f. and par.; John 21:15f.). It must be the way of the cross, "the Son of man must suffer . . ."

> Draw back, physician. . . . Healing is not for you. . . . Without your wound where would your power be? It is your very remorse that makes your low voice tremble in the hearts of men. The very angels themselves cannot persuade the wretched and blundering children of earth as can one human being broken on the wheels of living. In Love's service only the wounded soldiers can serve.[23]

Like Peter, who had finally to be told straightforwardly that his way was nothing less than satanic, there is much in us that would prefer it to be otherwise. We are attracted to the heroic, and to strong ideals like friendship, *esprit de corps*. This is even accentuated for all of us who belong to triumphant cultures. As Koyama says, "A strong Western civilization and the 'weak' Christ cannot be reconciled harmoniously. Christ must become 'strong.' A strong United States and a strong Christ!"[24] A Christ trampled upon, "broken on the wheels of living," is not the Christ whose praises are sung by electronic religion or, for that matter, in the more bourgeois sanctuaries of our nations. Yet beneath our surprise and distaste for a "broken" Christ, beneath the *skandalon* of the cross, there is for us too—for the affluent, the wise of the world, the "have" peoples—a certain basic relief in meeting the broken Christ. If we let it, this relief can turn to gratitude and even joy. For we too know, in the depths of our souls, that we are lost and broken—that "We are all beggars."

The conquest of suffering begins just here, with this relief, this gratitude, this joy. To find oneself befriended in one's suffering is not only a more believable "answer" to the pain of suffering; it is also more profound. The world abounds in physicians who promise to heal every wound . . . from the heights of their personal and professional detachment. Of answers to the "problem of suffering" there is in fact no lack! Only, all of them flounder on the rocks of reality, at the cry of one starving or derelict child. The only satisfying answer is the answer given to Job—the answer that is no answer but is the presence of an Answerer. It does not matter that the Answerer brings more questions than answers; for the answer is not the words as such but the living Word—the Presence itself. The answer is the permission that is given in this Presence to be what one is, to express the dereliction that belongs to one's age and place, to share all of it with this Other: to trample! Faith is the communion of the spirit with this fellow sufferer, this One whose otherness lies in the fact that he will not turn away in the face of one's failure, or the failure of one's world.

This communion with the "pain of God" gives to the community of faith a courage which is not like the courage of the Stoic. For it does not merely resign itself to pain and walk on in silent, lonely nobility; rather, it *seeks out other sufferers*. For in the encounter with "the crucified God" this faith has learnt, is learning, that the *sharing* of suffering is the beginning of its transformation to wholeness and joy. The suffering of the church . . . has its foundations in this courage.

ACCEPTANCE AND TRANSFORMATION

"Give us," runs the famous prayer of Reinhold Niebuhr, "grace to accept with serenity the things that cannot be changed, courage to change the things which should be changed, and the wisdom to distinguish the one from the other."

The resurrection-courage that is given to faith in the presence of the crucified Christ is a courage both of acceptance and of transformation. Some things must be accepted. But Christian acceptance is not an easy resignation to the status quo. For in the ambiguous world where wheat and tares grow up together, where good and evil are impossibly interwoven, it cannot readily be discerned that a given experience or fact belongs quite simply to the divine ordering of things, the reality of creaturely existence, the suffering of becoming.

That death, for instance, inheres in the structures of finitude seems both reasonable and scriptural. But premature death? The deaths of hungry children? The deaths of persons on account of that dread cancer, 80 percent of which is said to be caused by environmental factors? The death of whole species of plants and animals on account of the increasing mechanization of life and the pollution of the biosphere?

Loneliness too, we have said, belongs to creaturely existence. It is in some real sense the *conditio sine qua non* of love, even the love of God. Rodrigues might never have heard the speaking Christ if he had not known the silence of God. Loneliness should be accepted. But the loneliness of the aged in our youth-orientated societies? Of prisoners in our prisons? Of people without work in our cities and towns?

Limits, too, belong to the creaturely condition. From another perspective they are, we said, not limits at all, but boundaries defining the possibilities of our legitimate glory as human beings. They should be accepted, and gladly. But the limits experienced daily by the two-thirds undernourished? The limits felt by women, by racial minorities, by the handicapped in a society which worships "fitness"?

To the suffering of becoming there also belongs a certain anxiety. It inheres in finitude. It has its place—even an important place. Without it we might not have war, but we would probably not have civilization either. A certain degree of anxiety in the adolescent does not worry the wise parent. Such anxiety should be accepted, with gratitude. But the anxiety of a meaningless life which drives alarming numbers of young persons in Canadian and American societies to suicide? The anxiety of those who at fifty or sixty are told there is no longer any work for them to do? The anxiety of a civilization psychically numbed by "future shock"?

There is a danger in all theory, all theology. It is that the mind will find a sort of "sabbath rest" in theory itself. This is understandable. The mind needs rest. Nothing is accomplished by a mind that is only restless, that finds no place to perch for a moment and contemplate the course of its flight. When it comes to a searing question like God and human suffering, a question that in fragmented and concrete ways touches most of us every day, we need to perch for a time on the resting place of Scripture and tradition, so that we can fly again.

But it is the purpose of flying that we rest. Theology leads inevitably (if it is true theology—*vere theologia!*) to ethics, the gospel, to the law, the indicative to the imperative. To contemplate the christological doctrine of a God who identifies with us in our brokenness; to find this satisfying, even moving; and then to close the book of reflection and go on living as before—this is a travesty of theology. Encountering the crucified Christ (as Peter is supposed to have done on his way out of burning Rome!) must mean wrestling with decisions about the *actual* suffering we encounter in our world. What is to be accepted, what can and must be changed! Where is transformation possible?

> . . . The call of the gospel to its proclaimers consists in discerning the signs of the times in word and action so that people within the circumstances of their own lives may respond to the impetus of the Holy Spirit and move life in the direction of its glorious destiny in the kingdom of God.[25]

The line between thought and deed is here invisible. It would be a misuse of the great privilege of theology if, befriended by a suffering God, we were to take refuge in the comfort of this gospel away from the actual suffering of the world in which we find ourselves, whose destiny is to become fully God's kingdom.

The gospel of Jesus as the cross-bearer, the bearer of the unbearable burdens, introduces all who hear it to a process: the process of bearing the burdens of others. To *know* that God participates in human suffering—*really* to know this—is to do it! To *believe* that nothing can separate us from this participating love—*really* to believe this——is to accept the gracious invitation of this crucified God to participate in our Lord's participation. The church is—*we* are!—a vital part of God's response to human suffering. For how many will the adequacy of God's response depend upon who *we* are?

Notes

1. Reinhold Niebuhr, *Faith and History: Comparison of Christian and Modern Views of History* (New York: Scribner's, 1949), 22.

2. C. S. Song, *The Compassionate God* (Maryknoll, NY: Orbis, 1982), 109f.

3. Frederick Buechner, *Lion Country* (New York: Atheneum, 1971), 247.

4. Gustav Aulén, *Christus Victor: An Historical Study of the Three Main Types of the Idea of Atonement*, trans. A. G. Hebert (London: SPCK, 1953).

5. Anselm, "Cur Deus Homo?" in *A Scholastic Miscellany*, ed. Eugene R. Fairweather, Library of Christian Classics, vol. 10 (London: SCM, 1956), 100ff.

6. See Peter Abelard, "Exposition of the Epistle to the Romans," in ibid., 776ff.

7. For a more detailed discussion of this theme, see Hall 1980c.

8. Kosuke Koyama, *Mount Fuji and Mount Sinai: A Pilgrimage in Theology* (London: SCM, 1984), 241.

9. Jürgen Moltmann, *The Crucified God: The Cross of Christ as the Foundation and Criticism of Christian Theology*, trans. R. A. Wilson and John Bowden (London: SCM, 1973), 72.

10. In the context of a discussion about Nietzsche's rejection of Paul's theology, Eberhard Jüngel makes the important point that *it is only in connection with love that power and weakness are not antithetical.* "For Paul, the Crucified One is weak, subject to death. But Paul does not celebrate this thought with melancholy, but rather thinks of it as the gospel, as a source of joy. What is joyful about the weakness of the Crucified One? The weakness of the Crucified One is for Paul

the way in which God's power of life is perfected (II Cor. 13:4). Weakness is then not understood as a contradiction of God's power. There is, however, only one phenomenon in which power and weakness do not contradict each other, in which rather power can perfect itself as weakness. This phenomenon is the event of love. Love does not see power and weakness as alternatives. It is the unity of power and weakness, and as such is certainly the most radical opposite of the will to power which cannot affirm weakness. Pauline 'theology of the cross' (*theologia crucis*) is, accordingly, the most stringent rejection of all deification of self-willing power" (*God as the Mystery of the World: On the Foundation of the Theology of the Crucified One in the Dispute between Theism and Atheism*, trans. Darrell L. Guder [Grand Rapids: Eerdmans, 1983], 206).

11. See Niebuhr, *Faith and History*, 128.

12. Moltmann, *The Crucified God*, 205.

13. Jürgen Moltmann, "The Crucified God," in *Theology Today* 31 (1974): 18.

14. Shusaku Endo, *Silence*, trans. William Johnston (Tokyo: Sophia University, in cooperation with Rutland, VT and Tokyo: Tuttle, 1969).

15. Shusaku Endo, *Life of Jesus*, trans. Richard A. Schuchert, SJ (New York: Paulist, 1973).

16. I have used this way of designating the theology of the cross tradition in my *Lighten Our Darkness: Towards on Indigenous Theology of the Cross*—a work in which I have discussed this tradition in much greater detail than is possible here, and with special reference to its applicability to our own sociological and historical context.

17. It is an interesting and provocative fact that the most compelling *artistic* treatments of the *theologia crucis* seem to come from Roman Catholic and Jewish authors. Among these I would name particularly Georges Bernanos's *Diary of a Country Priest*, Graham Greene's *The Power and the Glory*, and the works of Elie Wiesel, especially *Night* and *The Town Beyond the Wall*. It seems possible, if not probable, that this is related to the observation . . . that while a Protestantism distrustful of art tended to degenerate into rationalism and conceptualism, both Catholic and Jewish faith permitted and encouraged a wider exploration of the human terrain for analogies to revelation.

18. Kazoh Kitamori, *Theology of the Pain of God* (Richmond: John Knox, 1965), 46.

19. Endo, *Life of Jesus*, 71

20. See my article, "Rethinking Christ: Theological Reflections on Shusaku Endo's *Silence*," in *Interpretation* 33 (1979): 254ff.

21. Song, *The Compassionate God*, 115.

22. Johannes Baptist Metz, *Poverty of Spirit*, trans. John Drury (Paramus, NJ and New York: Paulist, 1968), 77.

23. Thornton Wilder, *The Angel That Troubled the Waters* (New York: Coward-McCann, 1928), 148.

24. Koyama, *Mount Fuji and Mount Sinai*, 242.

25. J. Christiaan Beker, *Paul's Apocalyptic Gospel: The Coming Triumph of God* (Philadelphia: Fortress Press, 1982), 19.

PART III

Ecclesiology and Ethics: Theology in the Context of Disestablishment

12

The Church and the Cross

This chapter serves as a transition from part 2, which focused on specific theological topics and doctrines, to this final part of the book, which looks more closely at issues of contemporary ecclesiology and ethics, particularly relative to the disestablishment of the churches and the Christian vocation of stewardship. Hall here, in an excerpt from The Cross in Our Context, considers how the theology of the cross informs contemporary ecclesiology. Following his work in God and Human Suffering, he here considers the nature of Christian suffering, not as the goal but as the consequence of faithful obedience. At the same time, however, he takes to task those manifestations of the church that take undue pride in their particularly devout obedience and thus what they see as their distinct suffering. For Hall, our understanding of what he calls the ecclesia crucis must be necessarily modest. It is important to remember that Hall's theology is distinctly relational and thus aimed toward the church; he is less concerned about "being" and more about "being-with."

Source: Hall 2003:137–55.

A Suffering Church?

What kind of ecclesiology—what doctrine of the church—emerges from the theology of the cross? There can only be one answer: the *theologia crucis* gives rise to an *ecclesia crucis*. Indeed it could be said that the whole purpose of this theology of the cross is to engender a movement—a people—that exists in the world under the sign of the cross of Jesus Christ: a movement and people called into being by his Spirit and being conformed to his person and furthering his work. A cruciform people.

Now this can sound very pious. And one has to acknowledge straightaway that much of the Christianity that *has* taken the cross seriously has left the impression that the ecclesiological consequence of the theology of the cross is the existence of an especially devout community of belief, conscious of the need to suffer, and rather too smugly certain that *its* suffering renders it particularly beloved of God. Not only a certain type of pietistic Lutheranism, but various sectarian groups that have emerged out of, or in reaction to, state Lutheranism, give evidence of a good deal of this sort of cross-conscious piety. Karl Barth (with perhaps too much Calvinistic smugness) attributed this to "Nordic melancholy," seeing it as a blend of the almost-natural "world sorrow" (*Weltschmerz*) of a people living a good deal of the time in the cold and the dark and a Christianity that expects to inherit eternal life only if life in this world is sufficiently gloomy: "No cross, no crown." One has a rather kindly if bemused portrayal of this kind of religion in the famous story by Baroness Blixen (Isak Dinesen), "Babette's Feast." There are certain equivalents of this dour piety in the religion of most northern peoples, including my own Canadian people, and on the whole it is not more objectionable than the blasé optimism of dwellers in more hospitable climates.

An ecclesiology that manifests such world sorrow is certainly able to *use* the theology of the cross—and it has and does. But I think it has often been a misuse. It is quite correct in perceiving suffering as a mark of the church, but its error is in its introversion and subjectivization of this suffering. In what follows I shall elaborate on that contention.

To begin with, we have to reckon with the fact (and it is a fact) that there is more in the New Testament about the suffering of the church than about any other single theme or issue of ecclesiology. Not only is this theme prominent in the recorded teachings of Jesus ("If any would follow me, let them take up their cross and follow"), but it is a recurrent subject in the epistles, particularly those of Paul. For example:

> Therefore, since we are justified by faith, we have peace with God through our Lord Jesus Christ. Through him we have obtained access to this grace in which we stand, and we rejoice in our hope of sharing the glory of God. More than that, we rejoice in our sufferings, knowing that suffering produces endurance, and endurance produces character, and character produces hope, and hope does not disappoint us, because God's love has been poured into our hearts through the Holy Spirit which has been given to us. (Rom. 5:1–5, RSV)

Or again:

For what we preach is not ourselves, but Jesus Christ as Lord, with ourselves as your servants for Jesus' sake. For it is the God who said, "Let light shine out of darkness" who has shone in our hearts to give the light of the knowledge of the glory of God in the face of Christ.

But we have this treasure in earthen vessels, to show that the transcendent power belongs to God and not to us. We are afflicted in every way, but not crushed; perplexed, but not driven to despair; persecuted, but not forsaken; struck down, but not destroyed; always carrying in the body the death of Jesus, so that the life of Jesus may also be manifested in our bodies. For while we live we are always being given up to death for Jesus' sake, so that the life of Jesus may be manifested in our mortal flesh. (2 Cor. 4:5-11, RSV)

Or again, this time from 1 Peter:

Beloved, do not be surprised at the fiery ordeal which comes upon you to prove you, as though something strange were happening to you. But rejoice in so far as you share Christ's sufferings, that you may also rejoice and be glad when his glory is revealed. If you are reproached for the name of Christ, you are blessed, because the spirit of glory and of God rests upon you. But let none of you suffer as a murderer, or a thief, or a wrongdoer, or a mischief-maker; yet if one suffers as a Christian, let him not be ashamed, but under that name let him glorify God. For the time has come for judgment to begin with the household of God. (4:12-17, RSV)

Passages like these describe a Christian life so foreign to the average North American congregation—and indeed, so foreign to the vast majority of Christian churches throughout Western Christendom—that it is hard for us to appropriate them or even to hear them. "Beloved, do not be surprised at the fiery ordeal that is coming upon you." It would be difficult, on this continent, to find even one Christian congregation that could immediately identify with this statement, except among African American congregations here and there, or perhaps among small churches comprised of indigenous peoples, or perhaps in certain gay and lesbian communities—in short, among minorities, who may for this reason be more truly Christ's church than the others. As for the average Protestant, Catholic, or Orthodox church, the prospect of a "fiery ordeal" is far from the minds of the people gathered for worship of a Sunday, unless, after September 11, 2001, they leap to the conclusion that America is suffering today because it is Christian—and that is a conclusion having neither scriptural nor sociological foundations. Such passages of Scripture as I have just cited, and countless others could be added, have indeed been heard in the churches—certainly among those churches that follow a lectionary. But they are heard and not heard; they pass over the heads of congregations without making any existential impact, because they seem completely discontinuous with the church as we have known it or with the life most of us lead from day to day. If anyone actually hears them, such scriptural statements can be attributed without much mental exercise to Christian beginnings; few are likely to think of them as belonging to the essence of the church.

Yet these and similar pericopes of Scripture describe a motif that is far from incidental to the New Testament's understanding of the meaning of "church." I repeat: no other single ecclesiological theme receives the attention that the suffering of the church receives in our textual sources. For centuries theology has maintained that the true marks of the church are the four that are named in the Nicene Creed: "one, holy, catholic, and apostolic church" (unity, holiness, catholicity, and apostolicity). Each of these *notae ecclesia* can find some biblical basis, but none of them can claim a fraction of the attention paid to the theme of the church's suffering in these sacred writings. They are all latecomers on the scene of Christian ecclesiology. The earliest and most prominent manner of discerning the true church and distinguishing it from false claims to Christian identity was to observe the nature and extent of the suffering experienced by a community of faith. Why? Because, of course, as Paul makes clear in the passages I quoted, if you claim to be a disciple of the crucified one you must expect to participate in his sufferings; if you preach a *theology* of the cross, you will have to become a *community* of the cross. Anything else would represent a kind of hypocrisy. A purely doctrinal or theoretical theology of the cross is a contradiction. This theology is only authentic—only "for real"—insofar as it gives birth to a community that suffers with Christ in the world. Nowhere does Christendom's difference from the New Testament church show up more glaringly than in the fact that the birth of Christendom in the fourth century CE brought about a species of Christianity that with rare exceptions could be practiced without any threat or hint of its being a process of identification with the one who was "despised and rejected."

It is only within the last sixty or seventy years, and only among a minority, that there has been any serious attempt to come to terms with this persistent theme of the Scriptures—a theme prominent in the Newer Testament but by no means exclusive to it. In fact, it is there in the *Newer* Testament because it is there in the Older. Think of the suffering servant passages of Isaiah, of the prophetic tradition (especially Jeremiah and Lamentations[1]), of the wisdom literature (especially Job): the theme is already fixed in Hebraic faith that the people chosen by God to represent God's way and will among the inhabitants of the earth will suffer in their pursuit of this vocation. And I think it behooves Christians today to admit finally that if some of us have at last begun to grasp this reality of our identity and our mission, it is because the whole people of Israel has suffered so excruciatingly in our own time—and, what is worse, has suffered on account of a climate of spiritual suspicion created by Christendom itself. On account of the Holocaust of the Jews, sensitive Christians have had to ask not only how their faith could have contributed to such an event but also why the Christian faith in its established form has been so conspicuously devoid not only of any sustained suffering but of the very contemplation of that biblical theme.

In terms of a recognition of the importance of the biblical theme within the precincts of Christendom itself, it is again necessary to look to Europe during the period of the Second World War. That great cauldron of human chaos and revenge brought to the fore some few Christian witnesses who were able to recognize in the "fiery ordeal" that fascism had brought upon the world some parallels with the earliest Christian communities. Dietrich Bonhoeffer's writings, especially his first major book, *The Cost of Discipleship*, were a poignant and searing cry to his fellow Christians in both Europe and the West in general to realize at last that the discipleship of Jesus Christ is a serious business; it is not all the sweetness and light of Sunday morning ritual, confirmation at age twelve, pretty weddings, solemn funerals, the pageantry of state occasions. It is a quest for and a witness to truth in the midst of societies that lie, for authentic goodness in the midst of societies that reward duplicity, for true beauty in the midst of societies that celebrate kitsch and sentimentality. Above all, it is a call to obedience in the midst of a society *and church* that offer "cheap grace." For many of us it was Bonhoeffer's work more than any other that caused us to consider anew—or for the first time, really—this unmistakable claim of the New Testament that the discipleship of Jesus Christ entailed suffering.[2]

But of course it was not Bonhoeffer alone who recognized this out of that devastating ordeal prior to, during, and after World War II. Countless German and other European Christians who were harassed, imprisoned, tortured, or killed in the camps of that regime left their testimonies to the *meaning* that they found in their sufferings because they could understand them as participation in the suffering of the church that is its baptismal and pentecostal birthright: Edith Stein, the brilliant Jewish woman who had become a Carmelite nun, killed at Auschwitz; Martin Niemöller, the renowned preacher of Berlin/Dahlem, one of the first Christians to be imprisoned by Hitler; Helmut Gollwitzer, one of the great theologians of the immediate past, prisoner of war for five years in Russia; Simone Weil, daughter of a secular Jewish family who became deeply Christian, one of the outstanding philosophic minds of our age, hounded by her times and by the Spirit of God to identify increasingly with the victims of poverty and oppression; and many others.

And then, beyond this testimony from Europe, the post-war period saw the emergence of theologies that came to be in the face not of war and overt violence so much as in consequence of the subtle oppression of economic, racial, class, and gender systems that quietly stifle human possibilities and destroy hope. Out of the sufferings of the progeny of African slaves, the poor of the world, women, those harassed because of ethnicity or skin pigmentation or sexual orientation, and other great or small divergences from the dominant and policy-making majorities of the planet, there have arisen new expressions of Christian faith that have been able to remain within the faith despite its majority expressions because they recognized their own condition in the biblical depiction of God's people as a people of suffering. The various theologies of liberation have their own particular stories to tell and their own causes to uphold, but they can relate to the theology of the cross at least in this: they can find in the biblical testimony to a suffering church a genuine point of contact with their reality.[3] Unlike the churches of the possessing peoples of the earth, for whom the New Testament's description of a suffering church remains an anomaly or a merely historical narrative, the communities that have given us these theologies speak from experiences that place them far nearer to the scriptural account of the people of God than are we dwellers in the developed nations of the Northern Hemisphere. And they have helped some of us to notice and to try to appropriate this much-neglected theme of the church as a community of the cross.

THE CHARACTER OF CHRISTIAN SUFFERING

If I were asked to state in a single thesis what this theme is all about, I would borrow a sentence from the first Christian theologian who talked about it more than anyone else, Paul: "While we live, we are always being given up to death for Jesus' sake, so that the life of Jesus may be manifest in our mortal flesh" (2 Cor. 4:11). In what follows, I shall elaborate on this thesis in two observations: (1) The end (*telos*—inner aim) of the suffering into which faith is plunged is *life*-oriented, not death-oriented. (2) This suffering is a necessity that comes with faith, but it is not merely a foregone conclusion, as though it were predetermined or destined; moreover, it has more to do with the suffering that is outside the community of discipleship than with our own personal or ecclesiastical suffering. I want to expatiate a little on each of these subthemes.

ITS ORIENTATION TOWARD LIFE

It seems to me very important to distinguish Christian suffering from the phenomenon that Sigmund Freud named the *Todestrieb*—literally, the drive to death, or, as it is usually stated in English, the death wish. There *is* a drive to death in human nature under the conditions of historical existence, as is evidenced by the high rate of suicide in countries that, from every external point of view, offer unusual opportunities for self-development. Sartre claimed that the reason why most of us suffer from acrophobia (fear of heights) is that in such situations we have actually to *decide* at the semiconscious level not to jump! In other words, there are situations when the fascination with nonbeing—what Keats called "half in love with easeful death"[4]—is accentuated, rising far enough into our consciousness that we have actually to suppress it.

Earlier in my life, I read a good deal of the martyrology of the early church. I would have to say that these accounts often come very close to ambiguity precisely at this point. One frequently senses in the souls of those being put to the test the extremity of the tension between their religious convictions and their psychological confusions. They may speak humbly or perhaps heroically of their faith, for which they are ready to die, but their words and actions also betray a kind of dogged determination to have their day with the lions. Combined with a highly personalistic and sometimes even a romanticized pietism that desires (as Paul once put it) "to depart and be with Christ" (Phil. 1:23), the *Todestrieb*, which on biblical grounds is more demonic than divine, is often only slightly concealed by the martyr's excessive zeal for the "crown" beyond the "cross." Even though the acts of the martyrs are later, rather idealized accounts of these events, they sometimes attest to the genuine humanity of those charged with judging the persons accused. Certainly some of these judges were on the side of life; they are appalled by the prospect of having to condemn decent, law-abiding, and often young people to death. Yet the prospective martyrs seem determined to go all the way—their youth, family, rationality, and all the rest abandoned in favor of the apparent glory of a martyr's death. Time and again, one's sympathies are with the judges, who in many cases were persons both of fairness and compassion. It is not for nothing that the early church had to warn its members not actually to *seek* martyrdom!

Obviously that warning did not imply a negative judgment against those who had been martyred already. The same church can acknowledge that "the blood of the martyrs is the seed of the church" (Tertullian). But the warning against seeking martyrdom indicates a recognition on the part of the church that martyrdom is by no means always "for the right reason"—a telling phrase from a modern literary source (T. S. Eliot's play *Murder in the Cathedral*)[5] that treats exactly this same problem. Christianity, so long as it remains true to its own sources, cannot embrace any of the heroics of death, including those associated with war or various causes, because its orientation is toward life. Life should not be easily or lightly thrown away. Christianity has this life-orientation from its parental faith, Judaism, a religion that, unlike *many* other religions of the human species, never succumbs to the subtle whisperings of death—*even when it is hounded to death and rounded up by death and shipped to factories whose sole product was the transformation of the living to the state of death.* One of the most astonishing facts of human history, surely, is that a people whose whole recorded history is one of suffering at the hands of other, more powerful peoples manifested and still manifests the most intense and jubilant commitment to life—a people whose most cherished motto is "To life" (*l'chaim*). Christianity did not and does not embrace that type of life commitment with the consistency of Judaism, for Christianity has been intermingled with other strains of human longing and frailty; but there is enough of a memory of the life affirmation of the children of Abraham and Sarah in this "grafted on" community of faith (Rom. 11:17ff.) to resist, on the whole, the pull of oblivion that is the answer to life's trauma entertained by many, including not only a few contemporary cults but many ancient faiths (such as, some would say, that of ancient Egypt).

For biblical faith, death is "the enemy" (1 Cor. 15:26)—as the Apocalypse also insists (Rev. 21:4)—"the last enemy," waiting for its final eradication by "the Lord and Giver of life." This is why the theology of the cross must never become, or seem to harbor, a glorification of death. And this is why, when the cross *has* been turned into such a glorification, it is right that it should be resisted—as some feminists and others in our time have done. To the surprise of many, Jürgen Moltmann began his book on the theology of the cross with the sentence, "The cross is not and cannot be loved."[6] With this short sentence, Moltmann writes a great question mark over all cross-inspired pietism, heroism, and sentimentality, such as one has in many much-loved hymns ("In the cross of Christ I glory," "I shall cherish the old rugged cross," etc.). To such sentiments one wishes to say a qualified yes, but always with this caveat: be careful! The symbol at the center of our faith must not be turned into an apotheosis of death, including the death of Jesus. Golgotha, rather, is a courageous *facing* of death and a *confrontation* with death—with "the enemy."

Here God confronts the enemy and oppressor of life with a view to death's eschatological overcoming. This enemy, like all great enemies of life, can only be overcome from within. This is the permanent truth of the ransom or classical theory of the atonement.[7] Death must be faced, undergone, entered into—if it is to be challenged, defeated. Hence the *second* sentence of Moltmann's book on this theological tradition reads: "Yet only the crucified Christ can bring the freedom which changes the world because it is no longer afraid of death."[8] What Paul calls "the sting of death" (1 Cor. 15:55-56) is removed in faith through the grace-given courage to confront death's mockery of life openly. . .

This, however, constitutes no camouflaging of the grim *reality* of death. The theology of the cross "calls the thing what it actually is" (Heidelberg Disputation, thesis 21). Death is death, not sleep, not an automatic translation into the realm of the immortals, not the after-all quite beautiful thing that the funeral industry on this continent has so cleverly made of it. Death is real. For biblical faith it is perhaps even God's creature and servant, like Satan. At the very least it only has its reality and its (penultimate) power within the *providentia Dei*; that is, it has its purposes. Like the Bible's other negatives—evil, sin, the demonic—death too can serve, under God, life's positives. Where would love be without death? It belongs to the heart of love to know that the beloved like oneself is mortal, that we love only under the conditions of *chronos* and mortality. Genuine love, as distinct from mere infatuation or passion, contains a large measure of compassion borne of the recognition of our common finitude. So death is not *wholly* despised in this tradition—which is why we do not end up with a dualism, life/death, good/evil, darkness/light, and so forth.

The great objection of the Bible is in fact not to death in itself and as such; it is to the power of death over life—a power given it not by God but by *us*, by human beings, who in their state of "finitude in anxious self-awareness" (Tillich)[9] are fixated upon death. This anxious preoccupation with mortality detracts from our capacity fully and joyfully to enter into life. If you like, God's problem with death is not death itself but our human fascination with and temptation to and anxiety concerning death. Not death but our death wish or (which is the other side of the same thing) our nervously deliberate avoidance of the thought of death: that is the thing that the gospel of the crucified one wants to eradicate. And we do not learn this only from the resurrection accounts; it is there all the way through the biblical witness. The cross, which through the illumination and spiritual power of the resurrection becomes for us "gospel," *is* gospel, good news, because it frees us from the *bondage* to death and decay that is our spiritual condition. It does this through confrontation—through causing us to face and to enter into the negating reality that, because it is repressed in us, exercises an inordinate influence in our lives. The power of death—"the sting of death"—is a power that it has chiefly because it is so deeply concealed in our psyche. When Paul in Romans 6 writes of our baptism into Christ's death, he surely has in mind precisely this debilitating concealment and the profound need in all of us to be able at last to bring to consciousness this confining, draining, subconscious awareness of our total vulnerability, our nothingness, that we expend so much psychic energy holding down. The God of Israel and of Jesus the Christ wants *life* for us, and we are kept from life on account of our preoccupation with death and all that death stands for by way of life's negation. So, says Paul, we are thrust down beneath the waters of baptism—we are brought that close to death—so that we may at long last face it and see through it to the life that is God's gift for us. We notice that death, here liturgically enacted in the baptismal rite, is only the means to another end:

> Do you not know that all of us who have been baptized into Christ Jesus were baptized into his death? We were buried therefore with him by baptism into death, *so that as Christ was raised from the dead by the glory of the Father, we too might walk in newness of life.* (Rom. 6:3-4)

What we should pause to consider here is that this kind of neurotic fixation on death—which is "the sting of death"—must be applied not only to individuals but to whole societies. Our society, perhaps more than any other in history, is engaged in a massive denial of death. (And remember that for biblical faith *death* does not just refer to the termination of life, biological death, but stands symbolically for a whole Pandora's box of fears and negations that become particularly virulent when they are repressed or denied.) This was the point of one of the most insightful books written in our era, Ernest Becker's *The Denial of Death.* The more fixated the human spirit is upon its mortality, its vulnerability, its nothingness or apparent insignificance, the less capable it is of participating freely and joyfully in the life that it has been given. And this condition is most grievous, most overwhelming, when it is covered up with a show of shallow positives. Individuals whose sense of well-being depends upon a rigorous silencing of every thought of their own mortality are very difficult and sometimes dangerous people to be around. But what of a whole society whose well-being—whose way of life—depends upon the constant reassurance that the happiness it seeks is in no way threatened by the limitations that creaturely life places upon us? Such a society, says Becker, could be problematic, especially for those in its immediate sphere of influence or those within its own midst who are beyond pretension, the reality of whose condition precludes repression. When an entire culture is held in the grip of a worldview in which death is allowed no voice, death's power over life is immensely increased.[10] Such a society is greatly in need of (shall we say?) liberation, and at least in this respect the ancient atonement theology called the "classical theory" or *Christus Victor*[11] ought to be pondered anew by Christians who ask what their mission might be in this highly developed society of ours—this society that perennially searches for "the enemy" *outside itself* because, perhaps, it half recognizes how painful it would be to confront the enemy within.

Faith in the crucified one, which means both trust in him and conformity to his death and life, delivers us from the sting of death—not as a once-for-all deliverance but as an ongoing liberation. Or, to say the same thing in another way, such faith frees us from the kind of *self*-preoccupation and morbid anxiety that hold us back from the abundant life that the Creator intends for our creaturehood. And such faith is brought about (if I may put it in this no-doubt childish way) when the divine Spirit takes us by the hand, so to speak, and puts us into the company of the crucified one, where we are caused to face, finally, our utter vulnerability, mortality, and impermanence but in the company therefore of one who befriends us and shows us that this ending is also a beginning, that *this* death is the entrance into newness of life. Luther, as usual, understood all this when he said:

> The fear of death is merely death itself; he who abolishes that fear from the heart, neither tastes nor feels death. . . . The dream I had lately will be made true: 'twas that I was dead and stood by my grave, covered with rags. Thus am I long since condemned to die, and yet I live.[12]

So, in summary, the theology of the cross takes death very seriously—unlike, for instance, the Socratic tradition, which thinks of death as the soul's release from the body—but it does not glorify either death or dying. Because of the commitment to life on the part of the whole tradition of Jerusalem, this faith has more in common with Dylan Thomas's "Do not go gently into that dark night" than it has with some modern psychological schools that urge death's acceptance—schools that may be more Stoic than Christian. Even Jesus did not "go gently." There is no Hamletian "to sleep, perchance to dream" in the passion narrative. The literature of the Judeo-Christian tradition (so long as it remains the *Judeo*-Christian tradition) takes death so seriously as the end that it can only counter this ending by a beginning that is *not* found tucked away within this ending in some natural way but must be introduced *de novo* as God's possibility for us, not a possibility residing already within us. Grace and not nature counters this ending.

But it *is* countered. And its countering is already *anticipated* existentially and eschatologically whenever trust in the God of Golgotha takes us beyond the incapacitating fear of death and offers us some semblance of new life—some new courage to live (*Mut zum Leben*). As the negative in biblical thought is *always* present for the purpose of serving the positive (think of the role of Satan in Job), so death is there in order to enhance life and the beauty and joy of life, and in some sense death has to be gone through before life can be experienced in something approximating its fullness. Just as light presupposes the experience of darkness, and love of lovelessness and aloneness, and hope of despair, and faith of doubt, and so on, so life becomes the miracle it is only as we confront its antithesis. But the end, always, the bleakness of the *means* notwithstanding, is the positive pole in this dynamic—the yes, not the no. Therefore a pietism of the cross that ends by basking in unrelieved, morbidly enticing sorrow must certainly be seen as a contradiction and misrepresentation of the theology of the cross.

Suffering as Consequence of Obedience

The second generalization of my opening observation was that *the suffering of the church is a necessity that is laid upon faith but not as though it were an unavoidable fate; moreover, this suffering has more to do with the human situation outside the community of discipleship than it does with our personal or corporate condition as church.* Now to elaborate.

There are those who complain of Christians that they are much too interested in suffering. They ought to be listened to! Nietzsche was one of them; the great contemporary Jewish author, Elie Wiesel, is another; and one can hear this complaint also from some Christian feminists. The source of the complaint is of course related to the first point that I have been making, namely, that there are some forms of the church that manifest a certain fixation and glorification of suffering. But the objection also relates to the fact that the connection between true faith and suffering seems to be so deterministic, allowing for no decision on the part of the faithful. Feminism has been especially critical of this, because such a theology has been used to persuade women of their duty to accept their lot as long-suffering wives and mothers, in much the same way as this theology has been used to keep enslaved races or economic groupings from complaint or revolt.

It is true of course that both the Newer Testament and some very important theological traditions accentuate the theme of *necessitas* in relation to our theme, the suffering of the church. When these traditions are informed ones, they make once again the important connection between Christology and ecclesiology. The Christ, too, as he is presented in the Gospels, was conscious of a necessity carrying him ever closer to his passion and death: "The Son of Man must suffer and be rejected"—the so-called predictions of the passion. The suffering of the church is seen and should be seen under this same *necessitas*.

However, over against those who feel that such a necessity is the equivalent of a kind of fatalism, let it be remembered that Jesus in the Gospels is conscious not only of this "must," which he clearly associates with the will of God, but also of the fact that he himself is left to decide the matter. He is not simply born to suffer: he is born as one whose gift for compassion and justice will probably in the natural course of events lead to great suffering, but he is not presented as one following a script written by Another. Were he such a one, he could in no way be considered (as Paul considers him) the second Adam—the only other human fully free, like the first Adam, actually to *choose* not to sin (*posse non peccare*) (Romans 5). Jesus' decision for the cross, which he makes only with the greatest difficulty precisely because he is perfectly free *not* to make it, is a voluntary decision on his part, and this same volition belongs, in some real measure, to the community that Jesus calls the body of Christ (*soma Christou*). The suffering of the body of Christ is therefore by no means a fate, and where it is genuine (as in the case of Bonhoeffer, or of Simone Weil, or of Martin Luther King Jr.) the element of choice is prominent and vital to it. The church does not *have* to suffer, as if there were no other possibility—indeed, the fact that the historic church has so regularly and characteristically managed to *avoid* suffering ought to set to rest any insistence that Christians always and necessarily suffer. *However*, whenever the church has made good its claim to Christ's discipleship, it has at least known the *call* to suffer. And again let me repeat (because it can never be said often enough): called to suffer not because suffering is good or beneficial or ultimately rewarding (I think Paul can actually be criticized a little for giving that impression in Romans 5), but called to suffer *because there is suffering*—that is, because God's creatures, including human beings, are already suffering, because "the whole creation groans."

The point is: the suffering of the church is not the goal but the consequence of faith. For faith, we said, is that trust in God then frees us sufficiently from *self* to make us cognizant of and compassionate in relation toward the other—in particular, the other who suffers, who is hungry and thirsty, who is imprisoned; the other who "fell among thieves"; the other who knocks at our door at midnight in need. The church is a community of suffering because it is a community whose eyes have been opened to the suffering that *exists*. The first assumption of this ecclesiology is not that the church should suffer but that it should be (in Simone Weil's sense) "attentive"—namely, attentive to the suffering that is simply there and that is usually bypassed by the world, as in the parable of the Good Samaritan. The Bible assumes that human and creaturely suffering is perennial and manifold. If the church does not see this suffering and if, seeing it, it does not take the burden of it upon itself, then its whole life must be called into question.

This is why Luther insisted that among the so-called marks of the church there is only one that is indispensable—only one whose absence would automatically call into question everything else claimed by such a church, including its unity, holiness, apostolicity, and catholicity. As von Loewenich writes:

> Luther lists cross and suffering among the marks of the church. In his book *Of Councils and the Church*, 1539, Luther counts seven marks by which the church can be recognized, and he would prefer to call them the seven sacraments of the church, if the term 'sacrament' had not already taken on a different meaning. . . . As the seventh mark of the church, Luther mentions "the holy possession of the sacred cross" . . . suffering; a church of which that cannot be said has become untrue to its destiny.[13]

This seventh mark of the church, surely, is one that ought to exercise a good deal of critical guidance today as the churches struggle to overcome their internal conflicts and their penchant for excessive concern over their own institutional survival. Surely the only survival in which the church as *Christ's* body can be interested ultimately is the survival of God's groaning creation. The whole ethic of justice, peace, and integrity of creation, which the World Council of Churches tried two decades ago to make central to ecclesiastical and ecumenical concern, is not a mere addendum to Christian faith and life but stands at the center of our identity as communities of Christ's discipleship.[14]

I do not wish to be heard to say that the condition either of the individual Christian or of the Christian community as a whole is of no great concern to this tradition. Against any such claim, the whole high priestly prayer of John 17 would have to be read: "'I am asking on their [the disciples'] behalf,'" Jesus prays. "'I am not asking on behalf of the world, but on behalf of those whom you gave me, because they are yours'" (v. 9). We all suffer, individually and corporately. To be human is to suffer. Some of our suffering is integral to our creaturehood; without it we could not become fully human.[15] And some of our suffering as Christians and as churches is integral to our becoming mature disciples of the Christ—it belongs to what the tradition named *conformitas Christi* (being conformed to Christ). One dimension of the suffering of the church, therefore, is its appropriation and internalization of the pain involved in being identified with the crucified one—what the Reformers called its "continuing baptism" into his death.

But this side of the suffering of the church can be badly distorted if it becomes interesting in itself. It is for this reason that I claimed at the outset of the chapter that where the theme of Christian suffering *has* been acknowledged in certain Christian (especially Lutheran) traditions, it has too often been marred by introversion and subjectivization: "See how I suffer, see how we suffer, life is a cross," etc.

The necessary corrective to this kind of melancholy self-preoccupation on the part of Christians and churches is their being made newly conscious of the suffering that lies *outside* their own persons and communities. Surely if it is truly Jesus Christ whom we follow, that is the direction in which we must move; for in the scriptural sources we never hear of a Jesus preoccupied with his own pain. Even on the cross itself he is conscious, chiefly, of the pain of others—of the thieves on either side, and of the pathetic little group of his followers standing beneath the cross, devastated.

Christians, we have maintained, are those who through confrontation with death are given a new freedom from the sting of death and so a new freedom *for* voluntary service to others. Surely if this claim has any truth in it, then it is not our own suffering but the suffering of the world beyond us that must claim our attention. Indeed, is not the whole purpose of our liberation from excessive personal anxiety the creation within us of a new consciousness of and care for others? Just here we encounter the transition from theology to ethics. The theology of the cross is intended to give rise not only to an ecclesiology of the cross, but to an ethic, the essence of which is the attentiveness to human and worldly suffering that is made possible in those who have been and are being delivered from self.[16]

The completion of ecclesiological doctrine under the aegis of the *theologia crucis* is thus relegated to the discussion of Christian ethics. This, unfortunately, has been avoided too often in Christian thought concerning the nature of the church. Ethics have too often been appended (tacked on) to ecclesiologies arrived at without much reference to the worldly calling of the church. When this happens in the name of the theology of the cross, however (as it sometimes has), an enormous contradiction has been perpetrated. For a church that has its being in its ongoing identification with the crucified Christ is, under the very terms of that ongoing identification and not as a second step, thrust into solidarity with the suffering creation . . .

Notes

1. For a fascinating contemporary commentary on the much-neglected book of Lamentations, see Kathleen M. O'Connor, *Lamentations and the Tears of the World* (Maryknoll, NY: Orbis, 2002). An early sentence in the book sets the tone: "For readers who begin from a place of suffering, Lamentations is a book of comfort" (p. 3).

2. See my essay on Bonhoeffer in Hall 1998a:63–74.

3. The possible documentation for this observation is of course too extensive to cite; however, I would like to direct the reader to three works which illustrate, in three quite different ways, the point being made: (1) a book by Mary M. Solberg, who was inspired to explore Luther's *theologia crucis* by her work in El Salvador during that country's brutal civil war (*Compelling Knowledge: A Feminist Proposal for an Epistemology of the Cross* [Albany: SUNY Press, 1997]); (2) the multiauthor volume edited by Walter Wink, *Homosexuality and the Christian Faith: Questions of Conscience for Churches* (Minneapolis: Fortress Press, 1999), which sensitively documents the plight of gay and lesbian persons and the recovery of "biblical fidelity" (Ken Sehested); (3) Walter Brueggemann, ed., *Hope for the World: Mission in a Global Context* (Papers from the Campbell Seminar; Louisville: Westminster John Knox, 2001), especially the essays of H. Russel Botman (South Africa), Damayanthi M. A. Niles (Sri Lanka and United States), Ofelia Ortega (Cuba), and Janos Pasztor (Hungary).

4. John Keats, "Ode to a Nightingale," stanza 6.

5. T. S. Eliot, *Murder in the Cathedral*, in *The Complete Poems and Plays* (New York: Harcourt, Brace, 1930), 196.

6. Jürgen Moltmann, *The Crucified God: The Cross of Christ as the Foundation and Criticism of Christian Theology*, trans. R. A. Wilson and John Bowden (London: SCM, 1973), 1.

7. See Gustav Aulén, *Christus Victor: An Historical Study of the Three Main Types of the Idea of Atonement*, trans. A. G. Hebert (London: SPCK, 1953).

8. Moltmann, *Crucified God*, 1.

9. Paul Tillich, *Systematic Theology*, 3 vols. (Chicago: University of Chicago Press, 1951–63), 2:29ff.

10. Ernest Becker, *The Denial of Death* (New York: Free Press, 1973).

11. Aulén's *Christus Victor* is as relevant today as when it was written half a century ago; for the atonement theory that it challenges, that of Anselm, is as dominant today as it was then.

12. Martin Luther, *The Table Talk of Martin Luther*, ed. Thomas S. Kepler (New York: World, 1952), 320f.

13. Walther von Loewenich, *Luther's Theology of the Cross* (Belfast: Christian Journals, 1976), 127.

14. See D. Premen Niles, ed., *Between the Flood and the Rainbow: Interpreting the Conciliar Process of Mutual Commitment (Covenant) to Justice, Peace, and the Integrity of Creation* (Geneva: World Council of Churches Publications, 1992).

15. See Hall 1986a.

16. See Larry Rasmussen's "An Ethic of the Cross," in his *Dietrich Bonhoeffer: His Significance for North Americans* (Minneapolis: Fortress Press, 1990), 144ff.

13

The True Church

Confessing the Faith, the final volume in Hall's trilogy on Christian theology in a North American context, is concerned with "the doctrine of the church, or ecclesiology; the nature of the church's calling as a confessing body, or missiology; and the character of hope to which the being and work of the church points, or eschatology" (1996:22). Following somewhat the pattern of Professing the Faith, Hall looks at the church—which he refers to as "the disciple community"—in historical, critical, and constructive perspectives. He first explores the contours of the church, not only according to its traditional self-understanding, but also what those boundaries look like when translated into the North American context, where the breakdown of the church into thousands of denominational and sectarian expressions constitutes something of a scandal, compromising the message of the gospel. Caught between this challenge and the context of disestablishment, Hall thus proposes a new way of understanding the church relative to society, focusing especially on its minority status. This chapter is comprised of three noncontinuous sections from the book's second chapter, "Contours of the Church," that focus especially on those aforementioned issues.

Source: Hall 1996:65–70, 97–101, 122–27.

PARAMETERS OF THE DISCUSSION

BOUNDARIES

. . . What we want to ask [here] is in some ways a simple question, but history has made it complex, and its complexity is nowhere more conspicuous than in Protestant North America, where literally thousands of denominations and sects[1] and vague affiliations announce that they are the church. Our question will be phrased in this way: What may legitimately be regarded as "the Christian church"?

From ecclesiastical history, as well as the history of doctrine, we have inherited so many direct and indirect answers to this question that the result is rather bewildering. Perhaps, however, we can classify the answers in such a way as to facilitate our further reflections on the question. This history presents us, let us say, with two extremes, with a spectrum of possibilities between the two. On the one hand, ecclesiastical conservativism insists that the boundaries of the true church may be drawn up quite strictly. It will, of course, depend upon the specific type of conservativism under consideration—for instance, whether it is of the conventional Roman Catholic or the fundamentalist-Protestant variety; but what is true of all such ecclesiologies is that the question of boundaries is really not a question. It has been determined in advance what the boundaries are and shall be; therefore the church need not concern itself with an ongoing attempt to *decide* where and what they are. Its identity is always quite certain. As with individuals who "know who they are," this is obviously a very satisfying, comfortable position for any institution to assume, and particularly for those who bear authority within such institutions. The agony of identity does not affect such churches, and this, undoubtedly, is part of their popular appeal.

The weakness of this position is also evident, however; and today it has become more obvious than in the past, to the point that many who have membership in such closely defined communities of faith find it increasingly difficult to sustain their own certitude. For in the pluralistic society they are bound to encounter others who, although "not of their fold," entertain many religious and ethical ideas disturbingly similar to their own; and this naturally raises for the sensitive among such communities the question of why their boundaries must be so exclusive of others. For such persons, the well-established, conventional limits of the "true church" begin to assume purely institutional, theoretical, or even artificial proportions. They appear to have little or nothing to do with substance, but only with form—perhaps only nomenclature. It was one thing to maintain the exclusive veracity of Latin or "Roman" Christianity when it occupied an almost monopolistic position in pre-Reformation Western Europe; it is something else to do so in a postmodern North America in which most of a person's waking hours are spent in company with others, the majority of whom do not share his or her explicit convictions.

At the other end of the spectrum we encounter the most broad-minded forms of Christian liberalism, which is as inclusive in its description of "church" as staunch conservatives are exclusive. In fact, historically as well as psychologically, the two positions often constitute reactions to one another.

Appalled by the rigidity of an ecclesiology and church polity that insists that it alone is legitimate, Christian liberalism is driven toward a posture that is more and more universalistic. Correspondingly, as liberalism gains ground in churches, those who are fearful of the open-endedness of such a conception of the church become all the more adamant in their definition of ecclesiastical boundaries.

In our historical context, this particular polarization has been demonstrated very graphically during the past hundred years with the emergence of Christian fundamentalism. With the inroads made by historical-critical methods of biblical interpretation and other aspects of the Enlightenment mentality and scholarship, many conservative Protestants were drawn into a biblicistic reaction, culminating in the Niagara Conferences of 1895 and beyond, and issuing in the delineation of five so-called fundamentals by which the true church should be defined.[2] In turn, the continued growth throughout the twentieth century of fundamentalist or semifundamentalist forms of Christianity, including movements of the same within most of the once mainline denominations themselves, has inspired in those who could not accept such closed systems ever more inclusive, democratic conceptions of Christian boundaries, to the point of erasing boundaries altogether.

The apparent appeal of the latter position is signaled by two adjectives in the previous sentence: "inclusive" and "democratic." It belongs to the spirit of our present context to wish to appear as inclusive and democratic as possible. To exclude is bad; to include is good. That everybody should participate in decision making is good; that decisions should be reserved for an "elite" is bad. In this respect, liberalism has become the order of the day—a reality that is regularly demonstrated by self-styled radicals who claim to despise liberalism while depending entirely on the language and tactics that religious and cultural liberalism introduced into our discourse. Not to be open, inclusive, tolerant, and democratic in such a society is to invite scorn from all sides of the popular culture. Consequently, a Christian liberalism that on the grounds of theological ideas such as the universality of the divine *agape* can both reflect and foster such values can seem reasonable, or at least inoffensive. Even where religious faith of every kind has become suspect, the secular mind is glad enough to find its predisposition to liberality corroborated by what can still be regarded as avant-garde religion.

But this position is also becoming less viable. Even Christians of a basically liberal mindset are caused by the plethora of churches and sects all calling themselves Christian to wonder whether there are any limits whatsoever. As [Eugene] Bianchi and [Rosemary Radford] Ruether point out, "a dialogical church does not mean a debating society in which everything goes and nothing is decided or acted upon."[3] Whether overtly or covertly, a liberalism that is theologically nondiscriminating implicitly denies authenticity to Christian groups that are plainly restrictive. As for more serious Christians, they have long realized that the ultraliberal "position" ends by being no position at all. If there are no boundaries to the church—if everyone is to be included—then does the category "Christian" or "church" have any content at all? Is it not simply a generalization covering humankind at large, humanity's actual differences notwithstanding? Is not such inclusiveness finally an absurdity? All are included—but in *what*, precisely?

As I have already indicated, these two positions do not exhaust the alternatives from which we may choose in determining how we should answer the question posed at the outset: What may be legitimately regarded as "the Christian church"? Nevertheless, the juxtaposition of these two extremes, which are not only theoretical but descriptions of actual positions operative in our context, establishes the parameters of the discussion. Our own response will be informed by these parameters. At least we know what we shall have to avoid.

On the one hand we shall want to avoid the kind of exclusivism that results from the perpetuation and hardening of conventional forms of orthodoxy which, however hoary with age, have their origins in very shaky biblical and theological premises, and today are falsely offensive—that is, they substitute the false scandal of arbitrary criteria of authenticity for the genuine *skandalon* of the gospel that offers any church "legitimacy" only conditionally and as a matter of "sheer grace."

On the other hand, we shall have to avoid the kind of inclusivism that has been imposed upon Christianity by liberal relativism, and which ends in the ridiculous spectacle of a system of "belief" that is both contentless and directionless—that is, indeed, no confessional stance at all but only a vague attitude of tolerance that is, ironically, incapable of taking seriously the views of the "others" whom it is so fearful of excluding.

Both of these extremes must be avoided by a theology of the church that insists that the church is a "confessing church"; because both are incapable of confession. . . . Ecclesiastical conservativism is in danger of being so confined to its prescribed boundaries that it cannot go beyond them long enough to discover the world in which, and for the sake of which, its confession has to be made. Christian liberalism can be so devoid of boundaries that its flamboyant participation in the world makes no difference, finally. Professing nothing in particular, it can only repeat the opinions it already finds there. And since those opinions are in fact capricious and in constant flux, the church that is governed by such an orientation is pathetically bound to boundaries that are in the end more arbitrary than anything conceived by Christian exclusivism.

INDIRECT SELF-DEFINITION

By a process of elimination, we have arrived at the conclusion that if any community intends to be the church it must have some sort of self-definition, some sense of its own identity, some awareness of its boundaries; and that this must be derived from its own sources and not imposed upon it arbitrarily. . . . [W]e recognize that any discussion of the church's "own sources" must refer immediately to its God-given identity as the "body" of Jesus Christ, its "head"—an identity in which it is sustained by the Holy Spirit. We may speak of this as the church's "trinitarian foundation." If, beyond this, it is necessary to spell out the boundaries of the church more explicitly (and evidently it is), this must not be done in such a way as to minimize the significance of that one source and ground of its life. The danger of all very *direct* and *definitive* articulations of the boundaries of "the true church" is precisely that: that they will usurp this trinitarian source, if not in theory then certainly in practice, thus becoming criteria of authenticity that are no longer answerable to anything beyond themselves and their ecclesiastical guardians.

It is possible however to define the boundaries of the church *indirectly*. This may, of course, be done *via negativa*, by saying what the church is *not*. I shall make some use of this approach in what follows; but by itself it is not very satisfactory.[4] One may say that the church is not (for example) the religious dimension of the culture, or the established cult of the West, or a sectarian society, or "institutional religion," or a democratic "debating society" (Bianchi and Ruether), and so on; but unless one also risks defining the church more positively, these negative statements beg many questions. I shall take the risk.

There are, I think, two ways in which it is possible to offer the kind of definition of the church that avoids both conservative rigidity and liberal relativism—or to put the matter more positively, that retains the dynamic character of the life of the disciple community as the body of the living Christ while providing certain regulative clues concerning its character. One of these ways—the more familiar of the two—is by discussing the so-called marks of the church as these are identified by the four qualifying adjectives in the third article of the Nicene Creed: "one, holy, catholic, and apostolic." . . .

Another way of outlining the contours of the church indirectly is by considering its *relationships*, including its internal as well as its external relationships. All entities, including institutions and movements, are implicitly defined by their relationships. A nation is what it is as it stands vis-à-vis other nations, neighboring states, stronger and weaker peoples, enemy nations, empires or commonwealths or the trading blocs of which it may be part, and so on. Nations are also busy defining themselves in the manner in which they work out their internal relations: how their citizens relate as individuals to the community; how different linguistic or ethnic or racial groupings within the nation treat one another, and so forth.

Similarly, the contours of the church are determined by its relation to entities external to itself with which it must necessarily enter into relationship: its host society, the state, other religions, and the like. And its boundaries are also being determined by its way of working out its internal relations: the relation of individual members to the whole community; the relation of the church to the churches; and, perhaps most important, the relation of the church to the "kingdom" or realm of God that it proclaims and anticipates in its life. The discussion of these relations will occupy the successive sections of this chapter.

In all of this, our intention is to describe the disciple community *theologically*. This is not an exercise in history or sociology but in doctrine. Since it is a *contextual* theology we are engaged in, we have, of course, to relate this doctrine to the empirical realities of church and society in our context. For the most part, this will result in a critical assessment of the church as we actually find it in our society, for (let me say this in advance) I do not see how we can contemplate the church *theologically* without being led repeatedly to the conclusion that what is, by grace, altogether *possible* for this community is being thwarted at nearly every turn by the actual patterns of ecclesiastical behavior in this transitional period in the life of "Christendom." . . .

The excerpt below, which considers the disciple community relative to its denominational expressions, follows another section that looks at the traditional marks of the church—"one, holy, catholic, apostolic." But Hall also asserts that the Protestant church has added to these the criteria of word and sacrament, and that the "mark of the cross" is essential to the church's self-understanding (see chapter 12, above).

The Old Problem—and Its New World Complications

The church, we have said, must have *some* sense of its own identity, and therefore some boundaries. When the boundaries are too rigidly fixed, they tend to deny in principle the trinitarian foundations of the church—that it is

God's people, the body of the *Christ*, called into and sustained in its being by the *Spirit* who "blows where it wills." On the other hand, where there are no boundaries at all, the tyranny and confusion of the ever-changing agendas set for "religion" by the world are more problematic than the opposite danger.

The question immediately raised by these reflections is whether the boundaries of the church, Christ's church, are to be equated with the boundaries established and acknowledged by institutions called churches. Is the church (capital C, as it were) identifiable with the churches—and only with them? Is it necessary to be a member of one of the churches to be within the church of Jesus Christ? Does being in one of the churches *guarantee* that one is a member of the church? Are we to understand the old dogma that there is no salvation outside the church (*extra ecclesiam nulla salus*) to mean that those who are not members of the churches, or perhaps of one church in particular, cannot expect salvation?

This is a persistent question in Christian doctrine, partly inherited from ancient Israel, partly an inevitable problem for any movement that assumes an institutional status, and partly having specific pertinence to the Christian movement. Already, in the disagreement between the Jerusalem disciples and Paul, evangelist to the Gentiles, the problem concretized itself: Does membership in the *koinonia* of Christ's disciples presuppose Jewish birth, or at least circumcision? (See Galatians 2, 5, 6, and so on.) In another form, it is present in the Johannine literature: There are already those, apparently, who claim the status of Christian but whose fellowship is determined by "spirits" other than that spirit that confesses Jesus Christ. In the Apocalypse, with its astringent "letters to the churches" (chs. 2 and 3), we certainly encounter attitudes and assessments that would cause us to question any easy identification of Christ's church with the churches.

Very soon in its history, the young movement discovered that this incipient questioning of the Newer Testament would have to become a major area of reflection and decision making. It preoccupies the Apostolic Fathers, and the great Theological and christological decisions of the fourth and fifth centuries are almost impossibly intermingled with it. Who speaks for "the church"? How is the true church to be distinguished from heretical movements and sects? By now it is assumed by most thoughtful Christians, apparently, that there can be no question of an *equation* of the Church with the churches, or whatever may call itself "church" or the equivalent.

Thus begins the setting of boundaries—a necessary activity, but, in the end, perhaps far too successful. The early church tasted the potential and actual chaos that the boundary-less situation courts, and it reacted in the usual way: by drawing up boundaries, by bolstering them more and more, and sometimes by turning them into impenetrable bulwarks.[5] In the process, the *pneumatic* dimension of ecclesiastical existence was effectively curbed and, in certain situations, altogether expelled—in favor of the institutional dimension. *The* church became *this* church, meeting such-and-such criteria of theological orthodoxy and observing such-and-such systems of government, worship, and so forth.

This equation of the church with *this* church quite naturally occasioned protest. The Great Schism of Eastern and Western Christendom is one consequence of the overdefinition of boundaries. The protesting movements of the late Middle Ages, culminating in the Reformation of the sixteenth century, constitute another. When institutional boundaries become inflexible and exclusive, the Spirit will raise up children to Abraham out of stones (Matt. 3:9; Luke 3:8)—and peasants, and unheard-of scholars on the edges of the imperium.

But the vicious circle does not end there. In turn, the churches of the Reformation, tasting very soon the same chaos that was tasted by the pre-Nicene church, found it necessary to become definitive. And again, it was the pneumatic dimension that suffered most—both in the exclusion of those groups that were most affected by what they deemed to be the presence of the Spirit, and in the crystallization of dogma and form within the Lutheran and Reformed communions, resulting in the Protestant Orthodoxy of the seventeenth century and following.

And therefore, yet again, the pneumatic element had to assert itself over against the age-old institutional need to identify the church quite strictly with its institutional expression. And even the Augustinian-Protestant idea of the *ecclesia invisibilis* (church invisible) did not prevent this hardening from happening. In fact, one must ask whether the distinction between the "visible" and "invisible" church did not remain at the level of theory, and not praxis. It is comforting for the protesting element at the height of its protest against the rigidly defined and ordered church to cry that the true church is known only to God; but history intimates that as soon as the protest *becomes* the church, it is likely to behave toward *its* protesting elements in precisely the same way it was itself treated.

In any case, this sad but perhaps inevitable history repeated itself, *mutatis mutandis*, in the protest of the Spirit-enthused pietistic, activistic, and other groupings of Christians against the established Protestant (and Anglican) churches, particularly in the eighteenth century. Many of them, like the Wesleyans, wanted desperately to believe that the Spirit would still be welcomed *within* the well-bounded church—that the principle *semper reformanda* still applied. But the church that has determined in advance that its belief and its form and its polity are correct—are indeed of the very *essence* of church—is not easily moved; and therefore these later protestors and reformers had to form their churches outside the establishments, or as barely tolerated *ecclesiola in ecclesia* (little churches within the church).

And they in turn. . . . But there is no need to go on. We are *living*, in North America, with the consequences of these developments, and with further divisions and permutations bound up with our own continental Protestant history. The venerable problem of the church and the churches is accentuated in North America on account of the fact that the controls inherent in the old European situation, controls that evolved over centuries and were deeply entrenched, have been almost wholly absent in our religious history. As is well known, certain ecclesiastical bodies have *tried* very hard to import to these shores the kinds of ecclesial boundaries that took shape in their European histories, together with the systems of guardianship thereto pertaining. But these efforts are foreign to the spirit of freedom and experimentation that has characterized our context from the outset.[6]

The historical and theological advantage of the legally disestablished or nonestablished status of the church in the so-called New World has been that the pneumatic dimension of ecclesial foundations has enjoyed a greater liberty here, for it was not continuously thwarted by strong church authorities backed up by even stronger states, armies, and executioners. The disadvantage of our situation is the other side of the same coin: without many effective institutional restraints, the boundaries of the church have been paper boundaries at best, giving no serious opposition to allegedly Spirit-inspired Christian movements and groups that insisted upon very different kinds of boundaries.

As a result, the ancient question of the relation between the church and the churches is augmented for us, and from time to time the augmentation assumes almost tragic proportions (Waco, Jonestown). It is not only the quantitative difference between the parental Old World and the New World in this respect (the fact that we have so many more churches); for here Engels' Law applies: at a certain point, a change in quantity introduces a change in quality. To have (as in western Germany) three of four churches claiming the status of church, most of them rather modestly so, is one thing; to have fifteen hundred or (according to some statistics) four thousand denominations making this claim, many of them without the least modesty, is something else! What it means, in fact, is that the setting of boundaries seems to almost everyone except the most die-hard fundamentalists an exercise in futility; for no boundaries whatever, under such circumstances, can be made to stick. Why bother, then, even considering them? Let it be! If it ends with every individual having his or her own private sanctuary, so be it. Is such individualism not in any case the general preference of our society?[7]

But serious Christian theology cannot let it be. For the fragmentation of the church is not only an institutional scandal, it is a theological scandal—a scandal of faith. This faith, after all, is centered in the belief that, through the judging love and loving judgment of God in Christ, reconciliation, mutuality, communality, "oneness" has been made possible.[8] The "dividing wall of hostility" (Eph. 2:14) has been broken down; we are able to respond in love to love given. Unity here does not imply uniformity, but it does imply mutuality; but this gospel is rendered *incredible*, quite literally, unbelievable, in a situation in which Christians not only give no evidence at all of such mutuality but adamantly exclude one another, some openly, some more subtly. The question about the relation of the church to the churches, therefore, far from being passé in our context, is raised to existential heights never experienced in Old World settings, the wars, hostilities, and bloodshed of that European past notwithstanding. With so many *churches*, what can "the church" possibly mean? North American denominationalism is simply a *skandalon*—and not even a false scandal, but a real one. It literally betrays the gospel and makes a mockery of Jesus' high priestly prayer "that all may be one" (John 17).

Must we not conclude, moreover, that the scandalous character of this Christianity is particularly the responsibility of the older, formerly mainline denominations? While the absurdity of the situation may be more visible in the newer, "sectarian" groups, with their wild claims to ultimacy, the greater guilt for it must surely be laid at the doorstep of those from whose treasure houses of doctrine and experience wisdom might have been drawn—might still be drawn—to ameliorate this poverty of understanding. Instead, for the most part these denominations have tacitly withdrawn from the discussion, practicing a merely token ecumenism, and at bottom nurturing a "live and let live" liberality that, however admirable in its civility, has lost all touch with theological foundations and the wisdom they in some measure contain. . . .

The final excerpt comes from a section on the relationship between the church, society, and the state, which begins with a consideration of both the triumph and the humiliation of Christendom, a topic that informs many of Hall's books and essays. The two chapters that follow will explore the implications of disestablishment more specifically for mission and identity.

THE QUEST FOR AN ALTERNATIVE WAY OF CONCEIVING OF THE RELATION BETWEEN CHURCH AND SOCIETY

The Pauline image of the church as Christ's body is indispensable not only because of its dominance in all types of historic ecclesiological dogma, but also for its intrinsic worth: it is, as we have seen, a holistic metaphor, joining together all or most of the aspects of the doctrine of the church, which are otherwise all too easily fragmented. . . . [I]t is for this reason more than a "metaphor." Yet it is also *only* a metaphor, and like all metaphors it has its limitations.

One of the most serious of these limitations is that it can lend itself to triumphalistic forms of ecclesiology, and, under the conditions of Christian establishment, it has regularly done so. If one considers, for example, the ecclesiastical bravado conveyed in the lyrics of the popular nineteenth-century hymn "Onward, Christian Soldiers" (especially when they are set to the militant tune by Sir Arthur Sullivan), and of the manner in which this hymn is able to incorporate the "body" metaphor to its advantage, one has a concrete instance of what I mean:

Like a mighty army moves the Church of God,
Brothers, we are treading where the saints have trod.
We are not divided, *all one body we—*
One in hope and doctrine, one in charity.

Onward, Christian soldiers . . .

Apparently not even the blatant fact of the scandalous divisions of Christendom in all the areas named (eschatology, doctrine, and ethics) deterred the author of these words from promoting the "one body" imagery, for it suited his purpose so well. A "mighty army" must be unified if it is to go "forward into battle" and "prevail" "against the foe" . . . and so on.

It tells us more than almost anything else about the character of Christendom that this image of the church not only dominated Christian imagination (a thing that could be thought reasonable enough in view of its exceptional development in the Scriptures) but that it seems to have excluded other images that present a very different picture of the Christian movement. . . . [T]he Johannine image of the bride and the bridegroom . . . in the Apocalypse leaves us with certain questions about the suitability of the "bride" (church). . . . [T]he Gospel of John's "vine and branches" imagery (ch. 15) . . . , when combined with the Pauline image of the grafted-on "wild olive shoot," introduces a radically critical dimension in the face of all Christian "boasting." But beyond these epistolary images, we may ask why the references to his "little flock" contained in Jesus' own recorded discourse of the Synoptic tradition have been so consistently ignored or trivialized.

In the Sermon on the Mount, which falls directly after the Beatitudes having to do with the blessedness of suffering (and themselves, as we have seen, explicitly instructive concerning the life of the disciple community in society), Jesus addresses his followers thus:

> You are the salt of the earth: but if salt has lost its taste, how shall its saltness be restored? It is no longer good for anything except to be thrown out and trodden under foot by men.
>
> You are the light of the world. A city set on a hill cannot be hid. Nor do men light a lamp and put it under a bushel, but on a stand, and it gives light to all of the house. Let your light so shine before men, that they may see your good works and give glory to your Father who is in heaven. (Matt. 5:13-16; par.)

Three things are remarkable about these statements from the vantage point of our present topic: first, both the image of salt and light refer to something small; second, both are intended to do something for the larger entity with which they are associated; third, both are capable of failing to do so and therefore may be judged worthless.

a. *The Church as Minority.* Salt was a precious commodity in the ancient world and well into our own period. So the fact that it is "small" in relation to the food that it is intended to season does not detract from its qualitative importance. All the same, there is no mistaking the fact that this is a minority image. One does not want a whole plateful of salt!

It is similar with the metaphor of light—although, in the age of hydroelectricity, this is more difficult for us to grasp. We are used to brightly lighted rooms, offices, public places. When we think of cities, we think of great centers of light. Our metropoloi are so ablaze with artificial light that they light up the sky for a hundred miles around. But Jesus and his followers did not live in such a world. Light for them meant a modest light, the light of humble oil lamps, surrounded by much darkness—as the Prologue of John assumes: "The light shines in the darkness . . ." What is conspicuous, because it is so immense, is the darkness—"the encircling gloom" (John Henry Newman). Even a little light "lightens our darkness" (Cranmer); the deepest darkness cannot overcome even a candle (John 1:5). That is true—but only those who know the darkness know, profoundly, its truth. We should not therefore conclude that with the metaphor of light and the city of light we are led toward the imperial church! The light remains a little light, and the darkness remains immense.

For corroboration of this point, we could turn to two other images that Jesus employs—not, in these instances, to speak about his followers but about the greater reality at the center of the message to be broadcast by his followers, that is, the Reign of God. Even this reality, which greatly exceeds the disciple community as such, is likened to things that are by nature small in relation to that which they qualify: yeast (leaven), a mustard seed, one precious pearl, and so on (Matt. 13:31ff.; par.). Only a little yeast is needed: as Paul notes on two occasions (1 Cor. 5:6; Gal. 5:9), "a little leaven ferments the whole lump of dough." The mustard seed is "the smallest of all seeds," although it becomes "a tree." The pearl metaphor, of course, introduces another main thought (value), but it is again a minority image. And we could find many others in this literature, for they all grow out of the language of election, the remnant, and the covenant.

That this is so is, of course, no accident. Jesus was a Jew! The whole story of Israel is the story of a minority, both in its ancient and its modern form. Israel is conscious of itself as "a few" in relation to "the many." It is "called out" from the nations—chosen. The covenant, as it is presented in the continuity of the Adamic, Noachic, and Abrahamic sagas, assumes the minority status of this people. So does the concept of election. When it is faithful, Israel does not understand its election as a matter of privilege but of responsibility, because it is essentially a *representational* concept:

> Now therefore, if you will obey my voice and keep my covenant, you shall be my own possession among all peoples; for all the earth is mine, and you shall be to me a kingdom of priests and a holy nation. (Exod. 19:5-6)

—an affirmation repeated, this time about the church, in 1 Peter 2:9.

Out of this tradition of Jerusalem, Jesus quite naturally assumes that the "people of God" will be a minority in relation to the vast multitudes of earth's peoples, and that it will be *distinct*. Its distinction as such a minority is *by no means* an end in itself. To think so is to confuse the tradition of Jerusalem with that of Athens, which frequently thinks in elitist terms. "Elect" and "elite," as we have said before, are not synonymous, even though they both assume that "there only will be a few." The key question is: What is the *purpose* of this few? This leads to the second observation above.

b. *The Christian Minority Exists for the World Majority.* For the tradition of Jerusalem that Jesus so faithfully represents in these sayings, there can be no question here: the election of the few is a means for the salvation of the many. "And by you all the families of the earth will bless themselves" (the Abrahamic covenant, Gen. 12:2-3).

We should not be surprised, therefore, that the images contained in the Synoptic verses cited above without exception convey precisely that message. The salt is for the food; the light is for the darkness; the yeast is for the dough; the seed is for the growing of a bush large enough for the birds to nest in; the pearl is for the enhancement and concretization of beauty; and so forth and so on.

The principle being invoked through these images (to reduce all this to abstracts which may, in the end, be far more constricting than the images themselves!) is one that is steadfast throughout the length and breadth of this tradition: *through the particular to the universal.* Or, to state the same thing another way, *history is to be taken seriously.* Obviously enough, the God of this tradition wants to reach the whole creation, indeed to save "all" (a word which turns up again and again in that very literature, the Pauline, that develops most systematically the Newer Testamental version of the concept of election and the covenant). God's love is universal in its orientation—intended for creation in its entirety, and in the entirety of its existential distortedness. But God can communicate with "all" only through the medium of "some"—unless God would resort to an act of re-creation that would in effect annul existing creation. The universal judgment and love of God must pass through the experience and vocation of particular people.

Is it essential, then, that there should only be a few such people? Without being adamant on the subject, we may nevertheless answer: Probably. At least, this same tradition is obviously very wary of majorities, especially powerful majorities. There are always empires *on the edge of Israel's existence,* and Israel itself, in the persons of some of its more ambitious kings, is tempted by the imperial dream—a fact that undoubtedly lies behind the prophetic critique of the whole concept of kingship. But Israel is prevented from achieving anything remotely resembling an imperial status—and there can be no doubt that its *God* has a hand in this! Even though Israel, with its wisdom, its self-knowledge, its organizational genius, its traditions of justice, its respect for the "stranger," and so on, certainly *deserves* the imperial status more than the mostly barbarian peoples that achieved it, it is prevented from realizing such an ambition. That way is barred—and not only by the greater nations round about. Why?

Because there is a prophetic wisdom at work here that recognizes very well *the temptations of power*. There are things that majorities cannot and will not do and never have done. One of those things is that such majorities will not be vigilant against the oppression of minorities—will indeed *create* and *maintain* minorities, for their majority status is dependent upon that. Even at the level of *justice*, then, majorities cannot be trusted; and when it comes to *love*, the prospect of majorities being used in *that* service is beyond contemplation. Empires do not love. Perhaps nations cannot, either, and that is a thought entertained not only by Jesus and the Christians but already by the prophets of Israel itself. It is, by Jesus' own summing-up, precisely divine love (*agape*) that must be entrusted to human representation, and therefore it may well be that "there will only be a few." This, however, should not lead to mathematics!—as it does far too frequently with the guardians of the doctrine of election. The concentration here is not upon the messengers but upon the message. It is the quality of the message that has to be considered, not the quantity of the messengers.

c. *The Tentativeness of the Church.* The last sentence is illustrated beyond my powers by Jesus' own words about salt and light: "But if the salt has lost its taste, how shall its saltness be restored? It is no longer good for anything except to be thrown out and trodden under foot by men." Again: "Nor do men light a lamp and put it under a bushel, but on a stand . . ."

There is an assumption here that we have met before (for example, in connection with 1 Corinthians 10 and the question of presumption): not only is "the people of God" for Jesus a minority concept, a people called out and apart, not only is it "there" for the world from which it is distinguished by its message, but if it loses touch with that message, as it may in fact do, it is no longer significant in the economy of God.

The ministry of the church is a public ministry. We have said from the outset that the Gnostic temptation to privacy and ghettoization is anathema to this tradition. The *evangel* with which this community is entrusted is intended for "the world." To that end, as we saw in considering the mark of "apostolicity," the disciple community is "sent out." But it is sent out with a gospel that it has not learned from the world to which it is sent. To hear that gospel, it has had to be separated from the world, and to sustain its hearing of that gospel—a contextual gospel, about a love that is "new every morning"—it has *continually* to be called out, distinguished from the majority. Only so will it have salty salt; only so will its light be real and not ersatz light. To repeat, with high-sounding theological accents, the "plastic words" (Uwe Pörksen) that it has learned from its world will by no means prevent the church from being insipid.[9]

Here we have come to the core of the whole discussion of this relation. The recognition of the original disciple community concerning its distinction from the rest of society, a recognition that is perhaps beginning once more to dawn upon the church at the end of the Constantinian era, is a consequence and aspect of a more significant recognition and reality: namely, that the message it has to proclaim is a *different message*. The distinction is not to be located in the church itself, that is, in these people, with their various peculiarities and propensities, their talents for this and that, their insights and crafts and capacities. They are for all intents and purposes no different from anyone else—with the possible exception of the fact that they may have begun to realize something of the distance between what they are and what they are called to be. When the case for "distinction" between church and society is based on the *church's* difference from the rest of society, it is a pathetic case, whatever it turns out to be. What distinguishes the church from the world of which it is a part is that it has heard, is hearing, and hopes to hear a Word that comes from *beyond* this world but is intended precisely *for* this world and will make all the difference to it. This Word alone makes the church distinct from society, and when adherence to this Word is lost there is no longer any distinction at all. The salt has become insipid, the light is hidden under a bushel.

The theo-logic of these three observations needs to be taken very seriously by churches (our own) that are being denied their ancient majority status vis-à-vis their "host society." . . . [I]t is quite possible that their emergent *minority* status is opening to them a possibility they have scarcely if ever known heretofore. But this will only occur if they become infinitely more concerned to hear that Word than they have been throughout most of their history. That Word, if it is heard, will carry them, *in spirit*, farther away from their "host societies" than they have ever been (John 21:18). But, conversely, it will send them back into their same societies, *in the flesh*, in ways they have seldom undergone.

Notes

1. In the United States (and similar observations could be made about Canada), from the 1830s onward, "a unique situation developed. The distinction of church and sect disappeared. The church had commonly been established, the sect disestablished, but now all religious groups in the

United States were disestablished. Hence, from this point on, the American churches are commonly called not sects, but denominations. Again, the sect has frequently been dissociated from the culture, but the denominations in this country have created the culture. The Congregationalists did so in New England, the Anglicans in Virginia and the Carolinas, the Methodists in the Middle West, the Baptists in the South, the Lutherans in the central North, and the Catholics around the Great Lakes and in the old Spanish areas of the South." Roland Bainton, *Christendom: A Short History of Christianity and Its Impact on Western Civilization*, vol. 2 (New York: Harper & Row, 1966), 165–66.

2. They are: (1) the verbal inerrancy of Scripture; (2) the divinity of Jesus Christ; (3) the virgin birth; (4) a substitutionary theory of the atonement; and (5) the physical resurrection and bodily return of Christ.

3. Eugene C. Bianchi and Rosemary Radford Ruether, *A Democratic Catholic Church: The Reconstruction of Roman Catholicism* (New York: Crossroad, 1992), 115.

4. Christopher Morse, in his recent *A Dogmatics of Christian Disbelief* (Valley Forge, PA: Trinity Press International, 1994), 314–15, lists twenty-two misconceptions of the church.

5. Most notoriously, the Donatists of the fourth century, in the name of "holiness," wanted the church closed against all who had in any way apostatized during the persecutions, or even persons who communicated with traitors ('betrayers'). The statement of Augustine to which reference is made several times in this series ("Many who seem to be without are in reality within, and many who seem to be within yet really are without," from *De baptismo*, v. 38) was inspired by his opposition to the Donatist position.

6. Concerning the attempts of Anglican bishops from England to import to northern Canada the regulations they learned in the motherland, a witty Canadian clergyman, the late Ray McCleary, remarked in the presence of Reinhold Niebuhr: "Their gaiters did not go well with moccasins."

7. See their discussion "The New Voluntarism" in Wade Clark Roof and William McKinney, *American Mainline Religion: Its Changing Shape and Future* (New Brunswick, NJ: Rutgers University Press, 1987), 40ff.

8. See Lewis S. Mudge, *The Sense of a People: Toward a Church for the Human Future* (Philadelphia: Trinity Press International, 1992), 210.

9. "If the Christ and culture issue is not raised, then the gospel has become domesticated. There is no sense of distance between the church and its environment, no friction between what is and what might be that ignites the passions of repentance and transformation, no transcendent vision that illumines the dark places of the present while projecting a splendor yet to be. In other words, the gospel is betrayed and the church is boring" (Jack Stotts, *Insights* [Fall 1993]: 4–5). See also Wolfhart Pannenberg, *Christian Spirituality* [Philadelphia: Westminster, 1983], ch. 4, "The Absence of God in Theological Perspective," 71–92).

14

The Object of Disestablishment: Mission and Service

A primary message to the churches in much of Hall's work from the beginning has been: "Disestablish yourselves!" Hall is not alone in expressing this imperative, of course, but few have gone the extra step of answering the essential question, Why? To what end? Or, as he writes, "What then is the mission of a church that can no longer count on its favored status in Western civilization to ensure its meaning and its continued existence?," to which he answers, "(a) to begin at last to recognize the radical incompatibility of Christian establishment with the biblical and best traditional conceptions of the Christian movement, and (b) to explore the possibilities of Christian witness and service from a position outside or on the edge of the dominant culture." Put more bluntly, he says, "The greatest dangers to human welfare in today's global village are all of them products of, or backed by, religions driven by immodest claims to ultimacy. A Christianity that still hankers after Christendom . . . can only increase the reign of death that is tearing our planet apart."[1] This excerpt from Confessing the Faith explores this issue of mission more closely.

Source: Hall 1996:248–56.

. . . To what end are Christians asked to disentangle their movement and message from the cultures with which they have been identified? What purpose is served by the deliberate disengagement of the Christian faith from the values and pursuits of the dominant culture in North America? Why would anyone feel that the message of the divine Spirit to the churches in our field of concern is to disestablish themselves, rather than waiting to be disestablished, further "sidelined"? After all, any such deliberate dissociation must prove, in practice, a painful thing. Like any divorce, Christian efforts to define the church *over against* the culture will inevitably introduce disquiet and tension into what has been, all things considered, a rather comfortable if on the whole innocuous relationship.

Why, then, should it be undertaken at all? Could one not just let the matter be, assuming that it will happen in the future, as it has in the past, that here and there, in spite of everything, a few individuals will make their tortuous way through all the bric-a-brac and tinsel of the Christian religion to the gospel that originally inspired it?

This is the first temptation, and it is an insidious one. For most of us who get so far as to entertain such thoughts know that breakthroughs of that nature do occur; that for all its falseness, Christendom has always been the bearer of treasures that transcended its sins. Besides, we are reasonable people, not fond of conflict, craving acceptance and by no means wholly disinterested in the progress of our own careers! There is not a preacher alive who would not prefer to hear approving comments after his or her sermons, rather than being told Sunday after Sunday that the sermon was disturbing—or even "thought-provoking."

An allusion to the sermon in this connection is not incidental, for if the task of disestablishment is one of theology, then, given the character and program of most congregations, the sermon will have to be one of the primary occasions for the implementation of such a task. Similar necessities, however, are laid upon other lay and clerical officers who have responsibility for shaping the future of the churches. And in all of us the temptation to hesitate, to wait, to carry on in the usual way—in short, inertia—is strong. In all honesty, we must face the probability that one of the main reasons that the task of disestablishment has been so long delayed is that human beings such as ourselves are always sorely tempted to refrain from instituting any significant changes in the status quo until there is no other alternative—that is, usually, until it is too late.

Here again, however, Rahner's "must" confronts us. The Spirit of God may be resisted, and regularly is. But there is also something called irresistible grace, and not infrequently it takes the form of the niggling awareness that not to act may be to miss the one real opportunity for "doing the truth" that shall ever come one's way.

Those who overcome the temptation to passivity are sometimes confronted by a second and greater temptation. This is to undertake the task of disestablishment with a vengeance, relishing this exercise in "rightly dividing the word of truth" (2 Tim. 2:15, kjv), enjoying "the judgment [that] begins at the household of God" (1 Peter 4:17), perhaps even taking pride, secretly, in one's own purity, thinking oneself God's scourge, almost another Christ, throwing out the tax collectors and corrupters of the temple.

This response is not as infrequent as may be thought. There is a palpable anger against the churches today. It is conspicuous in society at large, highlighted by court cases and lawsuits amounting to millions of dollars in many denominations. But it is also present within the churches, where it is often hard to distinguish personal hurt from legitimate complaints about institutional injustices. In addition, there are many whose depth and sincerity of Christian conviction engender in them a terrible impatience with "bourgeois Christianity." They can only castigate or dismiss false Christendom. Such an attitude is easily mistaken for enthusiastic participation in "the task of disestablishment." But all it accomplishes, usually, is the alienation of the self-appointed judges from those in relation to whom a more compassionate witness to *God's* judgment could have made a difference.

A third temptation, the most subtle of all, is a refinement of the second. Perhaps it could be described as an objectification of the latter, an exercise whereby subjective distaste for empirical Christianity is qualified by reputedly objective theory—by theology! One may have recourse to the Reformation's concept of the church invisible, for instance. Or one may want to turn to the prophets, who "hate and despise your feasts and take no delight in your solemn assemblies" (Amos 5:21). With a little scriptural and doctrinal knowledge, this temptation can seem the very command of God.

What I am referring to is, of course, the approach that understands the disestablishment of Christianity from Christendom as an end in itself: pure Christian faith must be separated from the chaff and dross of religious history. "Come out from among them, and be ye separate, saith the Lord." (2 Cor. 6:17, KJV). "What has Jerusalem to do with Athens?" (Tertullian). God is *totaliter aliter* ("wholly other") (R. Otto, K. Barth). If American culture, this strange combination of personal charm and imperial aggressiveness, has contorted the image of the Christ, giving him the aura of a figure out of Disneyland, or the Pentagon, or both, then "Christ and culture" (H. R. Niebuhr) must be decisively separated. The political implications of the religious clause of the First Amendment must be supplemented, from the side of faith, by theological implications: Jesus Christ has nothing in common with "the American way"; Jerusalem has nothing to do with Washington, Hollywood, or the countless "theme parks" devoted to "Christian America." The purpose of disestablishment is simply—to disestablish! What has been falsely joined together must be parted without sentimentality or regret.

This is the great temptation of serious faith in our social setting today, and it is not to be attributed lightly to self-righteousness on the part of those who succumb to it. Whoever considers deeply the culpability of *Christians* in our context—their active or passive embrace of economic policies that oppress the two-thirds; their acquiescence to racism, sexism, and bigotry of many types; their silence and conformity in relation to consumerism; the exploitation of the natural environment; the destruction of species and natural processes; and so on—whoever contemplates earnestly even Christian sins of omission, to say nothing of our positive compliance with the whole course of First World greed, may well be driven to the conclusion that Christendom as such is beyond redemption; that the only possible course of action is to shake the dust off one's sandals, take leave of the moral Sodom and Gomorrah that our civilization has become, and seek among the misfits and victims of our society, here or abroad, the true church. In short, disengaging itself from a corrupt and perhaps damned culture, its alleged "Christianity" included, is itself the only justification needed for the act.

Biblical as well as historical precedent may without difficulty be found for such a position. Are not many of the words attributed to Jesus himself reminiscent of it? And in every age there have been Christians who have followed that path: the stricter monastics, the Donatists, the Cathari, Savonarola, some among those whom Luther called the "*Schwärmer*" (enthusiasts), holiness sects in our own time. Perhaps ironically, as the formerly sectarian, pietistic, and Bible-Christian separatists move toward greater identity with the dominant classes and structures of authority (the aforementioned Christian Right), not a few within the once-mainline churches are experiencing such estrangement from those classes and structures that they are increasingly attracted to separatist postures vis-à-vis their former hosts. Did not even Rahner speak of the "sect" quality of the diaspora church?

Understandable as this may be, I do not think that it is biblically or theologically defensible. As an exercise in *strategic* theology, that is, as an interim measure geared to equipping the *koinonia* for more faithful discipleship, it may be both justifiable and, in some situations, necessary. But the danger is nevertheless always present in such an approach that it will so absolutize the command of Christ not to be "of" this world that it will cease to hear his equally absolute command to "go into" the world—a command which, as we have seen, decisively qualifies the first, for it is nothing less than the inner aim (*telos*) of the command to "come apart and be separate."

There is only one legitimate rationale for the task of disestablishment, and that is to enable a new and different *kind* of relationship with those persons, classes, and institutions from whom and from which some kind of independence of identity is sought. As I have put it elsewhere: the purpose of disengaging the disciple community from its host culture is nothing more—and nothing less!—than to reengage that same culture.

Let me emphasize: *that same culture.* It is no doubt a great temptation for those who have been smitten by the gospel and by the often abysmal differences between the beliefs and lifestyles to which Christ calls us and the pursuits of white middle-class North Americans—a temptation to look upon one's own people as the enemy. I intend to question in this connection no one's ministry; yet precisely because many of the most clear-thinking and committed Christians in our context have in fact or in effect abandoned their own white middle-class culture and its historic cults, the process of the latter's decline has been denied the benefits of the kinds of purposing that it might otherwise have received. This is even more noticeable among professional theologians than where clergy and active laity are concerned. Those among our middle-class professionals who have not wished to be detached academicians and "religionists" have often turned to liberation theologies of the Third World, or concentrated their attentions on minorities within our own society, rather than engaging in the steady, difficult work of attempting to bring about in our dominant culture and its Christian expressions a metanoia of spirit and mind that might, in the end, make a far greater difference also where "the victims" are concerned.

This certainly does not imply that ministry among the poor, marginalized, and oppressed is invalid when it is taken up by white middle-class Americans or Canadians. Such an idea would be patently absurd. What I lament is the fact that so many of those most equipped by their personal background, training, and faith to minister to the culture and *cultus* that has reared them have failed to concentrate their insights and energies on the "conversion" ([Peter] Berger) of that same element. It is not that all whom I have in mind have abandoned that context physically. Removal to other parts of the world applies only to a minority, and in most cases, in my experience at least, these persons seem genuinely called to such mission and service abroad. But there is a way of abandoning the whole by concentrating on this or that part of the whole—taking up this or that cause, identifying with this or that particular interest group and, in the process, often not only failing to keep the larger society and church in mind, but coming to perceive it as "the problem," or as being insensible of judgment and inured to change.

Too many promising seminary graduates leave academia with the impression that they have become utterly different from the people who nurtured them. They are ready to repeat Isaiah's complaint that he dwells in the midst of "a people of unclean lips," but not his acknowledgment that he is himself one of them (Isa. 6:5). Too many clergy mount their pulpits quietly believing that the people they are about to address are incapable of sharing their profound critical insights—and believing, too, that the people are unaware of this attitude in their preacher! Too many pastors, having failed to learn the distinction between the *skandalon* of the gospel and "false scandals," imagine that they have struck the very core of the gospel's offense when their congregations object to their uncompromising use of inclusive language or take umbrage over their sexual preferences and moral conduct. It seems to many Christian professionals, who have got hold of the latest disavowal of some central Christian doctrine or symbol, that their very vocation in the church is to shock and ostracize every middle-aged male, every conventional housewife, every entrepreneur; and to uncover the latent homophobia, racism, sexism, and so forth that is allegedly rife in the whole waspish institution (wasps being the only remaining group who may be scorned publicly). A certain disappointment is to be noted in some clerical circles when evidence of middle-class generosity and compassion is brought forward. In view of the almost universal denigration of "typical" North American Protestantism that is found in the theological works most widely read by seminarians, it is perhaps no wonder that such attitudes are as prevalent as they are. Educationally, the great disservice that has been done by liberationism, especially when it is taken up by the relatively affluent, is that in its necessary concentration upon the plight of victimized peoples and groups, it has left the impression that the only thing to be said about the nonvictims is that they are victimizers. I do not take this to be a fault of the theologians of liberation, especially those working in "developing" world contexts; it is the fault rather of the educators and the educated in our own context who are naïvely prepared to leave the whole task of theology to those who represent oppressed minorities. So long as that particular context called "dominant culture," or "middle-class Protestantism," or "wasp," or whatever else it may be named is left out of the theological spectrum; so long as the only "interesting" theology, biblical interpretation, ethics, and practical theology is done by persons outside or inside that context who view it only from the vantage-point of its more blatant sins (which are many!), we shall continue to produce clergy and teachers of the faith who are so conditioned to disdain their congregations that their only function will be to participate in the "deconstruction" of the church as an end in itself.

By comparison with the theological literature and pedagogical influences that have dominated the professional Christian ethos in North America since approximately the mid-1970s, much of the earlier theological work of this century, including many now almost forgotten works of the 1960s and early 1970s, managed to combine deconstruction with creative reconstruction, and to do so in relation to the churches of "the dominant culture." None of this theology was easy on the churches. Neo-orthodoxy, a misnomer (as we have seen) for a movement whose aim is hardly to be confused with the desire to rekindle in Christians a passion for "orthodoxy," was at least as critical of the ecclesiastical endorsement of capitalism and the class system as liberation theology—and often more contextually relevant. All of the major exponents of that movement were accused of socialism—and they were socialists! Drawing upon biblical criteria, the "neo-orthodox" confronted conventional Christianity with the discrepancy between the Bible's radical conceptions of sin and salvation and the church's bland reductions of both. Although its leading representatives may all be criticized for having failed to develop feminist, ecological, racial, interfaith, and other themes that have since become mandatory, they all (in their responses to war, Stalinism, technology, anti-Judaism, and countless other issues of their epoch) demonstrated very concretely the necessity for what has since been named "contextuality" in theology, and for a *praxis* that was by no means all theory.

And they called the churches to account for their failure to do so. The theological memory of the churches, including their academic "wing," is extremely short. Each generation of scholars also manifests a certain, no doubt human need to chastise its forerunners for their omissions and shortcomings. But even in many areas in which they are currently accused of failure and myopia the major theological voices of the first part of this century were hardly as neglectful as a later generation [preferring to pass along unexamined stereotypes of past schools of thought instead of reading original works] makes them out to be.

For instance, Karl Barth's creation theology still has much to teach the ecologically minded theologians of today, and Tillich's conception of "the spiritual community" may be the most fruitful background for those who are newly conscious of religious pluralism. As for feminism, it is unfortunate that many of the women who were actually working alongside men in the World Council of Churches and elsewhere (to name only a few, Suzanne de Dietrich, Olive Wyon, Ellen Flessemann-van Leer, Ursula Niebuhr, Hulda Niebuhr, Charlotte von Kirschbaum, Marie-Jeanne Coleman, and Dorothy Sayers) seem to have been forgotten or categorized as compliant and lacking in gender-consciousness. In most areas of human concern, the theological community of the period between World War I and 1960 could be regarded, in fact, as setting a high example for the humanization of private and public life. Moreover, the example was felt within the churches because, while it was critical of them in ways that might astonish even the more disdainful of ecclesiastical life today, this community demonstrated a remarkable and consistent sense of responsibility toward the churches, as the very existence of the World Council of Churches testifies.

More lamentable than neglect or ideological caricaturing of the earlier theologians whose impact and literary output guarantees that they are not wholly forgotten even when they are seldom carefully read, is the fate of the Christian writers of the period from 1960 to c. 1975. These persons, of whom many were Americans (William Stringfellow, Stephen Rose, Gibson Winters, Bill Webber, Don Benedict, Harvey Cox, Joseph Haroutunian, Joseph Sittler, Peter Berger, Hans Hoekendijk, Albert van den Heuvel, and Paul Lehmann, to name only a few) were in almost every instance particularly concerned about the doctrine and life of the church. They wrote excellent and often poignant ecclesiological studies and tracts that combined biblical, doctrinal, and sociological-practical perspectives and insights in a way that is exceptionally rare today, when a more specialized approach has come to dominate the literature that actually reaches the churches—one, namely, that is particularly weak both biblically and theologically. Like their teachers and forebears, with whom they often quarreled but from whom they had learned much,[2] they made the churches their special focus—not chauvinistically, because they had the kinds of concrete concerns for society that demanded more of the churches than they were giving—but expecting the churches, nevertheless, to be capable of change.

Why has this work been neglected—some of it forgotten? The short answer is that it was displaced by the dramatic, media-catching movements the theology of the "death of God," of liberation, black theology, feminist theology. But there is no reason it could not have been combined with most of these movements (as it was in Martin Luther King Jr., for example) to produce a more holistic theology than any of them by themselves could possibly achieve. Surely the deeper reasons for the neglect of this earlier and truly contextual work have to do with (a) the unwillingness of North American churches and their leadership[3] during the same period to subject themselves to so explicit a critique, and (b) the abandonment of the churches by academic theology, much of it newly admitted into the universities and colleges, which could live its own life apart from the churches by fixing its attention upon issues that, despite their seeming concreteness, were in many cases more adaptable to abstraction than were the concerns of the earlier authors.

Be that as it may, the body of literature produced between 1960 and approximately 1975, much of it dealing with the *problématique* of the Christian movement at the beginnings of its contemporary North American awareness of the metamorphosis we have discussed here, really did set the tone for reforming the church along the lines of a new appreciation of its mission and worldly service. It knew that Christendom was ending and that Christianity could only emerge out of the ashes of that form of the church through much painful purgation. But it did believe that Christianity could emerge out of those ashes, and therefore it took very seriously the existing ecclesiastical structures.

Peter Berger, although perhaps more articulate than some because of his expertise in both theology and sociology, is nevertheless representative of much of this literature. For that reason I have devoted considerable attention to his *The Noise of Solemn Assemblies*. And while . . . his analysis naturally dates itself at some points, its basic challenge seems to me still entirely relevant.

Nowhere is its relevance more pertinent than in connection with the present subject, the "why?" of the task of disestablishment. I have expressed my own answer to that question in the formula: disengage in order to reengage. Berger, using the language of freedom that he may have learned from the school of Barth and Ellul, makes essentially the same point:

What is required in our situation is a new sense of the freedom of the Church. A free Church does not mean a community that is radically detached from culture, a sort of un-American enclave living on the margins of society. But a free Church *will* mean a measure of disestablishment. In relating to the culture, a free Church will pick and choose. Neither its affirmations nor its denial of cultural values will be absolute. In such an attitude of freedom, the Christian community *can then engage itself with the social dynamics of the rapidly changing American situation.* Such social engagement may not lead to dramatic changes in the nature of society. But it will mean a change *from the passive to the active mood in the churches' relationships with the society.* In the measure that this happens, the functionality of the religious institution previously analyzed will be damaged. As, indeed, it should be from the viewpoint of Christian faith.[4]

Or again:

As Christians free themselves from the bondage of the as taken-for-granted religious establishment, they become free to engage society at all of its local points. *Disestablishment is the very opposite of a retreat into a Christian ghetto.* It is rather the presupposition to a fully contemporary and fully conscious Christian mission in modern society.[5]

The parallels with what I have written both here and elsewhere will be obvious.

Notes

1. Douglas John Hall, "Cross and Context: How My Mind Has Changed," The Christian Century 127, no. 18 (September 7, 2010), http://www.christiancentury.org/article/2010-08/cross-and-context.

2. For example, in his *God's Revolution and Man's Responsibility* (Valley Forge, PA: Judson, 1965), 10, Harvey Cox writes, "We all stand today in the shadow of Karl Barth. That is why there is such an emphasis in this book on man's responsibility responding to God's holy initiative."

3. It should be noted that this period (1960–1975) was also the era during which, following the corporate model, head-office church bureaucracies began to expand exponentially and the "secretariats" of the denominations began to assume leadership, filling the vacuum of leadership on the part of the courts of the churches.

4. Peter Berger, *The Noise of Solemn Assemblies: Christian Commitment and the Religious Establishment in America* (Garden City, NY: Doubleday, 1961), 138–39. (My italics.)

5. Ibid., 157. (My italics.)

15

The Ethic of Resistance and the Ethic of Responsibility

Hall asserts, following his early theological influence, Karl Barth, that Christian theology and Christian ethics are inseparable. The reason for this is at least twofold: contextual and missional. First, as he writes in Thinking the Faith, "The split between theology and ethics is not only a false one, but one which has contributed much to the reputation for timelessness earned by a doctrine-centered theology that did not speak both from and to its historical context" (1989:75). Second, writing in Professing the Faith, he says, "While it is our ethic that most conspicuously is being tested for its adequacy in the 'postmodern' world, it is in reality our theology—as the foundation of that ethic—that is being weighed in the balance" (1993:17). Here, in this excerpt from Confessing the Faith, Hall suggests what this contextual, missional ethic might look like—a vision that mirrors the purpose of disestablishment described in the previous chapter.

Source: Hall 1996:332–40.

RECOVERING THE PROTEST IN PROTESTANTISM

. . . Christian theology when it is true to its biblical and best historical traditions, is already ethics. . . . There are, however, certain explicitly ethical directives in our Protestant heritage that ought to inform the Christian life as the disciple community takes leave of its establishment status and moves into a diaspora situation that is bound to seem strange and produce in most of us a sense of confusion and loneliness.

Without pretending to exhaust the possibilities, the two ethical directives I wish to develop in this connection could be understood as principles or guidelines for an attitude and posture of the disciple community in diaspora vis-à-vis its host culture. As such, they stand in a certain dialectical

227

relation—therefore a certain tension—with one another, chastening one another so to speak, while at the same time informing one another. As the [title above] indicates, the two principles are, first, the belief that, in relation to the pursuits of the classes and forces that chiefly determine our social context, it will be necessary for the disciple community in its disestablished state to draw upon the prophetic tradition of resistance; second, that as the bearer of a gospel that is grounded in God's "suffering love" (*agape*) for this world, the disciple community is obliged to develop an ethic of public responsibility as the undergirding rationale of its resistance.

We consider first the ethic of resistance.[1] Resistance ought to be a familiar theme to Protestants, and the fact that on the whole it not only indicates how very respectable Protestantism soon became, and remained. If the emphases in our pronunciation of the word were removed from the first syllable and placed on the second (Pro*test*ant), we would come closer to our origins; for the term was first used (at the Diet of Speyer, Germany, in 1529) to designate the minority of princes who were "against the proceedings of the emperor and the Catholic princes."[2] Unfortunately, about the only aspect of this heritage that remains in most Protestant circles is that the word "Protestant" has a distinctly anti-Catholic connotation; but while the original protest, as well as much subsequent activity on the part of Protestants, was directed against Rome, the significance of the nomenclature theologically has little to do with anti-Catholicism. As Wilhelm Pauck writes in *The Heritage of the Reformation*,

> Protestantism is a spiritual attitude, grounded in the living faith that God has made himself known in the person of Jesus of Nazareth and expressing itself ever anew in ways of life and thinking which reflect this faith as a proclamation of the glory of God transcending all human limitations and sufficiencies. *The Protestant spirit is a spirit of prophetic criticism. Its norm is the gospel of the God of love who liveth in a light no man can approach unto and yet is nearer to us than breathing, closer than hands or feet, and who has disclosed himself in Jesus who was born in a manger, had no place where to lay his head, and died on a cross.* No form can adequately express this content of the faith in revelation. No liturgical or ecclesiastical or theological form of this idea of revelation can be final.[3]

As Pauck's excellent summation indicates, Protestantism, historically and classically understood, implies an a priori polemic against all pretension to finality of doctrine and understanding; and just this is the reason that Paul Tillich spoke of "the Protestant principle" . . .

But Protestantism is not only a protest against doctrine put forward as final truth, it is also a protest against power masquerading as ultimate. In the name of the Ultimate, Protestantism resists the contingent, finite, and penultimate that pretends to ultimacy. The ethic of resistance has its foundation in this determination, which Pauck rightly links with the traditions of "prophetic criticism."

The voice of resistance has never quite been silent in the Christian church. Had it been consistently repressed, the very act of "confessing the faith" would have been practically impossible, for, as we have defined that act, it always entails the recognition and denunciation of that which threatens the life of God's beloved world. The dimension of resistance is therefore inherent in faith's confession. . . . [E]ven where the confession may appear harmless to the uninitiated ("Jesus Christ is Lord"), it implies a polemic ("ergo Caesar is not!"); and with some historic confessions, of which the Barmen Declaration . . . is one, the negating or critical or resisting aspect is made quite explicit: Jesus Christ is Lord, and therefore *der Führer* is not. Fortunately, the ethic of resistance, and therefore of the right, timely confession of the faith, have never been wholly suppressed or repressed. The diaspora of today and tomorrow may draw upon this critical history, much of it submerged, as in fact minorities throughout the universal church have been doing today.

But let us not imagine that the broad history of Christianity (including Protestant Christianity) in the world has been the history of a resistance movement. To the contrary! Resistance has been the way of minorities, whose critique was usually directed not only against secular and other agencies of power but against powerful Christendom itself. And the reason this has been the case is . . . that . . . religions seldom resist when the social office they have accepted is to legitimize and confirm, or (as Peter Berger said of American Christianity) to refrain from offering any alternative to, the status quo. That is, so long as Christianity functions as an establishment, whether in the legal or the cultural sense, it is inhibited by its own relationship with power from pursuing an ethic of resistance. Especially where power seems favorably disposed toward the Christian religion, as appears still the case with us in North America, the whole idea of resistance is one that most Christians, being also decent people and loyal citizens, find difficult if not abhorrent.

Just here we must register a nuance, or perhaps an irony. The very history of resistance that is part of the lore of Christendom—all the way from the acts of the early martyrs to the resistance against fascism in the 1930s and 1940s, and in more recent times against the police regimes of Central America, South Africa, South Korea, and elsewhere—functions to discourage resistance in the less "dramatic" situations that are more regularly the context of the Christian life, as is the case with us in North America today. We tell ourselves that the apostles, saints, and martyrs of the faith were living under conditions wholly intolerable to both faith and reason. In this way we help to convince ourselves that the conditions of our own context do not warrant any such protest, for, by comparison with the extremes of life under Nero, or "Bloody Mary," or Stalin, or the death squads of El Salvador, ours is a context of peace, tolerance, and humanity.

The resisting voices of our context, however, think otherwise. While we may not have the obvious evils of death camps and gulags and the strict censorship of literature, they would say, we belong to a system and a world that creates oppressive conditions for many both beyond and within the boundaries of our nations. The social, political, and cultural realities that we have to resist are certainly less obvious than those celebrated in the sacred history of resistance, but they may be even more insidious for all that. It does and will require greater subtlety, vigilance, and insight to detect them. And it does and will require, especially, concern for the victims who are not seen, some of whom may even appear to be well-off.

In all of the once-mainline denominations within the United States and Canada today, there are such protesting voices. Their protest cannot be ignored; for some reasons which I shall mention presently, it has achieved a remarkably sympathetic hearing within all of the churches concerned. But it is also rejected by many within these churches. There is a resistance against the resistance. It seems to many to be exaggerated, excessive.

This resistance of the resistance is the inevitable harvest of centuries of Christendom, augmented by the mythology of American innocence, decency, and good will. We should not be surprised if the resistance is resisted—that Protestants on the whole, through the elevation of their forms of Christendom to the position of established religion, have little sympathy for any sort of protest.

Nevertheless, the resistance has made a greater impact upon once-mainline Protestantism in these past two or three decades than could have been predicted in (say) 1950. With the breakdown of Christendom, the ethic of resistance becomes a live option for more and more of those who remain within these formerly most established of the denominations. As members of these denominations recognize their effective distancing from the source of power and policy-making, they are also grasped by a new sense of freedom: they may pursue avenues of thought and action that are significantly different from the opinions and pursuits of the majority. Realizing that they are no longer obliged to confirm the "conventional" morality, they are ready to explore ethical questions from the perspective of their own faith. It may be difficult to "swim against the stream." Most of those about whom we are thinking had or have little or no experience of real resistance. Unlike the experience of twentieth-century European Christians, there has been no dramatic history of resistance in the established churches of this continent, although the antinuclear protest, the civil rights movement, the sanctuary movement, and some more recent forms of resistance have influenced minorities in all of the churches. Still, for many who begin to feel the necessity and the possibility of the way of resistance, it seems an entirely new approach to the Christian life. In congregations in which this new way achieves a certain momentum, there are usually divisions.

As with the whole matter of our transition from Christendom to diaspora, there is also at present a serious lack of informed Christian leadership helping people to locate in the Scriptures and theological traditions of their faith a rationale for the ethic of resistance. Significant numbers of laypersons in our liberal and moderate denominations are prepared to engage in some kind of protest—for instance, against the growing power of a new kind of "conservatism" that celebrates individual initiative to the point of leaving the powerless to their own devices. But this readiness to resist is seldom sufficiently informed and empowered by Christian reflection. The result is that in the absence of such Christian tutelage the incipient resistance that informs many congregations today has to look for its rationale and for sheer encouragement to sources that are external to the faith. The Christian protest is thus caught up in other movements of resistance that, although they may share certain proximate goals with Christianity, also usually incorporate assumptions and strategies that are not compatible with Christian obedience. Thus the potentiality for developing a more genuinely confessional church through a thoughtful, disciplined discipleship remains unrealized.

We are again brought face to face with the priority of theology. For without any theological basis and corrective, that is to say, pursued as "an ethic" or "way of life" or "lifestyle," resistance may become as questionable an approach as conformity. It may become little more than conformity to the program of some countercultural ideology. But this leads to the second principle, which, in my view, may act as a corrective to that tendency.

DISCIPLESHIP AS WORLDLY RESPONSIBILITY

The posture of resistance must be held in tension with another aspect of the Christian life that will prevent Christians from abandoning the stance of confessor for that of ideologue. That other aspect is the worldly responsibility that discipleship of the Christ entails. Discipleship is not a program, a lifestyle, an agenda. Christians are disciples of *Jesus Christ*, therefore of one who lives, who commands, who is committed to the life of the world, and who for all these reasons refuses to be encased in any system or moral code or "theology of." Discipleship as worldly responsibility means obedience to the living Lord in the midst of a living, changing world; the ethic that belongs to this life is a thoroughly contextual ethic. What is required today may differ much from what is required tomorrow; what is commanded here may differ much from what is commanded there.

Certainly, in obedience to Jesus Christ, the disciple community may be called upon to resist, and we have seen that resistance, according to the Protestant faith and experience particularly, is a highly probable dimension of every faithful act of Christian confession. But Christian obedience is not to an ethic of resistance, it is to Jesus Christ.[4] "The Protestant principle" has also to be applied to the ethic of resistance!

For when protestation becomes a way of life, it is just as guilty of usurping the ultimacy of the Ultimate as any other system or code of behavior. The ethic of resistance becomes an ideology when the source and the object of resistance have been obscured by the style of resistance as such. Protest as a means has been transmuted to protest as an end in itself. The source of *Christian* resistance is a Christ who wills not that the sinner should die but that he should turn from his wickedness and live; not that the evil world should perish but that it should be transformed. In short, life and not death is the object of this resistance; therefore, although the threat to life has to be resisted, that which enhances and sustains life has at the same time to be supported, fostered, edified. Resistance of evil without reinforcement of the good is incomplete. It is because good is possible that evil must be resisted. Because of the possibility of justice, injustice must be named and stopped. Because of the possibility of peace, war and war preparations and the mentality of violence must be confronted and converted to a statecraft and mentality of peace. Because of the possibility of creaturely harmony, the disintegrating forces at work in the biosphere must be resisted and other ways found of sustaining and enriching life. Resistance of evil is for the sake of the good; and the good is not a theoretical good, but one that has been revealed, lived, and is always being concretized; a good that has "already" triumphed although it is "not yet" fulfilled.

The responsibility of the church as the disciple community of Jesus Christ is thus a broad and complex worldly stewardship that, in practice, is extremely difficult to exercise wisely and with integrity, yet prevents many of the excesses and dangers of "easier" versions of morality. While it assumes that Christians will be especially critical of "powers and principalities" that try to acquire worldly sovereignty, and vigilant for the victims of these powers, its resistance will be tempered by the recognition that both oppressors and oppressed are human beings; therefore it will attempt to avoid divisions of the world into camps of good and evil—divisions that, however appealing to the ideological spirit, are simplistic and unredemptive. And while it must be assumed that the disciple community will seek and find others with whom (through the recognition of "middle axioms," perhaps) it may make common cause, it will also recognize the variety of motivation and goal with which people band together for specific purposes, and it will continue to listen to, and depend for courage and sustenance upon, its own particular Source and sources of wisdom . . .

To exemplify the latter: Christians who participate in the universal *agape* of God in Christ will know today that "the world" for which they have responsibility includes the nonhuman creatures and the natural processes that are threatened by human folly and greed. They will therefore be impelled by divine love to cooperate with all who share this concern for "otherkind." They will enter into such covenants knowing, however, that as Christ's disciples they are not permitted to embrace outlooks and actions that reputedly "save" some species and natural processes by jeopardizing the future of others, including humanity. In other words, the holistic or integrated concern for *life* to which faith in Jesus Christ leads precludes the kind of specialized moral concentration that leads to myopic and exclusivist positions that in their preoccupation with parts no longer ask about the whole. As Rosemary Radford Ruether writes, "We need a much more nuanced perspective, one that can acknowledge that the sources of [the ecological] crisis are complex, not unilinear from one source [Gen. 1:28]. . . . What we do not need is the simple either-ors that write off entire cultures and groups of people as discardable, a way of thought that is all too obviously the reversed product of that same dualistic culture that feminists and deep ecologists deplore."[5]

The holistic nature of the "responsibility for history" (Bonhoeffer) that discipleship of Jesus Christ entails means that Christians will normally be denied the satisfaction of feeling that their actions have wholly succeeded—that the dilemmas to which they addressed themselves have been met and resolved. On the contrary, they will understand that the ultimate resolution of any specific dilemma will await the larger resolution of history as a whole—in short, they will know that resolution as such is an eschatological category. The resolution that history awaits is contained for Christians in the symbol of the divine reign or "kingdom." While approximations of the "peaceable kingdom" are possible in the midst of history, and therefore disciples of Christ *resist* what others think is inevitable, neither do they court utopian ideals that so often prove the most implacable tyrants in their attempts to impose perfection upon life. Life is movement, and the object of the disciple community is to move into the future with "the Lord and Giver of Life," doing what it can today to implement the promise of that future, and realizing that much will remain to be done tomorrow.

We are speaking about the Christian life, and what we have just observed about it is a reminder of an aspect of the theology of the cross that is also, with the rest of that "thin tradition," almost totally unheard of in the "established" situation of the church. It is that the Christian life is a "hidden" life.[6] "For you have died," writes the author of Colossians (3:3), "and your life is hidden with Christ in God." Far from being a clear-cut and transparent life that is dedicated to a recognizable program and mode of behavior ("the Christian Right," "the Left," fundamentalism, liberalism, and so on), the life of discipleship is one that may involve many different and even apparently incompatible approaches, and may bring one into the company of many different and sometimes strange combinations of persons and groups. While the ethic of resistance suggests a typical stance, attracts predictable supporters, and repels equally predictable critics, the ethic of responsibility bears about itself a certain unpredictability that may to some seem capricious and to others flexible. This is because it flows from discipleship. It follows and does not lead. It is content to obey, so far as understanding and volition allow, the One who shepherds it, and so to do what must be done "this day," and to trust that it will be used for good. It is a matter of faith and not of sight. "For *thine* is the Kingdom . . ."[7]

In the diaspora situation, where Christianity is no longer something altogether evident and predictable, the hiddenness of the Christian life that is part of our Reformation heritage will be newly meaningful. If Christianity is not a program; if it involves one in the world in an unprotected and unfamiliar way—the way of the sojourner; if verbal confession of the faith is meaningful only where it can presuppose solidarity with the world on its own terms, then we shall have to discover not only the traditions of the hidden God, the ubiquitous Christ, and the anonymous Christian, but also Luther's concomitant teaching concerning the "incognito" character of the Christian life itself. The strict lines of demarcation between Christian and non-Christian disappear in the post-Christendom situation. This is undoubtedly a confusing experience for those who have been conditioned by establishment forms of the faith—as we all have! But, in the concept of the hiddenness and anonymity of the Christian life, we may discover a way of absorbing this experience into a theology of discipleship that frees us for obedience.

In introducing this segment, I affirmed that the ethic of resistance and the ethic of responsibility qualify and correct one another. Each contains its temptation to which the other may apply itself. We have seen that the danger of the ethic of resistance is that it becomes under certain conditions a whole way of life with its own rationale and its own satisfactions. It needs to be constantly reminded that faith is not faith in a style of life or a posture vis-à-vis "the dominant culture," but faith in one who lives and moves within a living and changing world.

The danger of the ethic of worldly responsibility, on the other hand, is that it will devolve into a mystical attraction to the whole that fails to address itself to the parts—that it will become an abstract commitment to "life" that is apt to overlook the specific threats to life that must be resisted by any confession of faith.

In the tension between the two (which are, of course, not two separable ethical positions but two dimensions of the one covenantal relationship), the church that is edged out of its established relation with its host culture will work out a manner of existing vis-à-vis its "world" that is both critical and constructive . . . a mode of disengaging that enables meaningful reengagement.

Notes

1. See Ched Myers, *Binding the Strong Man: A Political Reading of Mark's Story of Jesus* (Maryknoll, NY: Orbis, 1988), "Resistance," 452f.

2. Owen Chadwick, *The Reformation* (Harmondsworth, UK: Penguin, 1964), 62.

3. Wilhelm Pauck, *The Heritage of the Reformation* (Glencoe, IL: Free Press/Boston: Beacon, 1950), 142f. (my italics).

4. "Christ is not a principle in accordance with which the whole world must be shaped. Christ is not the proclaimer of a system of what would be good today, here and at all times. Christ teaches no abstract ethics such as must at all costs be put into practice. . . . For indeed it is not written that God became an idea, a principle, a programme, a universally valid proposition or a law, but that God became man. This means that though the form of Christ certainly is and remains one and the same, yet it is willing to take form in the real man, that is to say, in quite different guises" (Dietrich Bonhoeffer, *Ethics*, ed. Eberhard Bethge, trans. Neville Horton Smith [London: SCM, 1955], 22).

5. Hall (with Ruether) 1995:86.

6. "God is a hidden God, faith is the evidence of things that do not appear, the life of the Christian is hidden. These three statements belong together in the most intimate way. One follows from the other. . . . Why is the life of the Christian a hidden one? Very simply because it is a life of

faith. . . . The Christian life is an object of faith and, as such, it is hidden. What we see is never the real thing; only God and faith see this innermost core" (Walther von Loewenich, *Luther's Theology of the Cross*, trans. Herbert J. A. Bouman [Belfast: Christian Journals Ltd., 1976], 114).

7. "In explaining the beginnings and the course of the Reformation to the people of Wittenberg after his return from exile in Wartburg castle, [Luther] said: 'All I have done is to further, preach, and teach God's word; otherwise I have done nothing. So it came about that while I slept or while I had a glass of beer with my friend Philip [Melanchthon] and with Amsdorf, the papacy was so weakened as it never was before by the action of any prince or emperor. I have done nothing; the word has done and accomplished everything. . . . I let the word do its work'" (Wilhelm Pauck, *From Luther to Tillich: The Reformers and Their Heirs* [San Francisco: Harper & Row, 1984], 9).

16

Stewards of the Mysteries of God
Preserving Classical Protestant Theology

Stewardship, the third of Hall's major concerns, was the focus of many of his books in the 1980s, most of which were published in partnership with the National Council of Churches in New York. Hall, drawing on the biblical images of the steward, worked in these books to retrieve the term from its distorted understanding and practice in the church in the thrall of Christendom. In so doing, he expanded its contemporary meaning from its monetary connotations and extended it to the entire mission of the disciple community, including care for creation, working for peace and justice, and nurturing life. In this closing chapter, excerpted from Bound and Free, Hall takes an apophatic approach to beckon Christians to embrace their vocations as theologians by taking seriously the call to be "stewards of the mysteries of God"—which entails doing the hard work of disciplined theological thought in this post-Christendom era.

Source: Hall 2005:106–21.

> *This is how one should regard us, as servants of Christ and stewards of the mysteries of God.*
> ——1 CORINTHIANS 4:1 RSV

The vocation to theology applies not only to individual theologians, but to the church as a community of theological discourse. In the United States and

Canada today, no work of corporate theology is more important than that of preserving the rightful heritage of Protestantism.

Protestantism—meaning classical Protestantism, the Protestantism that traces itself to the Reformation of the sixteenth century without being slavishly bound to its expressions half a millennium ago—as I see it is in trouble. One aspect of the trouble can be observed quantitatively, statistically. The [2004] *Encyclopedia of Protestantism* (a four-volume publication containing, by the way, no article on Protestant-inspired theology of stewardship) in its article "Statistics" presents a rather glowing account of the situation that can sound like a veritable success story with its heading "Protestants and Catholics Each Reach 1.5 Billion."[1] But when you examine the fine print, you can easily detect the flaw by which success stories quantitatively told are nearly always marred. The Protestantism that accounts for by far the greater share of this figure is what the encyclopedia calls "wider" Protestantism, as distinct from "core" Protestantism. This so-called wider Protestantism (we are informed) includes everybody who is not Roman Catholic or Eastern Orthodox but claims a Christian heritage. It includes, that is to say, a great deal of religious teaching and practice that has little or nothing to do with the Protestantism that came out of the sixteenth-century Reformation.

The great trouble in which classical Protestantism finds itself, however, cannot be glimpsed quantitatively, for it is a qualitative matter. Its problems are more conspicuous in developed societies like ours than in the newer churches of the Southern Hemisphere. Statistics can pinpoint some of its consequences, but they cannot get at the deeper matter of causation. For instance, it is common knowledge that conservative, biblicist, and fundamentalist forms of Christianity in North America have surpassed the growth and influence of the old "mainline" Protestant denominations. In the *Encyclopedia of Protestantism*'s article on Protestantism in Canada, which I find more honest than most such analyses, John G. Stackhouse concludes, "The general picture [at the turn of the century] was simply one of the increasing marginalization of Canadian Protestantism and of Christianity in general," even including the "relative success story of the evangelicals."[2]

Statistics will confirm that so-called true-believing forms of Protestantism have been particularly conspicuous in U.S.-American life, not least of all in the arena of politics, but they will not tell us what sort of Christianity this allegedly successful Protestantism is, nor why it appeals to a frightened public, nor how it stands vis-à-vis Protestant origins and the evolution of Protestantism. Nor will such analyses convey to us very much about the causes of the diminishment of the formerly most "established" churches in the United States and Canada. For instance, they will not help us understand the factors that have brought about our loss of nerve, our failure to educate our laity beyond the most rudimentary clichés of the tradition (if that), our assumption that we could carry on business as usual long after the whole Constantinian framework of our culture-religion had collapsed, and so forth. Statistics will not show how predictable it ought to have been decades ago that the automatic churchgoing of yesteryear would disappear as soon as the social structures and public moods that held it in place had been altered, as they were (vastly), nor how, in consequence, an alert Protestantism ought to have been working long ago to articulate for itself the "reason for the hope that is in us" (1 Peter 3:15 KJV).

In short, statistics will not demonstrate that the primary cause of the humiliation of classical Protestantism on this continent has been the failure of these old denominations to be "stewards of the mysteries of God" (1 Cor. 4:1) as those mysteries have been testified to in the traditions of the Reformation and its faithful interpretation in the best scholarship of the past four or five centuries.

Perhaps it is already too late to prevent the further erosion of the old Protestant churches on this continent. Frankly, as an ecumenical Christian who is quite prepared to spend his life in the multicultural and religiously pluralistic society that is our present social context, I am not overly anxious about the fate of specific denominations or even about the specific organizational form of a Christianity calling itself Protestant. But I am concerned that what the struggles of the Reformation produced by way of a better expression of biblical faith should not be lost to the world. And I am concerned that something might come to be and perhaps flourish that calls itself Protestant yet in essence has very little to do with that classical Protestant heritage and may in fact represent religious and moral assumptions antithetical to that heritage. I am concerned, too, that that heritage should not be reduced to the kind of traditional*ism* that is nothing but "the dead faith of the living." Stewarding the Protestant tradition means listening attentively to "the living faith of the dead" so that the present community of discipleship may find its way into the future.[3]

To do that, the community must always adapt the lessons it learns from the past to the realities of the present, many of which are entirely new and would not have been understood by the fathers and mothers of Protestant beginnings. Therefore, when I speak about "classical" Protestantism, I do not mean a Protestantism that is content simply to perpetuate the teachings of Martin Luther, John Calvin, Huldrych Zwingli, John Knox, and the others. Rather, I mean a Protestantism that has so absorbed those foundational traditions that it is able to deconstruct and reconstruct them in the light of the exigencies of the present and impending future.

It is no doubt foolhardy to attempt to name those foundational traditions; any such naming will involve a subjective element and leave many questions unanswered, particularly when it must be brief. Unless one risks such specificity, however, the entire subject will be left at the level of generalities and vague exhortations. So, comforted by the proverb that fools rush in where angels fear to tread (which has to be the motto of Christian theology done under the conditions of history), I shall take the risk of identifying what I regard as six paramount emphases of the Protestant tradition that we are called to steward. Each one of them, in typical Reformation fashion, is set over against temptations inhering in the principle under discussion—a temptation whose power is amply and perpetually demonstrated in the actual history of Protestantism.

CHRISTOCENTRISM (*CONTRA* CHRISTOMONISM)

The first principle of classical Protestantism that must be named is, of course, its being centered in Jesus, the Christ. Paul Tillich speaks as a true Protestant when he writes:

> Christianity is what it is through the affirmation that Jesus of Nazareth, who has been called "the Christ," is actually the Christ, namely, he who brings the new state of things, the New Being. Whenever the assertion that Jesus is the Christ is maintained, there is the Christian message; wherever this assertion is denied, the Christian message is not affirmed.[4]

The *per Christum solum* ("through Christ alone") of the Reformers precedes and gives the rationale for all their other priorities: *sola gratia, sola fide, sola Scriptura* (grace alone, faith alone, Scripture alone).

But this positive affirmation of the centrality of Jesus Christ in classical Protestantism must not be turned into a myopic spiritual singularity and exclusivity that rules out any concentration other than a formulary, doctrinaire Christology. The temptation inherent in Christianity's concentration on the Christ is the reduction of christo*centrism* to christo*monism*. And (according to H. Richard Niebuhr, for instance), that is precisely what North American Christianity has done. In defiance both of historic Christology and the doctrine of the Trinity, it has opted for a "divine" Christ whose humanity is strictly formal and, accordingly, for what Niebuhr called "unitarianism of the second person of the Trinity."[5] Perhaps the Reformers did not guard sufficiently against such a christomonistic distortion (which the late Dorothee Soelle in her

American sojourn remarked often becomes, in practice, christo-*fascism*). But subsequent Protestant experience has taught us that an exclusivist Christology leads inevitably to virulent supersessionism in relation to the parental faith of Judaism and (more recently) a total incapacity for dialogue with any other religious tradition.

The stewarding of God's mysteries here must mean guarding against this christomonistic displacement of the right and necessary Protestant emphasis on Jesus as the Christ.

THE PRIORITY OF GRACE (*CONTRA* VOLUNTARISM AND DETERMINISM)

Surely the second principle of classical Protestantism must be the priority of divine grace in human salvation. In a real way, this is where the Reformation began: with the rediscovery of the Pauline conception of justification, perhaps best expressed in Ephesians 2: "By grace you have been saved, through faith; and this is not your own doing, it is the gift of God—not because of works lest any[one] should boast" (vv. 8-9 RSV). Over against the tendency of religion, especially in its institutional expressions, to base belonging and acceptability on accomplishment, adherence to ritualized ecclesiastical practices, and "works" recognized by the authorities as "good," the Reformers insisted that God is the initiator and perfecter of our redemption. Even the act of faith itself is denied such priority, for faith must not be treated as a human work. The formula of the Reformation is not "justification by faith," as it is so often misleadingly stated, but "justification by grace through faith." This is a merciful doctrine, not only in its recognition of the graciousness of God, but also in its refusal to rank human worth on the basis of achievement. Justification theology has a leveling, democratizing effect in the church just for this reason.

But as history has regularly demonstrated, this principle, too, lives with inherent temptations. On the one hand, the emphasis on the sufficiency of divine grace tempts its champions to disregard human responsibility (on which all theology of stewardship rests). That, as Dietrich Bonhoeffer demonstrated in *The Cost of Discipleship*, is the temptation from the Lutheran side of the Reformation. On the other hand, the idea of divine sovereign grace too easily transmutes into a kind of religious determinism that is ready to attribute whatever happens, including human rejection of grace, to "the fore-ordaining will of God." This is the temptation from the Calvinist side. Both of these typical temptations stem from an apparent incapacity to hold together in creative tension the affirmation of God's grace and the recognition of human freedom and responsibility. That incapacity leads directly to a third important principle of classical Protestantism:

DIALECTICAL CHARACTER OF THEOLOGY
(CONTRA DOCTRINAL SIMPLISM)

Theology, in the classical Protestant mode, is a discipline of thought that is necessarily dialectical—ready to entertain polarities, ambiguities, paradoxes, including apparent opposites like prevenient grace and human freedom. Christian theology must do this for one very basic and unconditional reason: it deals with *living* realities—a living God, living creatures, lively and always changing relationships. The objects with which theology concerns itself are not objects but living subjects, and their interrelationships are complex and forever in flux. They do not stand still so that the theological observers can tabulate them once and for all. They do not lend themselves to definition in immutable propositional and dogmatic form. Karl Barth, who certainly cannot be accused of refraining from trying to be definitive theologically, stated both at the beginning and the ending of his long career that doing theology is like attempting to draw a picture of a bird in flight: the danger, almost the inevitability, is that one ends either with a bird permanently stuck in one position in an unchanging sky or else an unrecognizable oblong blur. I suppose one could say that "conservatism" courts the first danger and "liberalism" the second, but I am wary of using these categories at all.

This is why Protestant theology at its best has always had to be (as Barth also said) "modest"—indeed, "the most modest science"—and is constantly involved in self-criticism.[6] Theology can only point awkwardly toward the mystery of a livingness that it experiences but cannot contain. To do justice to this livingness, theology must resort to language that, especially to the modern scientific mind, seems imprecise and even inconsistent: the language of narrative, of poetry, of myth and symbol, the language of dialogue, in which every affirmation must be corrected by a qualification or counteraffirmation.

Thus, the vocation of theology in the Protestant mode has always been in a certain sense frustrating, for the human mind (including the mind of the theologian) wants finality. It wants fact, data, truth—and, by hook or by crook, it will get such, even at the expense of falsifying or ignoring the ongoingness and livingness of its subject. Moreover, in the contemporary scene, where the popular demand for finality is heightened by a pathological clamoring after *securitas* (security), this quest for certitude is vastly intensified. It is not surprising, then, that the most popular forms of Christianity on this security-obsessed continent and elsewhere today are those (most of them allegedly Protestant) that do not require continuous and profound contemplation of mystery but offer simple, immediate, and sloganized declarations of ultimate truth.

But nothing is more indicative of the plight of Protestantism in our time and place than the prevalence of just this "Protestant" simplism. The stewarding of God's mysteries (mysteries!) in such a context must mean struggling against this demand for the kind of finality that offers easy religious answers to difficult and unexamined human questions. *Life itself is not simple*, and a religion that accommodates itself to popular demand for unnuanced, undialectical, one-two-three assertions can appeal only to those who are comfortable enough physically and economically to be able to repress what they know very well to be true of life. Such persons may be very numerous in our "developed world" context; they may even be the majority. But a Protestantism that wants to win the whole world inevitably loses its own soul.

FAITH SEEKS UNDERSTANDING (*CONTRA* RATIONALISM AND IRRATIONALISM)

Classical Protestantism entertains an always-uneasy yet remarkably consistent mutuality between faith and reason. This, too, belongs to the dialectical thinking that characterizes this mode of theological thought. However, faith is not the consequence of human ratiocination. It is the human response to the revelation of the divine Presence; it is trust in the absence of clear evidence, what Paul calls "sight." I cannot bring about faith in myself or in others any more than I can bring about love. But if I find myself or another person yearning for something like faith, it is probable that the divine Instigator of faith is already at work.

However, once a person has entered into the faith relationship, the quest for understanding begins. And it is intense and relentless. *Fides quaerens intellectum*, declared Anselm of Canterbury: "faith seeks understanding." But the word *seeks* doesn't do justice to what is meant. Anselm's *quaerens* does not mean polite inquiry or having a mild interest in theology! Commenting on this phrase from Anselm's *Proslogion*, Karl Barth writes of "faith's voracious desire for understanding."[7] Faith, if it is really faith and not just spiritual froth, is *driven to* understanding—to the point that the absence of any quest for understanding must seem to this tradition to be evidence enough that faith isn't really present.

The stewarding of the Protestant tradition in this matter means maintaining a certain vigilance that the community of discipleship is not courting, on the one hand, a religious rationalism that reduces faith to a stained-glass intellectualism inaccessible to ordinary people or, on the other hand, a sentimental or apocalyptic irrationalism that settles for religious "feelings" and spiritual ecstasy. As Blaise Pascal once wrote, "If we submit everything to reason, our religion will have no mysterious and supernatural element. If we offend the principle of reason, our religion will be absurd and ridiculous."[8]

How multitudinous, where this principle is concerned, are the problems of Protestantism in our context! We could speak about the continuing allure of emotionalistic religion, ecstatic religion, spiritualism (including the spiritualism that has the name of being "new"). But before we attempt to clean up the houses of others, we should look to our own denominational houses. There we may find that the neglect of the pursuit of understanding indicates more about the demise of Protestantism than anything to be found in the realm of religious irrationalism—that and the equally damaging separation of academic theology from the ordinary discourse of congregations.[9]

It was not an incidental but a central affirmation and assumption of the Reformers that theology—the quest for understanding on the part of the faithful—is the work of the whole people of God. The Christian academy, whether of seminary or of university, exists for the sake of the church. "The true genius of Protestantism," wrote Ronald Goetz, "is to make extraordinary demands on very ordinary people."[10]

In North American Protestantism, because we have relied so heavily on our cultural form of establishment and because we have practiced great condescension toward the laity, we have made few demands of any kind upon church folk, least of all intellectual demands. It is not because the pews, or those potentially and actually present in them, are uninterested (though congregations are wonderfully adept at manifesting whatever is expected of them). Often, sitting in church during worship, I find myself irreverently thinking of John Milton's line from *Lycidas*: "The hungry sheep look up and are not fed." At a bare minimum, the stewarding of the mysteries of God must mean today and tomorrow a far greater effort on the part of clergy, "teaching elders," actually to teach. We are still—anachronistically!—pushing images of the minister as the CEO of the congregation, responsible for everything all the time, including the drumming up of enthusiasm for "stewardly" church giving, mostly a thankless task, since the whole exercise begs the question "Why?" The only answer to *that* question will be found—if it is found at all—in sermons and classes and study groups that are so seriously considered and worked upon that they can sometimes illumine the soul.

THE BIBLE (*CONTRA* BIBLICISM AND BIBLE ILLITERACY)

The *sola Scriptura* of the Reformation never meant that no other work of Christian tradition should have any importance for Protestantism, but it did and does mean that the canonical scriptures of the Older and Newer Testaments have priority. "Abandon scripture," warns Luther, "and God abandons us to the lies of human beings."[11] *In theory*, Protestantism everywhere, "core" and "wider" alike, makes the Bible central to the life of the church. But the nature of that centrality differs greatly in classical Protestantism from those forms of Protestantism that make the most noise about the Bible today. So-called biblical literalism—which is typically not a literalism of the biblical text but of certain doctrinal and moral presuppositions searched for (and, of course, regularly found) in the biblical text—is in fact antithetical to the kind of attention to the Bible that the main Reformers taught. Calvinism, to be sure, has frequently been the godparent of biblical literalism, but Calvin himself, the French Reformer schooled (as were Zwingli and Philipp Melanchthon) in humanism, would certainly never approve the kind of literalism that disdains critical interpretation of the text, especially of texts that are themselves only translations of original texts.

As for the approach Martin Luther took to Scripture, I suspect that it is scarcely known in most of our Protestant churches, even Lutheran ones, for it is a highly complex—indeed, wonderfully dialectical—approach and therefore goes counter to the kind of simplism to which I have already referred. On the one hand, Luther's theological method is extraordinarily informed by Scripture—and concretely, not merely theoretically so. On the other hand, Luther manifests an astonishing freedom with respect to the Bible. He is not above dismissing whole sections of it. For he is a master of a *contextually* sensitive exegesis (Barth might have called it "pneumatic" interpretation). Such an interpretation is conscious not only of the biblical testimony itself but of the present contextual realities, the *zeitgeist*, the pressing human questions that are brought to the contemplation of the text by anyone who is going to it under the impact of existential need. The authority of Scripture, for Luther, is its capacity to let us hear the *living* Word that always transcends without dismissing the written word. That is, through "the letter" we listen for "the spirit"—the deepest meaning—of the text for us, which surpasses yet never despises the biblical words.[12]

I have come to think that Luther's understanding of the Bible's role is the most important one for us to discern and emulate today—partly because, like so much of Luther's thought, it is so little known in the Anglo-Saxon Christian world. Yet all the Reformers have things to teach us still on this subject. Generalizing, it seems entirely clear that no major voice of the Reformation that gave Protestantism its start could condone either the biblical illiteracy of bourgeois Protestant liberalism *or* the biblicism of Christian conservatism. And that, I would say, is a very charitable way of stating the matter!

The stewardship of the mysteries of God, as these are vouchsafed to us in classical Protestantism, therefore requires enormous efforts on the part of the churches to achieve greater familiarity with the Scriptures, coupled with a critical questioning of the biblicism that is rampant on this continent and is unfortunately imitated today in many parts of the developing world.

FAITH IN DIALOGUE WITH DOUBT (CONTRA FIDEISM OR "TRUE BELIEF")

Faith, in the Protestant mode, is not a synonym for credulity. Like all of the major biblical categories (love, hope, sin, etc.—or even nouns like *God, humankind, world*, etc.), faith is a relational concept. It is another word for trust, and its application to God (faith *in* God) is in essence not different from its application to other relationships, such as when one says one has faith in one's life companion, one's child, or one's friend. Like these relationships, faith in God is always a matter of decision and is not a fixed quality but a response that demands continuous renewal.

As decision-in-response, faith lives with its own antithesis, doubt. There are, to be sure, moments of doubt's or of faith's ascendancy in the life of discipleship, both corporately and individually understood. Yet faith is itself an ongoing dialogue with doubt, for faith is denied the kind of ultimacy that is promised as the eschatological resolution of its internal tensions—the resolution that [the author of Hebrews] designates by the metaphor of "sight" (see, e.g., Heb. 11:1). As mentioned earlier, the Spanish philosopher Miguel de Unamuno said, "A faith that does not doubt is a dead faith."[13] Although Unamuno was not a Protestant and perhaps not even a Christian, he captured in this *bon mot* the nature of faith as Protestants of both the Reformation and later periods have understood it: as a living trust that achieves authenticity only where it manifests consciousness of the internal and external difficulties with which *all* trust, to be trust, must struggle.

The Reformation's *sola fide* is thus not a statement about Christian acceptance of religious "truths" in the absence of any clear proof. Rather, it is a statement about the centrality of an existential trust in God that is made in the full awareness of an ongoing temptation to existential distrust: "I believe, [Lord,] help my unbelief" (Mark 9:24 rsv). "There is no faith without an intrinsic 'in spite of,'" wrote Paul Tillich.[14]

There is a tremendous need for sensitive and informed stewarding of this Protestant understanding of faith—faith that is not credulity, not "true belief," not a spiritual possession, but an act of trust that entails honesty about its antithesis. I suspect that no practical teaching of Paul Tillich has been more accessible and important to thousands of people, both laity and clergy, than his teaching concerning the ongoing dialogue of faith with doubt. This teaching has liberated many from the tyranny of a fideism that made it impossible for them to be honest about their skepticism and unbelief, and that sent countless human beings in our time out of the churches because they were persuaded by Christian faith-talk that belief had to be all or nothing, and they could not claim the "all." Apart from Luther, who was uncommonly honest about his doubts, Reformation figures did not much develop this kind of thought about the nature of faith. Many later Protestants (including Karl Barth, who once said that he wished somebody would whisper to Paul Tillich that he should not take his doubt so seriously) have done little to counter the notion that doubt is inimical to the life of faith.

But the absence of the dialectic of faith and doubt in much of the tradition does not mean that it is absent from the whole or from the scriptural foundations. Job, Ecclesiastes, many of the Psalms, Jeremiah, Lamentations, and much else in the Old Testament, including the central image of Israel as "the one who struggles with God," is precisely about this dialectic. And what of the Gospels, which from first to last tell the story of Jesus' closest associates and their ongoing vacillation between loyalty and betrayal, trust and mistrust, in relation to their "Master"? Yes—and what of Jesus himself, who [on Golgotha] cries out in dereliction, feeling himself abandoned by the God in whom he trusted?

Nothing, I suspect, is more important in the stewarding of this tradition today than that pastors and teachers should take every opportunity to assure those in and around the churches that doubt and doubters are welcome in the community of faith. On this continent particularly, those who stand in the tradition of classical Protestantism cannot overestimate the manner in which religious certitude has defined for the populace as a whole the character of

Christian belief and belonging. Unfortunately, this is not confined to centers of fundamentalist, biblicist, and pietist religion. It also is present in many Christian circles that have the reputation of being liberal or moderate. To admit doubt, in a society like ours that rewards winners and in churches like ours that function to squelch negation of every kind, requires a great deal of honesty and personal courage.

CONCLUSION

In any full treatment of this subject, it would, of course, be necessary to go on—and on! For example, to establish concretely what the stewardship of the Protestant tradition must entail in our particular context, it would be necessary to speak about the relational character of the biblical conception of sin. Sin is probably the most misunderstood term in the Christian vocabulary. For centuries, it has suffered the worst kind of reductionism—namely, the reduction to "sins," nasty little thoughts, words, and deeds that we can confess and be forgiven for while we carry on with being the alienated human beings whose estrangement from God, neighbor, and self *is* the sin that generates all this nastiness and much, much worse.

It would be necessary, as well, to speak about the nature of redemption—which in the classical traditions of Protestantism is for the sake of the *whole* creation, not for the selfish end of getting a few precious souls into heaven. And in that connection, it would be necessary to address the bad, misleading, and utterly inadequate theology of atonement, a soteriology that took over the entire Western world ten centuries ago and is still (as Mel Gibson's film *The Passion of the Christ* has amply demonstrated) the only atonement theology we seem to know anything about: namely, the Latin satisfaction or substitutionary doctrine of the cross. Peter Abelard rightly insisted centuries ago that this interpretation of the meaning of the cross of Christ presupposes a very questionable conception of the nature of a God whom the Bible describes not only as loving but as *being* love. Truly, the Reformation failed to do very much about that Anselmic theory, and Calvin, alas, rather gave it a boost.

But Luther didn't, and we would be well advised (if we are serious about critiquing Mel Gibson's and other bloody ideas about the meaning of the cross) to return to the little seminal study of Gustav Aulén entitled *Christus Victor*.[15] Aulén demonstrates that the earliest soteriology of the cross, which Luther particularly favored, does not present the Christ as the innocent sacrificial victim who atones for all the sins of the guilty, but as the liberator of humankind from forces of oppression greater than our strength of will—an atonement theology that not only is behind the liberation theology of our own era (though perhaps unconsciously), but speaks far more directly to our condition in this society than does Anselm's explanation of the meaning of the cross. For we are not first conscious of ourselves as guilty, but as the superfluous pawns of technocratic and economic systems and fatalized mentalities that call in question any meaning that we might once have entertained.

It would be necessary, too, to speak about the church and how it is not called to be a religious institution or even another of the world's "religions." Rather, it is to be a movement that looks for the reign of God in the midst of historical chaos and uncertainty and so becomes, now and then, a harbinger of hope in the midst of a despairing age and a floundering creation. In the area of ecclesiology, we need to pay greater attention than mainstream Protestantism has yet done to the so-called radical wing of the Reformation—the Anabaptists and others who, already in the sixteenth century and beyond, knew what it meant to live outside Christendom.

One could go on! But I have said enough to establish the point. If we are ready to renew the Protestant commitment to stewardship (and stewardship is, in fact, a vital piece of the Protestant contribution to ecumenical Christianity), then it is essential that we begin by becoming more intentionally stewards of "the mysteries of God" as these have been vouchsafed to us in the traditions of classical Protestantism. I believe, as do many others, that so far as its "core" or "classical" expression is concerned, Protestantism in the West has been pushed further and further toward the periphery of our society. In my lifetime, the old, established denominations have been replaced in the public arena by manifestations of what calls itself Protestantism but could not endorse anything like the points I have been making in this review of the commanding principles of this tradition. In fact, much of this "wider" Protestantism represents a completely different approach to theology, morality, and the nature and mission of the Christian movement.

Most of us are shocked to note the extent to which our once most-established churches have been marginalized by the events of the past four or five decades. Though for the most part they are unworthy bearers of this classical tradition, they *are* the remnants of the Protestant witness in the Western world, and they are still looked to by many rather lonely souls in the rest of the world for some kind of guidance.

We may think we are fighting a battle that has been lost already. Certainly, no battles are going to be won by creating churches that are bigger, noisier, more communications-smart, better financed, and so on, but still lacking theological, ethical, and missiological substance. It is tempting to feel (I think every conscientious Protestant I know is frequently tempted to feel) that we are on the way out, if we have not already been summarily dismissed. Certainly it is folly to imagine that we are still at the center of things in either my country (Canada) or yours, though in the USA there is still an inordinate temptation in that direction.

But listen! From the edges, from the sidelines, it is possible for the once-mainline church to exercise a *prophetic* ministry, a *public* witness that it could not easily bring off and seldom did bring off when it was still an unquestioned part of the Establishment. Nothing has been more encouraging to me and other Canadians and Europeans of late than the manner in which important segments of all of the once-established Protestant churches of the United States, including the National Council of Churches, said no to the unfortunate war against Iraq, for which we are all reaping the whirlwind that its instigators sowed. I doubt the churches could have done that a century ago. Even with regard to Vietnam, many of them were still ambiguous enough in their loyalties to hold back from forthright protest.

What is needed now, surely, is a theological rigor and discipline that can give the necessary ideational and spiritual backing to this newfound moral courage of American Protestantism to go against the grain of institutions and classes that in the past have been its chief supporters. All is not lost with the Protestant (the *Protest*-ant) mainstream. In fact, it could be only now undergoing preparation for the ministry that has been its potential all along. Its sidelining *could* be the very sociological condition that is preparing it for a prophetic ministry—indeed, for the stewarding of history. But although that is the very purpose and rationale for stewarding "the mysteries of God" in their Protestant form, it is yet another topic.

Notes

1. "Statistics," *The Encyclopedia of Protestantism*, ed. Hans J. Hillerbrand (New York: Routledge, 2004), 4:1809–16.

2. Ibid., 1:347.

3. As noted earlier, the historian of doctrine, Jaroslav Pelikan, has wisely contrasted "traditionalism" and "tradition" in this way: tradition is the living faith of the dead; traditionalism is the dead faith of the living.

4. Paul Tillich, *Systematic Theology*, vol. 2 (Chicago: University of Chicago Press, 1957), 97.

5. See my discussion of H. Richard Niebuhr in Hall 1998a, esp. 98.

6. "Evangelical theology is an eminently *critical* science, for it is continually exposed to judgment and never relieved of the crisis in which it is placed by its object, or, rather to say, by its

living subject." Karl Barth, *Evangelical Theology: An Introduction*, trans. Grover Foley (New York: Holt, Rinehart & Winston, 1963), 10.

7. *Anselm's Fides Quaerens Intellectum* (London: SCM, 1960), 24.

8. Blaise Pascal, *Pensées*, no. 273.

9. This is an issue I address in Hall 2005: Introduction.

10. Ronald Goetz, "Protestant Houses of God: A Contradiction in Terms?" *Christian Century* (March 20–27, 1985): 299.

11. E. Theodore Bachman, introduction, in *Word and Sacrament*, pt. 1, *Luther's Works* (Philadelphia: Muhlenberg, 1960), vol. 35, pt. I, 116.

12. See my essay "The Diversity of Christian Witnessing in the Tension between Word and Relation to the Context," in *Luther's Ecumenical Significance*, ed. Carter Lindberg and Harry McSorley (Philadelphia: Fortress Press, 1984). The original German title of the essay, one assigned me, was "*Die Vielgestaltigkeit christlichen Zeugnisses im Spannungsfeld zwischen Wortgebundeheit und Kontextbezug.*" I think the German title captures more accurately the dialectic under discussion. It can be found in the German edition of the work, entitled *Ökumenische Erschliessung Martin Luthers*, ed. Peter Manns and Harding Meyer (Paderborn: Bonifatius und Lembeck, 1982).

13. Miguel de Unamuno, *The Agony of Christianity and Essays on Faith*, trans. Anthony Kerrigan (Princeton: Princeton University Press, Bollingen Series 85.5, 1974), 10.

14. Paul Tillich, *Dynamics of Faith* (New York: Harper & Row, 1957), 21.

15. Gustav Aulén, *Christus Victor: An Historical Study of the Three Main Types of the Idea of Atonement*, trans. A. G. Hebert (London: SPCK, 1953).

Bibliography

This complete listing of Douglas John Hall's books, of which he is the sole or co-author, is ordered according to year of original publication, with revised or reprint editions following. References to Hall's books in the text are keyed to this bibliography.

Hope Against Hope: Towards an Indigenous Theology of the Cross. 1971. Tokyo: World Student Christian Federation.

The Reality of the Gospel and the Unreality of the Churches. 1975. Philadelphia: Westminster. Reprint: Minneapolis: Fortress Press, 2007.

Lighten Our Darkness: Towards an Indigenous Theology of the Cross. 1976. Philadelphia: Westminster. Rev. ed. 2001 (rev. and with a foreword by David J. Monge).

The Canada Crisis: A Christian Perspective. 1980a. Toronto: Anglican Book Centre.

Ecclesia Crucis: Church of the Cross. 1980b. Chicago: United Church of Christ.

Has the Church a Future? 1980c. Philadelphia: Westminster. Reprint: Minneapolis: Fortress Press, 2009.

The Steward: A Biblical Symbol Come of Age. 1982. New York: Friendship Press. Rev. ed.: Grand Rapids: Eerdmans/New York: Friendship Press, 1990. Reprint: Eugene, OR: Wipf & Stock, 2004.

The Stewardship of Life in the Kingdom of Death. 1985. New York: Friendship Press. Rev. ed.: Grand Rapids: Eerdmans, 1988.

God and Human Suffering: An Exercise in the Theology of the Cross. 1986a. Minneapolis: Augsburg.

Imaging God: Dominion as Stewardship. 1986b. Grand Rapids: Eerdmans/New York: Friendship Press. Reprint: Eugene, OR: Wipf & Stock, 2004.

When You Pray: Thinking Your Way into God's World. 1987. Valley Forge, PA: Judson. Reprint: Eugene, OR: Wipf & Stock, 2003.

The Future of the Church: Where Are We Headed? 1989. Toronto: United Church Publishing House.

Thinking the Faith: Christian Theology in a North American Context. 1989. Minneapolis: Augsburg. Paperback reprint: Fortress Press, 1991.

Professing the Faith: Christian Theology in a North American Context. 1993. Minneapolis: Fortress Press.

God and the Nations (with Rosemary Radford Ruether). 1995a. Minneapolis: Fortress Press.

Confessing the Faith: Christian Theology in a North American Context. 1996. Minneapolis: Fortress Press.

The End of Christendom and the Future of Christianity. 1997. Valley Forge, PA: Trinity Press International. Reprint: Eugene, OR: Wipf & Stock, 2002.

Remembered Voices; Reclaiming the Legacy of "Neo-orthodoxy." 1998a. Louisville: Westminster John Knox. Reprint: Minneapolis: Fortress Press, 2007.

Why Christian? For Those on the Edge of Faith. 1998b. Minneapolis: Fortress Press.

Être image de Dieu: Le stewardship de l'humain dans la création. 1998c. Paris: Cerf/ Montreal: Bellarmin.

The Cross in Our Context: Jesus and the Suffering World. 2003. Minneapolis: Fortress Press.

Bound and Free: A Theologian's Journey. 2005. Minneapolis: Fortress Press.

The Messenger: Friendship, Faith, and Finding One's Way. 2011. Eugene, OR: Cascade.

Waiting for Gospel: An Appeal to the Dispirited Remnants of Protestant Establishment. 2012. Eugene, OR: Cascade.

What Theology Is Not: *An Exercise in "Negative" Theology.* 2013. Eugene, OR: Cascade.

Index of Names and Subjects

Index of Biblical References